Traditional Justice
and Reconciliation
after Violent Conflict

Learning from African Experiences

INTERNATIONAL
IDEA
INSTITUTE FOR
DEMOCRACY AND
ELECTORAL
ASSISTANCE

Traditional Justice
and Reconciliation
after Violent Conflict

Learning from African Experiences

Editors
Luc Huyse
Mark Salter

Contributors
Luc Huyse
Bert Ingelaere
Victor Igreja
Beatrice Dias-Lambranca
James Ojera Latigo
Joe A.D. Alie
Assumpta Naniwe-Kaburahe

I

© International Institute for Democracy and Electoral Assistance 2008

Reprint 2008

Applications for permission to reproduce or translate all or any part of this publication should be made to:

International IDEA
SE - 103 34 Stockholm
Sweden

International IDEA encourages dissemination of its work and will promptly respond to requests for permission to reproduce or translate its publications.

Cover photo: B. Dias Lambranca (During a nocturne healing session in central Mozambique, a *gamba* healer shows a bayonet, i.e. a healing instrument, to a female patient as a way to trigger the emergence of the *gamba* spirit in the body of the patient).
Graphic design: Trydells Form
Cover design: Kristina Schollin-Borg
Printed by: Trydells Tryckeri AB, Sweden

ISBN: 978-91-85724-28-4

Preface

A key question facing democracies emerging from civil conflict is how best to deal with the painful legacy of past—and in many cases all too recent—violence, while at the same time maintaining the fragile social harmony that often characterizes post-conflict societies. Should priority be given to bringing the perpetrators of past human rights violations to justice, thereby combating the culture of impunity that has come to characterize many civil conflicts? Or is it more important to start by focusing on measures designed to ensure that peace and stability, and with them the prospects for a country's longer-term recovery, are bolstered?

These are not easy questions, but the dynamics of contemporary conflict compels us to consider them. In regions afflicted by civil wars and violent upheavals, critical aspects of a country's post-conflict agenda rarely admit of easy, generalizable 'solutions'. Increasingly, the accepted wisdom is that the best resources—and hence the best 'answers'—to the many seemingly intractable dilemmas of managing the consequences of violent conflict lie within countries themselves.

In Africa in particular, an undervalued indigenous conflict management resource is to be found in the sphere of traditional social mechanisms. Prompted by the Rwandan experiment with Gacaca, a 'modernized' approach to an indigenous form of dispute settlement developed and applied in the aftermath of the 1994 genocide, international attention to the potential role of traditional mechanisms in reconciliation and transitional justice strategies has increased. Most recently in Uganda, debate over the respective roles of the International Criminal Court and the traditional reconciliation practices of the Acholi people in ongoing efforts to achieve a peaceful settlement of the country's two-decades-long conflict indicates that traditional mechanisms are increasingly in the policy spotlight.

There have been too few systematic attempts to analyse and assess the role and impact of traditional mechanisms in post-conflict settings. This report aims to address this gap by examining the role played by traditional justice mechanisms in dealing with the legacy of violent conflict in five African countries—Rwanda, Mozambique, Uganda, Sierra Leone and Burundi. These case studies are used as the basis for outlining conclusions and options for future policy development.

The report is intended to serve both as a general knowledge resource and as a practitioner's guide for national bodies seeking to employ traditional justice mechanisms as well as external agencies aiming to support such processes. It suggests that in some circumstances traditional mechanisms can effectively complement conventional judicial systems and represent a real potential for promoting justice, reconciliation and a culture of democracy. In addition, even in situations where communities are more inclined to demand straightforward retribution against the perpetrators, traditional justice mechanisms may still offer a way both of restoring a sense of accountability and of linking justice to democratic development.

At the same time the report also cautions against unrealistic expectations of traditional structures. It offers a sober, evidence-based assessment of both the strengths and the weaknesses of traditional conflict management mechanisms within the broader framework of post-conflict social reconstruction efforts.

Vidar Helgesen
Secretary-General
International IDEA

Acknowledgements

We are very grateful to our member state, Belgium, for providing the funding that made the ambitious project of which this report is a key outcome possible. Not for the first time, International IDEA owes an immense debt of gratitude to Professor Luc Huyse, lead researcher on the project who as well as authoring key sections of the report has lent his extensive knowledge and expertise to every stage of its development.

Additional thanks are due to Klaas de Jonge for research in the demanding initial stages of the project, to Stef Vandeginste of Antwerp University for his professional advice and assistance, and to Mark Salter of International IDEA's Democracy Analysis and Assessment Unit who has managed and shepherded the project through from start to finish. Thanks are also due to Eve Johansson for her professional input in editing this publication; to Andrew Mash for proofreading the final text; and to Florencia Enghel, International IDEA's Publications Manager, for ensuring smooth production of the final report on behalf of the Communications Team.

Last but not least, we acknowledge with gratitude and appreciation the key role of the country case study authors in bringing this project to fruition.

Contents

Chapter 3. Restorative justice and the role of *magamba* spirits in post-civil war Gorongosa, central Mozambique Victor Igreja and Beatrice Dias-Lambranca 61

Chapter 4. Northern Uganda: tradition-based practices in the Acholi region James Ojera Latigo 85

Boxes and tables

Acronyms and abbreviations

ACC	Anti-Corruption Commission (Sierra Leone)
ADF	Allied Democratic Forces (Uganda)
AFRC	Armed Forces Revolutionary Council (Sierra Leone)
AMETRAMO	Mozambican Association of Traditional Medical Practitioners
APC	All People's Congress (Sierra Leone)
ARLPI	Acholi Religious Leaders' Peace Initiative (Uganda)
BINUB	Bureau Intégré des Nations Unies au Burundi (United Nations Integrated Office in Burundi)
CDF	Civil Defence Forces (Sierra Leone)
CNDD	Conseil National pour la Défense de la Démocratie (National Council for the Defence of Democracy) (Burundi)
CNVR	Commission Nationale Vérité Réconciliation (National Truth and Reconciliation Commission) (Burundi)
CSOPNU	Civil Society Organizations for Peace in Northern Uganda
DDR	disarmament, demobilization and reintegration
DRC	Democratic Republic of the Congo
ECOMOG	ECOWAS Monitoring Group
ECOWAS	Economic Community of West African States
FDD	Forces pour la Défense de la Démocratie (Forces for the Defence of Democracy) (Burundi)
FNL-Palipehutu	Front National de Libération-Parti pour la Libération du Peuple Hutu (National Liberation Forces-Party for the Liberation of the Hutu People) (Burundi)
Frelimo	Frente de Libertação de Moçambique (Front for the Liberation of Mozambique)
Frodebu	Front pour la Démocratie au Burundi (Front for Democracy in Burundi)
HSMF	Holy Spirit Mobile Forces (Uganda)
ICC	International Criminal Court
ICTJ	International Center for Transitional Justice
ICTR	International Criminal Tribunal for Rwanda
IDP	internally displaced person
IRC	Inter-Religious Council (Sierra Leone)
KKA	Ker Kwaro Acholi (Uganda)
LRA	Lord's Resistance Army (Uganda)
LRM	Lord's Resistance Movement (Uganda)
MRND	Mouvement Révolutionaire National pour le Développement (National Revolutionary Development Movement) (Rwanda)

NGO	non-governmental organization
NPFL	National Patriotic Front of Liberia
NPRC	National Provisional Ruling Council (Sierra Leone)
NRA	National Resistance Army (Uganda)
NRM	National Resistance Movement (Uganda)
NUPI	Northern Uganda Peace Initiative
NURC	National Unity and Reconciliation Commission (Rwanda)
ONUB	Opération des Nations Unies au Burundi (United Nations Operation in Burundi)
Renamo	Resistência Nacional Moçambicana (Mozambican National Resistance)
RPA	Rwandan Patriotic Army
RPF	Rwandan Patriotic Front
RUF	Revolutionary United Front (Sierra Leone)
RUFP	Revolutionary United Front Party (Sierra Leone)
SLA	Sierra Leone Army
SLPP	Sierra Leone People's Party
SNJG	Service National des Juridictions Gacaca (National Service of the Gacaca Courts) (Rwanda)
SPLA	Sudanese People's Liberation Army
SPLM	Sudanese People's Liberation Movement
TRC	Truth and Reconciliation Commission (South Africa, Sierra Leone)
UCDA	Uganda Christian Democratic Army
UK	United Kingdom
UN	United Nations
UNAMSIL	United Nations Mission in Sierra Leone
UNDP	United Nations Development Programme
UNHCHR	United Nations High Commissioner for Human Rights
UNICEF	United Nations Children's Fund
UNLA	Uganda National Liberation Army
UNOMSIL	United Nations Observer Mission in Sierra Leone
UPC	Uganda People's Congress
UPDA/M	Uganda People's Democratic Army/Movement
UPDF	Uganda People's Defence Force
Uprona	Union pour le Progrès National (Union for National Progress) (Burundi)
USAID	United States Agency for International Development
WNBF	West Nile Bank Front (Uganda)

CHAPTER 1

CHAPTER 1

Introduction: tradition-based approaches in peacemaking, transitional justice and reconciliation policies

Luc Huyse

'Traditional justice mechanisms, such as *Culo Kwor, Mato Oput, Kayo Cuk, Ailuc* and *Tonu ci Koka* and others as practiced in the communities affected by the conflict, shall be promoted, with necessary modifications, as a central part of the framework for accountability and reconciliation.' This paragraph is article 3.1 of a preliminary pact on accountability and reconciliation, signed in late June 2007 by the government of Uganda and the rebel Lord's Resistance Army (LRA). It could be a major step towards success in the Juba peace talks that must bring an end to the long and cruel civil war in the northern part of Uganda. The explicit reference to traditional justice instruments in the context of peacemaking and justice is innovative. It is one of the strongest signs of the rapidly increasing interest in the role such mechanisms can play in times of transition.

Almost ten years earlier, Rwandans, battling the heavy legacy of the genocide, began scouting the possibility of mobilizing an informal dispute resolution tool, called Gacaca, for their transitional justice policy. Since then, thousands of such lay tribunals have been set up. They have identified and tried numerous men and women who were suspected of participating in the events of April–June 1994. The Gacaca justice and reconciliation activities have attracted worldwide attention. Academics have written countless articles and books. International non-governmental organizations (NGOs) and donor countries have provided generous funding. Examples of the ritual reintegration of ex-combatants in Mozambique and Sierra Leone were given a similar welcome. A hype was born.

The first part of this chapter examines the rise of traditional techniques in peacemaking, transitional justice and reconciliation policies. It then sets out the difficulties of terminology and methodology in investigating the actual performance of tradition-based instruments. The third part presents a comparative analysis of such practices in the five African countries that are the subject of the case studies in this book.

1. Traditional mechanisms in a broader context

When a civil war, genocide or a brutal dictatorship ends the inevitable question arises of how to deal with those who have committed grave human rights abuses. From the end of the 1940s to the mid-1980s, the answer was to look away from such painful legacies. This policy sometimes took on the appearance of a self-imposed silence, as was the case in post-Khmer Rouge Cambodia. Elsewhere, as in Spain after the demise of the Franco regime, amnesia was the outcome of a negotiated compromise between the successor elites, or impunity was established through formal amnesty legislation: Pinochet's Chile at the end of the 1970s is a striking example. The dominant strategy was to (try to) 'close the books'. This response is quite surprising. In the immediate post-World War II context the emphasis had been on accountability. A legal foundation was laid for the fight against impunity in the form of the 1948 Convention on the Prevention and Punishment of the Crime of Genocide and the four Geneva conventions of 1949. The tribunals at Nuremberg and Tokyo tried the leaders of the wartime German and Japanese governments. But this trend towards greater accountability for grave human rights crimes was not continued in the decades that followed. Silence, amnesia and amnesty were the rule, with the trials of the junta leaders in Greece (in 1974) being a notable exception.

> From the end of the 1940s to the mid-1980s, the dominant strategy for dealing with those who committed grave human rights abuses was to (try to) 'close the books' and look away from such painful legacies.

A major policy shift, both morally and politically grounded, occurred from the mid-1980s onwards. The global growth of a human rights culture blossomed into a new, now much wider, fight against impunity. International agencies such as the United Nations (UN) and the Inter-American Human Rights Court as well as large human rights NGOs cooperated to develop both the norm and the practice of a duty to prosecute crimes against humanity, genocide and war crimes. This in turn resulted in the establishment of the ad hoc tribunals of The Hague (for the former Yugoslavia) and Arusha (for Rwanda) and of the International Criminal Court (ICC), and in the gradual spread of the principle of universal jurisdiction. Moreover, the choice of retributive justice as a strategy has even been written into internationally brokered peace agreements, as in Guatemala, Sierra Leone and Burundi.

Concurrently, however, questions were asked about the applicability of systematic prosecutions in contexts where regime change is an extremely delicate and/or complex operation. Local political and civil society leaders pointed to the many political, social, economic and cultural contingencies that may make it impossible for their societies to fulfil the duty to prosecute. Doubts about the use of trials led to a search for alternative and/or complementary mechanisms to avoid the dangers of too much and of too little criminal justice. The South African Truth and Reconciliation Commission (TRC), with its principle of 'amnesty for truth', was a turning point. Moreover, the conviction arose that in most circumstances one tool alone would not suffice. A combination of measures and instruments was called for—limited amnesty or temporary immunity, vetting or lustration, a truth commission, and a few (token) trials. Such a mixture had and has to be innovative because of the uniqueness of each society that emerges from a violent conflict. What we are thus witnessing is the domestic appropriation of previously existing models of dealing with a painful past, with the aim of taking into account the numerous risks that trouble transitional societies. The overall result is the move from a de facto dichotomy (impunity *or* trials) to multiple conceptions of justice and reconciliation— state and non-state instruments; legal, semi-judicial and non-judicial techniques.

As part of this important development some post-conflict societies have now turned their attention to their legacy of indigenous practices of dispute settlement and reconciliation. The argument is that traditional and informal justice systems may be adopted or adapted to develop an appropriate response to a history of civil war and oppression. Kofi Annan, the then UN secretary-general, officially acknowledged this evolution in his August 2004 report on *The Rule of Law and Transitional Justice in Conflict and Post-Conflict Societies*: 'due regard must be given to indigenous and informal traditions for administering justice or settling disputes, to help them to continue their often vital role and to do so in conformity with both international standards and local tradition' (United Nations 2004: 12). This is the societal, political and academic context in which this report must be located.

> From the mid-1980s onwards, the global growth of a human rights culture blossomed into a new, much wider, fight against impunity. Concurrently, however, questions were asked about the applicability of systematic prosecutions in contexts where regime change is an extremely delicate and/ or complex operation. Political, social, economic and cultural contingencies make it almost impossible for a society to fulfil the duty to prosecute.

1.1. An ongoing debate

In the ongoing public debate on transitional justice, political leaders, members of civil society and academics are divided on numerous points. By far the most divisive question is how to balance the demands of justice against the many political constraints.

Those who emphasize the beneficial effects of prosecution bring forward two categories of arguments. One is victim-oriented: a post-conflict society has a moral obligation to prosecute and punish the perpetrators, because retribution is exactly what most victims want. It serves to heal their wounds and to restore their self-confidence because it publicly acknowledges who was right and who was wrong and, hence, clears the victims of any labels of 'criminal' that were placed on them by the authorities of the past or, indeed, by rebel groups or the new elites. Only trials, the argument runs, lead to a full recognition of the worth and dignity of those victimized by past abuses.

> By far the most divisive question is how to balance the demands of justice against the many political constraints.

A second set of arguments has to do with establishing and upholding peace and political stability. Prosecutions will avoid unbridled private revenge, it is said. Otherwise, victims may be tempted to take justice into their own hands. The risks then are vigilante justice, summary executions and spirals of revenge. In addition, such 'self-help justice' can trigger social and political disturbance. Trials also protect against the return of those who were the cause of the miseries of war and repression. The survival of a newly established regime depends on swift and firm judicial action against those who are responsible for the gravest violations of human rights. This is seen as a necessary protection against sabotage 'from within' and as a way of achieving some minimal physical security. In addition, criminal courts establish individual accountability. This is essential to the eradication of the dangerous perception that a whole community (e.g., 'the Hutu', 'the Tutsi') is responsible for violence and atrocities. This idea of collective guilt is often the source of negative stereotypes, which in turn may provoke more violence. Also, prosecutions are seen as the most potent deterrent against future abuses of human rights and the most effective insurance against sustained violence and atrocities. They can successfully break the vicious circle of impunity that causes injustice in many parts of the world. Finally, criminal action against perpetrators of war crimes, genocide and crimes against humanity is a duty under international law.

> The survival of a newly established regime depends on swift and firm judicial action against those who are responsible for the gravest violations of human rights. Criminal action against the perpetrators of war crimes, genocide and crimes against humanity is also now a duty under international law.

On the other hand, some question whether outright punishment is the appropriate response in any and every context. The end of a civil war or of a period of violent repression creates an intricate agenda—rebuilding the political machinery and the civil service, guaranteeing a minimum of physical security, disarming rebel movements, reorganizing the army, rebuilding infrastructure, reconstructing the economy, stabilizing the currency, establishing a non-partisan judiciary, organizing elections, healing the victims, repairing the damage inflicted on them and so on. Dealing with the perpetrators, possibly by means of criminal prosecution, is only one of many challenges. More often than not it will be impossible to tackle all tasks simultaneously. Choices have to be made. It is argued that the place of justice in general, and of trials in particular, on the post-conflict agenda depends on the particular conjunction of political, cultural and historical forces. Other problems and needs may be more important and/or more urgent than seeking justice through trials. In addition, prosecutions are ambivalent in certain transitional contexts. They can have highly destabilizing effects on a peace settlement or a fragile shift to democracy. In fact, precisely to avoid such an outcome, Latin American policy makers throughout the 1980s deliberately opted against trials.

> Other observers question whether punishment is the appropriate response in any and every context. Prosecutions can have highly destabilizing effects on a peace settlement or a fragile shift to democracy, and have intrinsic limitations. They may contradict the legal culture of a post-conflict society.

Moreover, prosecutions have some intrinsic limitations. They are perpetrator-oriented and do not give victims the full attention they are entitled to in order to be healed of the injustices they suffered. Trials identify individual guilt, not patterns of atrocities. Moreover, they may contradict the legal culture of a post-conflict society. Desmond Tutu, chair of the South African Truth and Reconciliation Commission, argues that Western-style justice does not fit with traditional African jurisprudence. It is too impersonal. The African view of justice is aimed at 'the healing of breaches, the redressing of imbalances, the restoration of broken relationships. This kind of justice seeks to rehabilitate both the victim and the perpetrator, who should be given the opportunity to be reintegrated into the community he or she has injured by his or her offence' (Tutu 1999: 51). Finally, there may be a whole range of practical shortcomings and risks. Evidence may have been destroyed. In many cases the criminal law system will be in shock, seriously crippled or perceived as an integral part of the old order. Lack of proof can lead to the acquittal of well-known perpetrators. Such justice, perceived as arbitrary, will seriously damage victims' trust in the whole system.

> More often than not it will be impossible to tackle all the tasks involved in establishing justice and rebuilding a country simultaneously.

1.2. The rise of a cross-cultural perspective

At first sight the debate is a clash between two opposing models. On the one side, full priority is given to prosecution. The tribunal is the gold standard. The international community, through its permanent ICC or via the principle of universal jurisdiction, must act if local authorities willingly or from sheer necessity abstain from retributive action. In all cases, professional judges play the principal part. More attention goes to the suspect than to the victim. The duty to prosecute is a stronger argument than the many contingencies the local context creates. International institutions such as the UN and large NGOs such as Human Rights Watch and Amnesty International deliver the growing-power for this model. At the opposite extreme is the choice of a strategy that tries to avoid the tribunal as much as possible. The centre of gravity moves from the courtroom to the hearing, from the judge to the local civil society leader, from a fixation on individual guilt to the search for societal patterns in atrocities, from legal retaliation to ritual reconciliation, from the internationally driven retributive impulses to the full acknowledgement of the opportunities the local context offers.

Using more analytical language, one can position the two models at the extremes of a continuum. At one end is a strategy that is initiated, organized and controlled by (national or international) state institutions. Its procedures are formal and rational-legalistic. The criminal court is the prototype. At the other end of the continuum are policies that are community-initiated and community-organized. They are predominantly informal and ritualistic-communal. The north Ugandan rite of stepping on the egg, exercised to reintegrate former child soldiers, is a striking demonstration of this type of approach.

There are, good reasons to correct the picture of two 'pure' strategies that differ on all points and are mutually exclusive. First, in real-world situations many transitional justice policies will combine, albeit to different degrees, ingredients of both extremes. The Gacaca, for example, has been highly formalized and can impose prison sentences, yet operates with lay judges. Second, the original approach of reasoning in absolute terms (to prosecute *or* to forgive and forget) has gradually been abandoned. An explanation for this development should run along a variety of lines. One is the relative success of the South African TRC, a creative mix of formal and informal procedures and of international norms and domestically designed techniques. There is also the growing awareness that broadening the scope of local variation is totally justified. That is exactly what Diane Orentlicher, a professor of international law and the United Nations' independent expert on combating impunity, meant when she recently wrote: 'Given the extraordinary range of national experiences and cultures, how could anyone imagine there to be a universally relevant formula for transitional justice?' (Orentlicher 2007: 18). In addition, planning post-conflict justice and reconciliation has become an intrinsic and unavoidable part of any peace negotiation process. There is therefore a real and major risk that a peace agreement that mandates prosecutions will kill the prospects for peace. The case of northern Uganda is a convincing demonstration of the difficult dilemmas local people and international facilitators then have to tackle.

> The South African Truth and Reconciliation Commission was a creative mix of formal and informal procedures and of international norms and domestically designed techniques.

1.3. Traditional justice and reconciliation systems: from a normative approach to a more realistic view

The shift in transitional justice paradigms has opened up ample space to discuss the role of traditional mechanisms. At first, the strengths of the formula (home-grown, locally owned, culturally embedded and so on) received overexposure. Awareness of the many weaknesses was not lacking, but they were too often kept in the shade. The outcome was a great deal of myth making, of discussing 'invented traditions'. The resulting knowledge gap produced decision making that was based on weak data, *ex ante* evaluation and speculation.

The mood changed as soon as the results of empirical studies started to circulate. This was most visible with regard to the Gacaca initiative. The programme ran into a multitude of operational problems. In addition, two dubious effects have been observed of what had been labelled a very promising model. The Gacaca courts were expected to drastically reduce the number of people in prison (*c.* 120,000) and to deal with the backlog of genocide cases. However, as is discussed in the chapter on Rwanda, questionable instrumentalization of the lay tribunals resulted in more than 800,000 men and women being put on the list of suspects. A second unwanted effect is that mutual trust between the two ethnic communities—the Bahutu and the Batutsi—has tended to decrease. However, the most important shift in perception and evaluation is the insight—now commonly accepted—that traditional techniques, in Rwanda and in other African post-conflict countries, have been greatly altered in form and substance by the impact of colonization, modernization and civil war. Normative approaches are thus gradually

The Gacaca initiative in Rwanda ran into a multitude of operational problems.

giving way to more realistic, empirically based assessments of the potential role of traditional mechanisms within the broader reconciliation and transitional justice policy framework.

The ambition of this book is to develop insights, based on case studies by local authors, which will both enlighten the debate and heighten awareness among all involved stakeholders, local and international, of the range of policy instruments and contextual resources available to them in the pursuit of sustainable peace in post-conflict societies.

With the results of empirical studies of traditional justice mechanisms, the most important shift in perception and evaluation is the now commonly accepted insight that traditional techniques have been altered in form and substance by the impact of colonization, modernization and civil war.

The next step now is to tackle the intricate problems that arise in the search for an acceptable terminology and methodology.

2. Investigating tradition-based practices: problems of terminology and methodology

'The term "traditional" with its Eurocentric connotations tends to suggest the existence of profoundly internalized normative structures.' It also refers to patterns that are seemingly embedded in static political, economic and social circumstances. But 'it must be borne in mind that African institutions, whether political, economic or social, have never been inert. They respond to changes resulting from several factors and forces'. Both quotations come from Joe Alie's case study on Sierra Leone (in chapter 5). They point convincingly to the problems that arise in any study of tradition-based justice and reconciliation instruments. Terminology is problematic. How justified still is the label 'traditional' if the mechanism is susceptible to almost continuous change? Are there any satisfactory alternatives? In addition, if the subject of the study is a constantly moving target, where should the focus of the observation be directed? Second, many questions of a methodological nature appear, such as how to avoid ethnocentrism in developing the key notions that will guide the analysis and whether it is at all possible for Western observers to interpret these phenomena in a basically sound way.

These are questions that cannot be avoided. This part of the chapter tackles them, but it cannot be other than an unfinished exercise.

2.1. A tricky terminology

In the section of his chapter on the substance of traditional practices in northern Uganda (chapter 4), James Latigo writes that there is still a need to carry on tracing the processes that led to the development of some of the original practices, to the decay of others and to the appearance of new ones, such as various forms of psychotherapeutic healing. Colonizing authorities and processes of modernization, civil war or genocide have had deeply disturbing effects on the original institutions so, strictly speaking, they are no longer traditional. The problem is that alternative terms also tend to provoke embarrassing questions. 'Customary' is too close to 'traditional'. Some prefer 'informal', so as to make the contrast with the formal and formalistic character of state justice institutions, but some of our case studies show that the mechanisms in question acquire formal attributes once they are more or less part of a transitional justice policy. This is firmly demonstrated in the case of the Rwandan Gacaca, as chapter 2 argues. A similar problem arises when 'non-state' is used as the adjective. Mobilization of these techniques in the context of a broader transitional justice policy tends to bring them into the sphere of influence of state authorities and institutions. No satisfactory generic term thus seems to exist.

This discussion is more than a purely terminological excursion. It puts a finger on a crucial aspect of traditional instruments today: they are hybrids and move back and forth between their origin and capture by the state.

This book retains the word 'traditional' as the key label, for want of a more accurate alternative. But we explicitly acknowledge the dynamic processes that drive the form and content of our subject. Each case study describes the life cycle of tradition-based justice and reconciliation techniques, thus confronting their actual format with prior states of affairs. The analysis in terms of strengths and weaknesses, however, focuses on the present characteristics and performance.

2.2. Methodological pitfalls and choices

Ethnocentrism is like nature: chase it away through the front door and it comes back through a window. It is a major source of misconceptions in viewing the practices of the outside world. This is a specific risk in any study of or report on tradition as a socio-political phenomenon in African societies. A strong tendency to romanticize persists, particularly in European and North American academic and NGO communities. What is more, some of the cultural barriers that block the line of sight are extremely high, as are language barriers. In his book *Trial Justice: The International Criminal Court and the Lord's Resistance Army*, Tim Allen, an expert on northern Uganda, shows how confusing some critical notions in the local idiom may be for external observers: 'in the Lwo language, "amnesty" and "forgiveness" are not distinct—the same word (*timo-kica*) is used for both. The Christian organizations and the "traditional" leaders were especially prone to confuse the two ideas, even arguing that there is an Acholi system of justice based on forgiveness which is superior to mere conventional law-making and enforcement. Rather naively, many NGOs have taken this at face value' (Allen 2006: 76–7).

To avoid these and other pitfalls, International IDEA has chosen to engage local authors for this project. The only exception is the chapter on the Rwandan Gacaca. Its author is a Belgian scholar who has spent lengthy periods of field research in the rural areas of that Great Lakes country. (The Rwandan experts who were originally involved in the project pulled out.) The other case studies have been written by Africans with an intimate knowledge of their own societies. The outcome, as their contributions demonstrate, is a set of well-informed and highly relevant country studies. These authors are in various degrees themselves actors in their society, not far-away observers who read and write from the comfort of a university or an NGO or a newspaper. A few have even been insiders to the conflict in focus. This results in firm, even provocative, opinions on the causes of the war that ravaged their country. They also have outspoken views on the role of traditional justice and reconciliation mechanisms. Some readers may find that, as a consequence, balance and neutrality have suffered. Our approach, however, has the advantage of injecting clarity into the debate on transitional justice policy choices. To further stimulate the dialogue, International IDEA will open its Reconciliation Resource Network website (http://www.idea.int/rrn) for discussions related to this book.

A case study depends to a great extent on the analytical frameworks that guide research and observation, especially if the ambition is to make the output as comparative as possible. To this end the team (the lead researcher, the other authors and the project leader) worked with a common checklist of issues and topics that was meant to cover the subject matter of the project. A draft of the list was presented and revised extensively at a meeting with the authors in Pretoria on 25–26 September 2006. It was agreed, however, that the list was not intended to be an operational straitjacket, since that would lead to so-called observation blindness. Society constantly shapes new forms and expressions of existing patterns. Only research instruments that are fully flexible will register novel appearances of, for instance, informal justice mechanisms. Victor Igreja and Beatrice Dias-Lambranca deliver a convincing example in their case study. Victims and offenders in Gorongosa, Mozambique, have used old models of healing and reconciliation to develop new rituals that are better suited to the actual post-conflict circumstances.

Two factors explain the choice of the five countries that are part of the project. They are sufficiently similar for comparison to be possible. All have a legacy of extremely violent conflict. At the same time, they represent a wide diversity in terms of the type and status of the domestic conflict (ongoing in northern Uganda, close to peace in Burundi, ended in the three other countries in focus), kind of transition, and degree of involvement of indigenous instruments in the transitional justice programmes of the country (formally integrated in Rwanda, officially linked to a truth commission, as in Sierra Leone, planned incorporation in Uganda, no explicit inclusion in Burundi and Mozambique). The choice of cases was also based in part on consultations with staff of the Belgian Ministry of Foreign Affairs, the project's funders.

3. Five African experiences

Traditional justice in general, particularly as it functioned in pre-colonial and colonial times, has been the subject of an abundant literature. The approach was and is anthropological or has its focus on the phenomenon of legal pluralism, that is, the coexistence of state and non-state forms of adjudication. Reconciliation rituals have also received a great deal of attention. The specificity of the International IDEA project, however, lies in its analysis of *the role such mechanisms play or might play in dealing with the legacies of widespread human rights abuses.*

3.1. The ambitions of justice after transition

Mention is made above of the complexity of the political agenda once a civil war or a repressive regime has ended. Dealing with the fate of victims and per-petrators is one of the huge tasks the successor elite and civil society have to tackle. They may enact amnesty legislation, prosecute offenders, establish a truth commission, seek reconciliation through local rituals, build memorials or develop a combination of these measures. Academics and practitioners have coined the term 'transitional justice' to cover the various policies for challenging a grisly past. This section examines the extent to which traditional techniques of dispute resolution fall within the range of that key notion.

> Which should come first after violent conflict—justice or the restoration of social peace?

To enable such an exercise, we first need a brief description of the goals of justice after transition.

3.1.1. General goals

The study of how post-conflict societies handle a legacy of grave human rights violations is relatively young. As a consequence, views on its core subject still differ. However, gradually a prudent consensus has appeared with regard to the minimum goals of transitional justice policies.

Two general objectives lie at the level of individuals and local communities. Healing the wounds of victims and survivors is the first. The second is aimed at social repair—restoring broken relationships between members of a group and between communities. The second general objective operates at the level of a society or of a nation as a whole. The main aim here is to prevent the recurrence of deadly conflict, not least by strengthening and/or creating institutions and processes tailored to the purpose.

Do these general ambitions feature in the traditional techniques that are the focus of this book? The answer is that they mostly do. Victor Igreja and Beatrice Dias-Lambranca see healing, addressing war-related conflicts and avoiding new aggression as inherently connected to local practices in Mozambique (chapter 3): 'By making use of available and accessible endogenous resources, war survivors were able to begin the paramount task of repairing their individual and collective lives'; and, elsewhere in this case study, 'In the social spaces that are thus created, the violence of the past is re-enacted: the grudges, bitterness and discontentment in the hearts of the survivors can be conveyed without the risk of starting fresh cycles of abuse and violence'. According to Joe Alie, in the chapter on Sierra Leone: 'Societal resources such as indigenous accountability mechanisms are very useful in peace building, especially after a violent conflict. They have the potential to facilitate the reintegration and healing processes, since the community members can easily associate with them'. Writing on the rich body of traditional practices of the Acholi people of northern Uganda (chapter 4), James Latigo shows how they can lead to the remaking of relations of trust, the restoration of social cohesion, and the prevention of gruesome new crimes.

> The general goals of justice after transition are healing the wounds of the victims and survivors, repairing the social fabric and preventing the recurrence of deadly conflict.

There is a growing conviction in political and academic circles that the general goals (healing the victims, repairing the social fabric and protecting the peace) are best pursued through a search for reconciliation, accountability, truth telling and restitution for the damage that was inflicted. These can be called the four *instrumental* objectives that all transitional justice policies must ideally have. Our report also sees them as the critical dimensions of tradition-based forms of conflict resolution after civil war and genocide.

3.1.2. Four instrumental objectives

The notions of reconciliation, account-ability, truth, and reparation are discussed below will be used here as the main gateways to a comparative review of tradition-based techniques in the countries that are part of the project.

> The four instrumental objectives all transitional justice policies must ideally have are reconciliation, accountability, truth and reparation.

Reconciliation

'The ultimate goal of traditional justice systems among the Kpaa Mende (and indeed among most African communities) is reconciliation.' This is one of Joe Alie's conclusions in the Sierra Leone case study. Local reconciliation activities are very often focused on the return of ex-combatants. *Curandeiros*, traditional healers, in Mozambique conducted reintegration rituals for ex-soldiers. Another example is the *moyo kum* ('cleansing the body') ritual in northern Uganda. During a meeting of the elders, men and women who have come back from captivity have their guilt washed away and may begin living together in harmony again. Caritas Makeni, an NGO working in Sierra Leone, 'successfully reunified child ex-combatants with their families. The latter sought to "change the hearts" of their children through a combination of care, support and ritual action. Usually, the eldest member of the family prayed over a cup of water and rubbed it over the child's body (particularly the head, feet, and chest), asking God and the ancestors to give the child a "cool heart," a state of reconciliation and stability in which the child is settled in the home, has a proper relationship with family and community' (Shaw 2002: 6).

The Liberia TRC Act of June 2005 has provisions for the employment of traditional mechanisms of conflict management. In Sierra Leone, too, TRC commissioners were able to 'seek assistance from traditional and religious leaders to facilitate its public sessions and in resolving local conflicts arising from past violations or abuses or in support of healing and reconciliation' (Sierra Leone, TRC Act, article 7.2). According to Tim Kelsall, a lecturer in African politics who observed hearings of this commission, it is clear that the addition of a carefully staged reconciliation ceremony to the proceedings was extremely significant. He writes that the ritual 'created an emotionally charged atmosphere that succeeded in moving many of the participants and spectators, not least the present author, and which arguably opened an avenue for reconciliation and lasting peace' (Kelsall 2005: 363). The *mato oput* ceremony in northern Uganda has the reconciling of victims and perpetrators as its central purpose. In Mozambique the *magamba* spirits create a socio-cultural context that allows individuals and communities to refrain from violence and re-establish broken relationships. In 1993, after a most gruesome period in the 'undeclared civil war' in Burundi, members of the Ubushingantahe—a local dispute resolution institution—tried to develop processes of reconciliation. They succeeded in several communities, but failed in the majority of the others. Reconciliation, although mainly seen as a way to national unity, was one of the stated objectives when the Gacaca tribunals in Rwanda became part of a broader transitional justice policy. Their actual experience, however, raises serious doubts about whether the outcome can be called successful.

Accountability
James Latigo writes in chapter 4 that the practice of *mato oput* 'is predicated on full acceptance of one's responsibility for the crime that has been committed or the breaking of a taboo. In its practice, redemption is possible, but only through this voluntary admission of wrongdoing, the acceptance of responsibility'. Similar principles apply in reconciliation rites that are performed in neighbouring regions of Uganda. In Mozambique, as the case study demonstrates, acknowledgement of guilt by the offender is a crucial element in the *gamba* spirit scenes. The reconciliation ceremonies of the Sierra Leone TRC were oriented explicitly towards the perpetrators accepting their wrongdoing. The *bashingantahe* in Burundi are not today dealing with the legacy of grave human rights violations, but the accountability component is very prominent in their customary dispute settlement sessions. The Gacaca mechanism in Rwanda originally had a certain tendency to record blame, although the restoration of social harmony was the first goal. The actual Gacaca is strongly oriented towards retribution.

The extent to which these rites require full accountability has become a key element in the discussion on the international law-based duty to prosecute. The argument is that a tendency to reconcile and even to forgive does not exclude the search for acknowledgement, responsibility and restitution. This is, at the moment, a core

> A tendency to reconcile and even to forgive does not exclude the search for acknowledgement, responsibility and restitution.

element in the debate on the role of the ICC in northern Uganda. It has also been invoked in the June 2007 Juba agreement between the Ugandan Government and the leaders of the Lord's Resistance Army.

Truth telling

Truth telling is an integral part of local dispute resolution practices in many African countries. This is clearly the case in the Mende society in Sierra Leone, as chapter 5 demonstrates. James Latigo's description of traditional systems of justice in northern Uganda shows how one of their objectives is to establish a common view of the violent collective history. Lars Waldorf, who ran Human Rights Watch's field office in Kigali from 2002 to 2004, notes that, when the idea of incorporating the Gacaca into the genocide trials was first discussed, local scholars proposed using the institution instead as a Rwandan version of a truth commission because its original version had the capacities to develop such a role (Waldorf 2006: 49). Truth seeking through ritual public narratives is extremely important in the case of Mozambique. After the civil war ended the political response was to bury the past and impose a curfew of silence. This culture of denial has prevented victims evoking their suffering and restoring their dignity. The *gamba* spirit ceremonies create opportunities for both victims and perpetrators to engage with the past. In Burundi, members of the Ubushingantahe are expected to develop conditions that are conducive to the establishment of the real facts in a dispute. However, while truth telling may be integral to many traditional mechanisms, the actual form it takes is not necessarily the 'Western' public/confessional model of the South African TRC.

Reparation

All the authors of our case studies indicate that traditional mechanisms in their countries require the performance of reparation for the victims. It is not, however, clear whether such reparation has sufficiently materialized in the context of dealing with mass violence. *Magamba* healers in Mozambique assert that to deal successfully with the legacy of the civil war offenders must repair the damage they inflicted. In Rwanda, the actual Gacaca legislation provides for two types of reparation. A fund has been set up to compensate individuals, their family or their clan, but it has not become operational. The other form is of a collective nature. It prescribes community labour (*travaux d'intérêt général*). This measure too has run into problems.

3.2. Two salient features

In 2002 Penal Reform International (PRI), an NGO, published a report on the role informal justice systems play in Sub-Saharan Africa—but without the focus on a post-conflict context. It contains a long list of ideal-typical attributes of such systems (see box 1). This list is highly instructive. The first two items refer to reconciliation and accountability and, via the term 'restorative', to elements of truth seeking and reparation—the instrumental objectives which were discussed in section 3.1.2. Next are six traits that give a concrete expression of their ritualistic-communal character, an aspect that marks a crucial difference with rational-legalistic instruments such as criminal courts. The remaining points on the list express yet another dominant attribute, namely that most processes are initiated and run by civil society actors—in distinct contrast with state-based models of conflict resolution.

Box 1: The ideal-typical attributes of informal justice systems in Sub-Saharan Africa

1. The focus is on reconciliation and restoring social harmony.
2. There is an emphasis on restorative penalties.
3. The problem is viewed as that of the whole community or group.
4. The enforcement of decisions is secured through social pressure.
5. There is no professional legal representation.
6. Decisions are confirmed through rituals aimed at reintegration.
7. The rules of evidence and procedure are flexible.
8. The process is voluntary and decisions are based on agreement.
9. Traditional arbitrators are appointed from within the community on the basis of status or lineage.
10. There is a high degree of public participation.

Source: Penal Reform International (PRI), *Access to Justice in Sub-Saharan Africa: The Role of Traditional and Informal Justice Systems* (London: PRI, 2002), p. 112, by kind permission.

3.2.1. Ritualistic-communal procedures

Western justice systems claim to encompass the principles of accountability, reparation and, albeit to a lesser degree, truth and the restoration of broken relationships. Modern and indigenous dispute resolution institutions thus pursue the same objectives. However, they differ, mainly with regard to the procedures they develop to reach these goals. The specificity of the *mato oput* ceremonies in northern Uganda and of the efforts to reintegrate former child soldiers in Sierra Leone is the use of ritualistic ingredients—stepping on an egg, washing away the evil past with holy water or oil, drinking the juice of a plant or a tree, evoking ancestors, provoking trance. Spirits dominate the scenario in Mozambique. As Victor Igreja and Beatrice Dias-Lambranca write,

People in Gorongosa, as in many other parts of Africa, live in a social world that traditionally practises the belief that the death of individuals through traumatic acts, or the breaking of taboos such as the killing of human beings without metaphysical and/or social legitimization, is an offence that requires immediate redress through atonement rituals. If wrongdoing is not acknowledged, the spirit of the innocent victim will return to the realm of the living to fight for justice.

Ritual elements are not completely absent in modern courts. Look at the solemn language, the robes and wigs of judges and advocates. But the dominant tone there is rational. Another critical difference lies in the absence of legalistic tools in almost all traditional justice practices. There is no professional representation and the rules of evidence and procedure are flexible. In addition, the logic of criminal law is different. It has to generate 'yes or no' decisions. The outcome of a trial must be 'guilty' or 'not guilty'. To arrive at such clear verdicts, criminal courts must have strict rules. They also limit the amount of information that is processed. However, during violent conflict the behaviour of perpetrators often falls into a grey area in which different forms of guilt and innocence are mixed. Child soldiers, forcibly abducted from their families and compelled to commit horrendous crimes in the course of the conflicts in Sierra Leone, Uganda and elsewhere, are a clear case in point. Courtrooms are not usually capable of the subtlety needed to deal with such complexities. A combination of palavers, the African way of prolonging discussions, and ritual events creates in principle more opportunities for exploring issues of accountability, innocence and guilt that are integral to the legacy of violent conflict. The actual Gacaca institution, however, is more ambiguous. Bert Ingelaere, the author of the case study in this book, notes: 'it is the repeated act of coming together in the Gacaca sessions, irrespective of what is done there in the sense of content, that seems to have a transformative influence on social relations with those encountered in those meetings. But the substance of the encounters is handled according to the purely prosecutorial logic which limits the discursive aspects normally connected with ritual doings or the dialogical and healing dimension of truth-telling processes'.

Even more important, perhaps, is the communal dimension. Guilt and punishment, victimhood and reparation are viewed as collective in most African societies. A community will be incited to accept responsibility for the deeds of a perpetrator or to engage in the healing of a victim. Modern justice systems are designed to identify individual responsibility. Moreover, trials only recognize criminal guilt, not political or moral responsibility.

> Modern justice systems are designed to identify individual responsibility, but guilt and punishment, victimhood and reparation are viewed as collective in most African societies. Moreover, trials only recognize criminal guilt, not political or moral responsibility.

3.2.2. Civil society as the main stakeholder

Sizeable components of transitional justice policies are initiated and organized by state authorities. Criminal prosecutions are the prototype. Even truth commissions often operate in the shadow of the state. The case studies in this book show that the centre of gravity is different in the case of almost all indigenous practices. Civil society in its various forms (traditional, cultural and religious leaders; elders; local NGOs and the media) normally sets the rules, appoints the key personnel (mediators, arbitrators, lay judges) and watches over the implementation of the decisions that are taken. In addition, there is in principle a high degree of public participation. Gacaca sessions at the level of the Rwandan hills are intended to attract large parts of the population (presence there is compulsory). Such broad sharing of experiences also typifies the other cases. Criminal courts, on the other hand, are much more distanced from those who were involved as victims or as offenders. This has led to complaints, particularly with regard to the ad hoc tribunals in The Hague (for the former Yugoslavia) and Arusha (for Rwanda), and to the permanent International Criminal Court. The perception of the distance of internationally instigated tribunals from the victim populations and the lack of direct access to these courts is sometimes framed in terms of questioning the basic legitimacy of such 'international' institutions for dealing with 'local' war crimes.

3.3. An impressive diversity

Up to this point in the comparative analysis the accent has been on the many similarities between the traditional mechanisms in the five countries. There is, however, considerable variation in content and form.

All indigenous justice and reconciliation practices are, strictly speaking, no longer traditional. But some are newer than others. The *gamba* spirit ceremony is an instance of a newly invented mechanism, based on existing ingredients. It was needed to fill the vacuum created by the culture of denial in Mozambique. War survivors in the Gorongosa area managed to develop their own socio-cultural mechanisms to attain justice and reconciliation in the aftermath of the civil war. The Juba agreement between the Ugandan Government and the rebel LRA stipulates that local justice instruments shall be promoted, '*with necessary modifications*' (emphasis added). This will change *mato oput* and other existing practices in northern Uganda. But the most radical transformation has hit the Rwandan Gacaca. Lars Waldorf writes: 'In fact, *gacaca* has always been an uneasy mix of restorative and retributive justice: confessions and accusations, plea-bargains and trials, forgiveness and punishment, community service and incarceration'. But its modernization by the actual regime has made it 'increasingly retributive, both in design and in practice' (Waldorf 2005: 422). Legislation has introduced legalistic procedures, state control and forced participation for the population. The Gacaca court of today is unquestionably an outsider in the context of this project.

Practices also differ in the way the objectives of reconciliation, accountability, truth seeking and reparation are ranked. Reintegration and cleansing rituals in Sierra Leone (as in Liberia) fully prioritize bringing together returning rebels, their families and their victims. In the *gamba* spirit case the emphasis is on truth telling, although the other goals are not absent. Accountability is the main intention in the Gacaca proceedings. The Ubushingantahe in Burundi involves a more or less balanced mixture of the four components.

Finally, substantial variety is caused by the broader context in which traditional mechanisms have to function. The Mozambican amnesty law creates an environment that is completely different from that in Sierra Leone, with the presence of a special court and a TRC. The next section explores this source of diversity.

3.4. Tradition-based mechanisms: from aversion to full integration

Publications on transitional justice have often tended to study amnesty legislation, trials, truth commissions and other strategies as if they operated in a societal vacuum. But, as a recent report notes, 'Strategic interventions or planned change in one part of a system affect all parts in reverberating pathways' (Baines, Stover and Wierda 2006: 3). Preference should indeed be given to a more comprehensive approach.

3.4.1. The need for a comprehensive approach

All regimes coming out of a devastating conflict are confronted with a formidable transition agenda. This raises intricate problems of prioritizing and sequencing. When to address a legacy of mass violence if basic needs in the areas of physical security, housing and so on remain unanswered? Or if the conflict has not ended yet, as in northern Uganda, will it be peace first or justice instead?

Given the volatility of an immediate post-conflict context, timing and sequencing in particular represent an extremely important but difficult dimension. Policies must not come too soon or too late. Questions and challenges abound. *When* to develop justice and reconciliation activities? Decisions will inevitably impact seriously on the final outcome. To get the time as right as possible, policy makers must 'understand the times', that is, make an adequate reading of the forces that influence the transition agenda; be conscious of the importance of measures for the long term; and be aware that the mere passage of time will not ultimately heal all individual and collective wounds. Then, once the decision to tackle the crimes of the past is taken, what is the *proper timing*? Any policy needs a 'flight plan' to control the right sequencing of the steps and dimensions of the process. What should come first—healing initiatives, locking up leading offenders, starting cleansing and reintegration rituals, or saving vital documents for the future search for truth? Wrong sequencing may have undesirable effects. The threat of trials may incite suspects to destroy evidence. To give priority to truth telling may frustrate victims who are in urgent need of healing. Finally, what is the *appropriate pace*? Experience suggests that a rushed approach, as regularly advocated by national and international peacemakers and facilitators, will almost certainly be counterproductive. In the immediate aftermath of a

> When to develop justice and reconciliation activities? What should come first—healing initiatives, locking up leading offenders, starting cleansing and reintegration rituals, or saving vital documents? What is the appropriate pace? Experience suggests that a rushed approach will almost certainly be counterproductive.

civil war or of an inhuman regime, victims are too preoccupied with their own distress to develop firm views on how to reach justice and reconciliation.

The particular conjunction of political and cultural forces in and around the post-conflict country weighs heavily on prioritizing and time management.

Politics
A political system has a variety of relevant actors. Official authorities are crucial. The many groups and organizations that populate civil society form another important category. Both operate on the national, the local and the international level.

State authorities
The case study on Burundi clearly shows that the *bashingantahe* institution has not yet been accepted as a vital component of dealing with the legacy of an almost continuous and brutal conflict. There is no reference to that effect in the 2000 Arusha Peace and Reconciliation Agreement, it has no place in the law on the proposed national truth and reconciliation commission (commission nationale vérité réconciliation) and it is absent in the current negotiations between the government and the UN regarding the mandate and composition of the Burundian commission. This is partly due to an aversion that exists in the Bahutu-controlled government, where the *bashingantahe* are viewed as still in the hands of the Batutsi. Opposition also exists at the local level. Traditional leaders clash with those who received their authority through elections. The former mostly have to yield. The international community, in its role as a facilitator in the peace negotiations, has apparently not felt the need to counter these sources of resistance.

How to understand this outcome? Justice after transition is part of a broader objective a new regime has to pursue, namely to consolidate its authority and legitimacy, internally and vis-à-vis the outside world. This is a question of nation and state building. New or renewed control over the justice sector is a vital factor in these processes. In countries like Rwanda political leaders have formalized informal justice mechanisms, bringing them under closer scrutiny. Non-state actors and traditional authority structures (elders, lay judges and so on) are also important targets of 'state capture'. The politicization of the traditional leadership is often one of the consequences, resulting in problems of weakened credibility, inefficiency and corruption. This, in its turn, may considerably reduce the potential of the traditional institutions of conflict regulation, since they rest on these local leaders. In some instances the legitimacy of these tools has been compromised by the role that traditional leaders played (albeit often under duress) during the conflict.

> Traditional leaders clash with those who received their authority through elections. The former mostly have to yield. New or renewed control over the justice sector is a vital factor in nation and state building after conflict. Non-state actors and traditional authority structures (elders, lay judges and so on) are important targets of 'state capture'.

International instances

Where a brutal conflict has crossed borders the odds are that transitional justice policy will also have international ramifications. Charles Taylor, a Liberian and key perpetrator in the Sierra Leone civil war, had to stand trial in Freetown. (He was transferred to a tribunal in The Hague, the Netherlands, for security reasons.) In other cases a legacy of violence is internationalized because foreign countries or the UN have taken up the role of peacemaking facilitator. This happened in Burundi. As a consequence national justice and reconciliation strategies were developed according to internationally inspired models. Finally, there is the influence of international law. Its insistence on the duty to prosecute may restrict the policy choices national authorities can make. This is currently a major point of discussion in northern Uganda. Such pressure has been growing over time. When the civil war in Mozambique came to an end in 1992 an amnesty act passed without international protest. That would no longer be the case today.

> In some instances the legitimacy of the traditional institutions of conflict regulation, which rest on local leaders, has been compromised by the role traditional leaders played (albeit often under duress) during the conflict.

Civil society

All the authors of the case studies in this book put clear emphasis on the important part civil society has had, still has or might have in dealing with the grisly fallout from their country's wars. Local NGOs, separately and/or through networking, try to influence the decision-making processes of national and international authorities. The majority of the churches in Gorongosa (Mozambique) totally discouraged ideas about achieving retributive justice. The Inter-Religious Council of Sierra Leone was involved in some of the hearings of the TRC. The National Council of Bashingantahe in Burundi has lobbied for inclusion and involvement in the post-war policies of the government. Victims' associations in Rwanda pressure the authorities in questions of accountability and reparation. The Northern Uganda Peace Initiative (NUPI), a network of associations, has strongly supported the use of *mato oput* and cleansing ceremonies. Other local NGOs in the region, however, are fighting for criminal prosecutions. Opinions thus diverge. Such variety in viewpoints is not an exception. It is an important feature of civil society in most post-conflict countries.

International NGOs such as Amnesty International and Human Rights Watch are not absent in the debate on transitional justice policies. In the course of their vigorous lobbying for an effective ICC and for the extension of universal jurisdiction they have tended to put a robust emphasis on retributive justice. Doubts about the justification of traditional practices abound.

Culture

No Future Without Forgiveness is the title of Desmond Tutu's personal memoir of chairing the South African Truth and Reconciliation Commission. He argues that the conditional amnesty the TRC could grant was 'consistent with a central feature of the African *Weltanschauung* (or world-view)—what we know as *ubuntu* in the Nguni group of languages, or *botho* in the Sotho languages. ... A person with *ubuntu* is open and available to others, affirming of others, does not feel threatened that others are able and good; for he or she has a proper self-assurance that comes from knowing that he or she belongs in a greater whole' (Tutu 1999: 34–5). It is this fundamental attitude that opens the heart for forgiveness. This is mostly closely related to religious convictions. In their case study on Mozambique, Victor Igreja and Beatrice Dias-Lambranca write: 'Christian religious groups in Gorongosa rely entirely on unilateral forgiveness since God is considered to be the most important figure in the resolution of conflicts'. On the other hand, the practice of forgiving and forgetting may be widespread in Africa but it is not a general cultural given. The results of two surveys on peace and justice in northern Uganda were released in August 2007. One was conducted by the Office of the High Commissioner for Human Rights (OHCHR), with the participation of 1,725 victims of the conflict in 69 focus groups in the Acholiland, Lango and Teso sub-regions, and with 39 key informants to provide a degree of cultural interpretation of responses from the focus groups. The report concludes that perceptions on the virtues of amnesty, domestic prosecution, the ICC and local or traditional practices are very mixed (United Nations, Office of the High Commissoner for Human Rights 2007). The other survey, conducted by researchers from the Berkeley–Tulane Initiative on Vulnerable Populations and the International Center for Transitional Justice (ICTJ), produced similar results: there are high levels of support for a traditional approach, but a majority of interviewees wanted the perpetrators of grave human rights violations to be held accountable (forthcoming publication).

Cultural attitudes also have an influence on views on truth commissions. In his report on the TRC in Sierra Leone, Tim Kelsall argues that, in the absence of strong ritual inducement, the public telling of the truth 'lacks deep roots in the local cultures' of that country (Kelsall 2005: 363). A similar situation exists in Burundi and Rwanda.

3.4.2. How to merge different strategies?

Most of the countries studied as part of this project combine traditional justice and reconciliation instruments with other strategies for dealing with the legacy of civil war and genocide: in Mozambique with an amnesty act; in northern Uganda with an amnesty act and the intervention of the ICC; in Rwanda with the Arusha court, national tribunals and Gacaca meetings; in Sierra Leone with a special court and a truth commission. (Burundi is an exception to that rule. Its Ubushingantahe is neither formally nor informally involved in the actual programming of transitional justice.) How do these strategies interrelate? How can interpersonal and community-based practices live side by side with state-organized and/or internationally sponsored forms of retributive justice and truth telling?

(This is not a problem that is unique for Third World countries in general, or African post-conflict societies in particular. The search in Western Europe and North America for a justice mechanism that can complement a purely punitive approach has generated renewed interest in traditional non-state systems of dealing with crime. In Australia,

New Zealand, Canada and the United States traditional justice systems belong to the aboriginal heritage and have recently been revived. Interest in restorative justice programmes is on the rise in other Western countries but this is based more on progressive contemporary philosophies of justice than on a forgotten local tradition. One example is victim–offender reconciliation programmes. That formula has been used predominantly to handle fairly minor crimes, although initiatives in conflict contexts such as Northern Ireland have tried to extend the concept.)

Our case studies report a considerable diversity in the reception of traditional mechanisms. There is a clear aversion in most political circles in Burundi. Mozambique is a case of passive tolerance. It is, however, useful to remember that in such contexts certain dangers may emerge. Victor Igreja and Beatrice Dias-Lambranca write that '*magamba* and other similar post-war phenomena run the risk of being wrongly used by the national political elites. For instance, political elites can use the success of *magamba* spirits and healers as arguments to justify their option for post-war amnesties, impunity and silence'. Official recognition of the value of reconciliation and cleansing rituals has been the reaction in Sierra Leone. But their incorporation into the workings of the TRC has been rather weak. The June 2007 Juba agreement between the Ugandan Government and the LRA plans full integration of the *mato oput* ceremonies into the national policy on the war crimes of the past. Rwanda is the only country where a local accountability instrument has been wholly part of the official policy. This chapter has already mentioned the problems that arise in such situation.

> Most of the countries studied as part of this project combine traditional justice and reconciliation instruments with other strategies for dealing with the legacy of civil war and genocide. How can interpersonal and community-based practices live side by side with state-organized and/or internationally sponsored forms of retributive justice and truth telling?

* * *

This chapter has collected information on the similarities and differences between the tradition-based justice and reconciliation mechanisms in the countries in focus. An evaluation of their real or potential role after violent conflict is the subject of the concluding chapter.

References and further reading

Allen, Tim, *Trial Justice: The International Criminal Court and the Lord's Resistance Army* (London: Zed Books, 2006)

Baines, Erin K., 'The Haunting of Alice: Local Approaches to Justice and Reconciliation in Northern Uganda', *International Journal of Transitional Justice*, vol. 1 (2007), pp. 91–114

Baines, Erin, Stover, Eric and Wierda, Marieke, *War-affected Children and Youth in Northern Uganda: Toward a Brighter Future* (Chicago, Ill.: John D. and Catharine T. MacArthur Foundation, 2006)

Kelsall, Tim, 'Truth, Lies, Ritual: Preliminary Reflections on the Truth and Reconciliation Commission in Sierra Leone', *Human Rights Quarterly*, no. 27 (2005), pp. 361–91

Orentlicher, Diane, 'Settling Accounts Revisited: Reconciling Global Norms with Local Agency', *International Journal of Transitional Justice*, vol. 1 (2007), pp. 10–22

Penal Reform International (PRI), *Access to Justice in Sub-Saharan Africa: The Role of Traditional and Informal Justice Systems* (London: PRI, 2002)

Shaw, Rosalind "Remembering to forget: Report on local techniques of healing and reconciliation for child ex-combatants in Northern Sierra Leone" (USA: Tufts University, 2002), p. 6

Sierra Leone Truth and Reconciliation Commission, 'Reconciliation', Final Report, 2004, Vol. 3B, chapter 7, available at <http://trcsierraleone.org/drwebsite/publish/v3b-c7.shtml>

Tutu, Desmond, *No Future Without Forgiveness* (London: Rider, 1999)

United Nations, *The Rule of Law and Transitional Justice in Conflict and Post-Conflict Societies: Report of the Secretary-General*, UN document S/2004/616, 23 August 2004

United Nations, Office of the High Commissioner for Human Rights (OHCHR), *Making Peace Our Own: Victims' Perceptions of Accountability, Reconciliation and Transitional Justice in Northern Uganda* (New York: United Nations, 2007), available at <http://www.ohchr.org/english/docs/northern_Uganda_august2007.pdf>

Waldorf, Lars, 'Mass Justice for Mass Atrocity: Rethinking Local Justice as Transitional Justice', *Temple Law Review*, vol. 79, no. 1 (2006), pp. 1–88

CHAPTER 2

CHAPTER 2

The Gacaca courts in Rwanda

*Bert Ingelaere**

1. The Rwandan conflict

Before 1994, Rwanda was an almost unknown country hidden in the heart of Africa. On 6 April 1994, however, the aircraft carrying the then President Juvénal Habyarimana was shot down over the skies of the capital, Kigali. This signalled the start of a campaign of genocidal violence against the Tutsi minority ethnic group and the so-called 'moderate' Bahutu belonging to the majority ethnic group but opposed to the regime in place. In the space of 100 days, approximately 800,000 people died. These tragic events shocked the world and placed Rwanda on the global map. The Rwandan genocide took place in the context of a civil war and an attempt gone awry to introduce multiparty democracy. It was the violent apex of a country history marked by sporadic eruptions of ethnic violence as a consequence of the struggle over power (and wealth) over the course of time—a struggle grafted on to the Hutu–Tutsi ethnic bipolarity that marks the Rwandan socio-political landscape. The Bahutu are the majority ethnic group with approximately 84 per cent of the population, 14 per cent of the population are Batutsi and 1 per cent are Batwa.[1]

1.1. The distant origins of the conflict (up to 1962)

There is no general consensus on Rwandan history in pre-colonial times. There are two main interpretations of this period. One was propagated by the former (Hutu) regime, especially during the 1994 genocide; the other is supported by the current regime. Selectivity in the use of the available sources and the nature of the interpretation given to

* The author would like to thank Stef Vandeginste and Luc Huyse for their valuable comments on earlier drafts of this chapter. The final text has greatly benefited from their support. The usual disclaimer applies.
[1] The author has used the forms 'Bahutu' and 'Batutsi' rather than 'Hutu' and 'Tutsi' as being more faithful to the original language. Muhutu and Mututsi are the respective singular forms. The roots, 'Hutu' and 'Tutsi', have been preferred for the adjectival form.

crucial ancient institutions which structured the interaction between the different social groups, such as clientship (*ubuhake*) and forced labour (*uburetwa*), defines the reading of history. This section briefly sketches the main threads of these readings of history. The truth, as always, probably lies in between.

Before independence in 1962, the country was a kingdom. A Tutsi king (*mwami*) and aristocracy ruled over the masses, who were predominantly Bahutu. A central kingdom was engaged in the continuous endeavour to conquer and control surrounding territories in order to exploit the Hutu population. The Batutsi were pastoralists rearing large herds of cattle. They invaded the region centuries ago and managed to subjugate the Hutu population of agriculturalists, tillers of the soil. The Bahutu had equally, although earlier, migrated to the region that became known as Rwanda. But, while the Bahutu had come from other regions in the centre of Africa and were considered to be descendants of the Bantu race, the Batutsi were thought to originate from the North, being of Semitic or Hamitic origin. The Batwa were considered to be the original inhabitants of the region. This is one reading of the past.

Another version of this pre-colonial history, currently in vogue in Rwanda, rather than emphasizing the distinct geographical and racial origins of the groups inhabiting the country, stresses the unity of the people of Rwanda—the *banyarwanda*—and Rwandan citizenship based on a common thread—'Rwandanicity' (*Ubanyarwanda*), or 'Rwandaness'. Hutu and Tutsi were originally not racial categories, but socio-economic classes. *Abatutsi* (in the plural) was the name given to wealthier persons possessing cattle. Poorer families, with only little or no land, and no cattle, were referred to as the *abahutu*. Mobility was possible. A family obtaining cattle became 'tutsified'; those losing status degraded into a situation of 'hutuness'. Colonialism then further 'created' ethnic groups out of a perfectly harmonious society whose only divisions were socio-economic ones.

Less controversy surrounds the impact of colonialism on the social fabric of Rwandan society. The impact was decisive, but the idea that it also sowed the seeds of the genocide that was to happen is contested by some, while it is assumed by others. Rwanda was first colonized by Germany (1897–1916) and in 1919 it became officially a colony of Belgium. Several far-reaching reforms, and especially the method of indirect rule employed by the Belgian colonizer, were to alter Rwandan society. In line with the anthropological ideas of the time, the Belgians believed in the classification of races according to superior and inferior beings. They came to the conclusion that the Tutsi 'race' was more fit to rule than the Bahutu, who were inferior creatures only apt to be governed and to do manual labour. They used the Tutsi rulers to implement their colonial policies. The Tutsi power-holders adapted to this new situation easily since not only was alignment with the colonial ruler a prerequisite for staying in power, but it also sharply increased this power, their control of the (Hutu) population and, subsequently, their wealth. Racial identity—ethnicity—became institutionalized, for example, through the introduction of the ethnic identity card.

The year 1959 was marked by a social revolution—an event unimaginable a few years before—that became known as the 'Hutu revolution'. In a wave of successive events between 1959 and 1962, local Tutsi rulers were ousted from their communities (on their hills) and replaced through elections by 'burgomasters', predominantly of Hutu origin. Grégoire Kayibanda, a Muhutu, became the first president of Rwanda. These events were accompanied by violence against the Tutsi rulers and their families, and a first wave of Batutsi sought refuge in neighbouring countries. A second and larger wave followed in 1963–4, when the Batutsi of the first wave had regrouped and attacked Rwanda from Burundi and Tanzania. A significant number of Batutsi were killed in reprisal attacks and even more left the country as refugees. These attacks and the violent reaction of the Rwandan regime foreshadowed what was to happen 30 years later. The descendents of these refugees would form the bulk and backbone of the Rwandan Patriotic Front (RPF) and its military wing the Rwandan Patriotic Army (RPA) that attacked Rwanda in October 1990, seeking an armed return to their country.

1.2. Bahutu and Batutsi under the Habyarimana regime

The ideological underpinnings of the Rwandan republics (1962–73, under President Kayibanda, and 1973–94, under President Habyarimana) 'constituted both a reversal and a continuation of [these] long-standing psychocultural images' (Uvin 1998: 33) of the foreign, racially superior Tutsi pastoralist and native, subaltern Hutu cultivator which had been reinforced under colonial rule. Bahutu and Batutsi remained distinct categories after the social revolution, but Batutsi now became the inferior creatures in a newly regained 'natural order' of Hutu homogeneity. These ideas were institutionalized through a policy of ethnic quotas by which Batutsi were allocated 9 per cent of government positions (with no real power) and the same percentage of places in schools and at universities. But, despite these crippling opportunity constraints, the ordinary Tutsi population inside Rwanda lived without overt physical targeting during the height of the Second Republic.

A second legitimization strategy was based on the intertwined notions of 'development' and 'peasantry'. The image of Rwanda as an autarkic nation of peasants valuing 'manual labour' reverberated through Habyarimana's speeches. The single political party was denominated the National Revolutionary Development Movement (Mouvement Révolutionaire National pour le Développement, MRND), while the parliament was the National Development Council (Conseil National du Développement, CND). The president was the key political actor, but he exercised power together with an oligarchy of northern Bahutu, members of his and, mostly, his wife's clan. They constituted what became known as the Akazu (little house), controlling the state and its (monetary) privileges. The entire system was directed towards the maintenance of the status quo. In the pyramidal, hierarchical state structures, chains of command went deep into rural life. These institutional structures were to play an important role in mobilization and generating momentum during the 1994 genocide.

1.3. Civil war, multiparty democracy and genocide (1990–4)

A range of factors initiated a political transition in Rwanda. A wave of democratization accompanied the end of the cold war; French President François Mitterrand obliged francophone Africa to democratize in order to secure a continuation of economic assistance; a drop in coffee prices on the world market and the introduction of a structural adjustment programme resulted in a socio-economic crisis; and in October 1990 Rwanda was attacked by the Ugandan-based and Tutsi-dominated RPF rebel force, demanding a return to their country of origin and a share in power. These circumstances pressured the Habyarimana regime to initiate liberal reforms. A revision of the 1978 constitution heralded a fundamental change: multiparty politics was endorsed and political parties blossomed. At the same time, an external politico-military movement, the RPF, was fighting its way into Rwanda, claiming a share in power and forcing the incumbents to the negotiating table.

Converting to multiparty politics after decades of single-party rule and undertaking institutional reforms while at the same time waging a war in an overpopulated country turned out to be a daunting exercise. Three political currents/actors were at play during this period of transition: the presidential movement, being the elite in power; the internal 'democratic' opposition constituted by the newly created political parties; and the RPF and its supporters as the armed opposition. The internal opposition forces drove the political and institutional reforms. A new constitution allowing political parties to organize was followed by the installation of a coalition government. The opposition forces used this access to the state apparatus to reform the political system further and undermine the incumbent regime. The Arusha Peace Agreement was signed on 4 August 1993 after a year of negotiations: internal reforms were supplemented by a negotiated settlement on power sharing between the three political currents and on the integration of the rebel forces into the national army. The agreement entailed not only the further disentangling of the MRND from the machinery of state; it also implied that the incumbent elite, with the president and the northern Akazu at the centre, saw its privileged position slip away.

The Arusha Agreement was never implemented. Despite the peace talks and the agreement, Rwanda had 'settled in a war culture' (Prunier 1998: 108). Violence had become a way of doing politics, not only on the battlefield but also in the streets of Kigali and in the hills in the countryside. With the opening up of the political arena, the newly established political parties started to recruit members. Rallies were organized in the countryside where inspiring speeches and free drinks were aimed to convince the peasants to adhere to this or that political 'family'. In this atmosphere the once well-oiled, but totalitarian, machinery of state quickly fell apart. In areas where the invested authorities were (politically) ousted from their communities this created a power vacuum. In particular, the youth wings attached to the political parties played an important role in the terror campaign. The Coalition for the Defence of the Republic (Coalition pour la Défense de la République, CDR) had its Impuzamugambi ('those with a single purpose'), the Inkuba ('thunder') were the youth wing of the Democratic Republican Movement

(Mouvement Démocratique Républicain, MDR), the Social Democratic Party (Parti Social-Démocrate, PSD) had its Abakombozi ('the liberators'), and the ruling party, the MRND, had the Interahamwe ('those who work together').

Later, with the war continuing, the political process more grim and the peace talks contested, some of these youth groups would turn into outright militia, trained and armed by the army. They would spearhead the genocide together with the army and a large part of the administrative personnel. The term Interahamwe was originally restricted to members of the youth wing of the MRND and the militia that grew out of it. However, after the genocide, all those who had participated or were suspected of participation in the genocide received the qualification 'Interahamwe', even if they had never been an 'official member'. The expression was inflated.

While the insecurity caused by the political parties affected all ordinary citizens during these years of turmoil, the Batutsi were those most often targeted. They were called *ibiyitso*, accomplices of the rebel force, because of their alleged connection in conspiracy with the RPF—for one single reason: they were of the same ethnic identity which dominated the rebel group. Immediately after the start of the war in October 1990 a significant number of Batutsi were arrested throughout the country and locked up for a period. At regular intervals, and often in retaliation for RPF attacks or advances, massacres of Tutsi civilians were instigated. This not only echoed the 1963–4 revenge killings; it also 'established patterns for the genocide of 1994' (des Forges 1999: 87).

Although a peace agreement had been signed, President Habyarimana, under severe pressure from the hardliners, had no intention of implementing it. He referred to the agreement in a speech as a mere 'scrap of paper'. Preparations for a resumption of war were being made, on the side of the RPF as well. Both sides were engaged in destabilizing and terrorist activities and political assassinations. By early 1994, the enemy had been identified. Through intensive media and government propaganda, the enemy threatening the rule of the *rubanda nyamwinshi* (the great majority) became a threat to the rule of the Hutu ethnic majority. The (perceived) danger therefore was coming not only from outside, through the invasion, but also from within, from every single Tutsi citizen living in Rwanda, and by extension through every single Muhutu who was not in favour of the status quo of the reigning *rubanda nyamwinshi*. Stories and reports of the RPF massacring Bahutu along its way into Rwanda stirred the imagination and strengthened the fear. Thus it was felt/perceived that the threat had to be eliminated. The slogan 'Hutu power' (*Hutu pawa)* found its way through the hills; Batutsi were stigmatized as *inyenzi* (cockroaches).

In this highly explosive atmosphere, Habyarimana's aircraft was shot down when approaching the airport in Kigali as he was returning from a regional summit meeting in Tanzania. That same night, of 6 April 1994, a massive extermination campaign started. Events moved rapidly in the capital. Some rural areas reacted spontaneously to the call for action; others resisted for a long time and outside force was necessary in order to start the killings. The militia, the army, police forces and the bulk of the state personnel drove the killings throughout the country.

It is important to note that Bahutu who were not in favour of the genocidal campaign or were vehemently opposed to the Habyarimana regime, or were in some way connected to Batutsi, also became victims of the violence. What is puzzling, however, is the high level of involvement of ordinary citizens, the Hutu peasantry, who became involved in the genocidal campaign to track down, pillage and eventually kill their Tutsi neighbours.

1.4. The causes and dynamics of the conflict: the main paradigms of interpretation

A consensus has arisen in the vast literature available on the Rwandan tragedy on the fact that the genocide had little to do with apolitical 'tribal warfare' between ethnic groups. Nevertheless, the main paradigm used by observers to interpret the 1994 genocide is the ethnic character of the conflict: the majority ethnic group—the Bahutu—attempted to achieve the complete extermination of the minority ethnic group—the Batutsi.

Other paradigms focus on elite manipulation; ecological resource scarcity; the socio-psychological features of the perpetrators; and the role of the international community (Uvin 2001).

The 'elite manipulation paradigm' explores the desire of the Rwandan elite to stay in power. The RPF invasion and the following war, the international power-sharing agreement and the pressure for democratization followed by the birth of the political opposition all threatened the monopoly of power and the privileges of Rwanda's elite. This elite was ready to use all means to survive politically and keep a hold on the privileges associated with state power. This 'elite manipulation paradigm' fits neatly with the 'socio-cultural features of Rwandan society paradigm'. A powerful elite, desperate to stay in power, makes use of the highly centralized state structure, with command lines that go deep into rural life, to mobilize an 'obedient', 'conformist' and 'uncritical' army of peasants, even if this means slaughtering their neighbours.

Another paradigm focuses on the importance of 'ecological resources'. The argument is that Rwanda's resource scarcity, combined with the highest population density in Africa and high population growth rates, was fertile soil for genocidal violence.

The role of the international community has also received a great deal of attention in the past few years. The focus is mostly on the months preceding and during the genocide. The argument is that the nature of the (in)action of international stakeholders paved the path towards genocide, either intentionally—implicitly—or unintentionally. It is also argued that the long-standing presence of the international community in Rwanda in the form of development enterprise fuelled the momentum of the genocide through its apolitical and socially and culturally ignorant presence in the country.

Macro-level paradigms for explanation fail to capture the dynamics and experience of violence at the local level. Apart from the need to understand the general causes of the conflict in order to prevent a recurrence, it is equally important to explore the conflict dynamics at the lowest levels of society. We have already mentioned the degree of involvement of ordinary citizens in the looting and killing. It is important to understand the unfolding of the genocide in small, face-to-face communities, since the bulk of the transitional justice work is being done at this level through the Gacaca courts. The court system is designed to operate at the lowest units of society, as we argue below. Comparative micro-analysis of the genocide demonstrates that the violence unleashed at the macro level was appropriated and fundamentally shaped by the micro-political matrixes and social formations in which it took hold. Genocide, although shaped from above, was significantly reshaped in a highly differentiated terrain of local social tensions and cleavages, regional differences and communal or individual particularities. The genocidal violence reflected both the goals of the supra-local forces and factors—mainly the Hutu–Tutsi cleavage mobilized by political actors for political purposes—and their local shadows—struggles for power, fear, (intra-group) coercion, the quest for economic resources and personal gain, vendettas and the settling of old scores (Ingelaere 2006).

1.5. Post-genocide Rwanda

The RPF took over power on 4 July 1994 and ended the genocide. The defeated government and its armed forces fled to the neighbouring Democratic Republic of the Congo (DRC) and a large part of the population followed. The consequences were felt way beyond the Rwandan borders and caused regional instability and insecurity for years to come. Although the genocide machine came to a halt after 100 days in July 1994, violence remained the order of the day. Fieldwork in Rwanda reveals that Rwandans have known a decade of violence between 1990, with the start of the civil war and the introduction of multiparty politics, and the end of the 1990s, when overt hostilities on Rwandan soil ceased. From 1996 onwards, after the violent dismantling of the camps in the DRC, the defeated government forces and the Interahamwe militia attacked northern Rwanda from their basis in the DRC. This came to be known as the war of the infiltrators (*abacengezi*), in which hundreds—most probably thousands—of civilians were killed. Since it was difficult to distinguish infiltrators from civilians, the RPA gradually resorted to brutal counter-insurgency strategies to pacify the region.

The RPF as the military victor was able to set the agenda for post-genocide Rwanda without much constraint. President Paul Kagame has repeatedly indicated that he 'wants to build a new country'—a wish that needs to be taken literally. Liberation from a genocidal order is one of the underlying ideological vectors and legitimization strategies. A bold social engineering campaign has been instituted in the post-genocide period in order to translate into practice the vision incorporating the following set of ideas. The RPF can be seen as aiming to create the *true* post-colonial Rwanda. The colonial powers distorted the essence of Rwandan culture and this colonial mindset sustained the first two republics. Rwandanness or Rwandanicity, not ethnicity, should define relations between state and society. Building or (re-)establishing this unity of Rwandans goes together with eradicating the 'genocide ideology'. Reconciliation, an element that had begun to dominate the post-1994 ideological framework by the end of the 1990s, is also couched in terms of unity, while the overall objective of justice for genocide crimes (in the sense of accountability) has been one of the cornerstones of the regime. Home-grown traditions derived from the Rwandan socio-cultural fabric need to replace imported, divisive practices. Gacaca is one of them. These institutions are seen as part of what is called 'the building of a democratic culture' that is in essence conceived as being 'closer to the consensus-based type of democracy' (Rwanda 2006a: 151).

> The Gacaca courts are part of the policy of creating a true post-colonial Rwanda and restoring unity. Home-grown traditions need to replace imported, divisive practices.

The choice and installation of the Gacaca courts fit perfectly into this vision. They are a home-grown, almost pre-colonial resource; the courts are meant to fight genocide and eradicate the culture of impunity, and they need to reconcile Rwandans by (re-)enforcing unity.

2. The 'old' and the 'new' Gacaca

The Gacaca court system as it currently functions in Rwanda is often referred to in terminology and descriptions as if it were identical, or at least similar, to the 'traditional' conflict resolution mechanism known as the Gacaca. However, the relation between the 'old' and the 'new' Gacaca is not one of identity, and not even one of gradual continuity. There is a difference in kind. An essential change marks the installation of the Gacaca courts after the genocide. The resemblance lies in the name, a similar orientation in the most general sense, and common features, but one needs to look beyond these most visible elements of similarity to understand the true nature of the 'old' and the 'new' institution and capture the rupture with the past. The 'new' Gacaca courts are in the truest sense an 'invented tradition'. While any 'traditional' institution transforms over time due to social change in general, discontinuity prevails in the case of the Gacaca. State intervention through legal and social engineering has designed and implemented a novelty, loosely modelled on an existing institution.

This section will therefore not focus on the 'gradual' evolution of the Gacaca, but will first highlight what is known about the 'old' institution, focusing on it at close range at different periods, and then turn to the system that is dealing with genocide crimes. The

> The 'new' Gacaca courts are an 'invented tradition'. State intervention through legal and social engineering has designed and implemented a novelty, loosely modelled on an existing institution. There is a difference in kind between the 'old' and the 'new' Gacaca.

distant history of the Gacaca suffers from the same problem as that highlighted above related to Rwanda's ancient history in general. There are not many sources available and opportunities for twisting or manipulating the evidence are rife. We summarize the main threads of the ancient institution and its gradual change over time by relying on the few written sources that are available. These sources are complemented by information disclosed by older people during interviews collected during fieldwork in all the regions of Rwanda.

Our understanding of the Rwandan context and the functioning of the Gacaca court system is based on 18 months of fieldwork, carried out between July 2004 and April 2007, in several rural Rwandan communities. Through a range of methods—(participant) observation, life-story interviews, semi-structured interviews, group discussions and survey questionnaires—the author and his Rwandan collaborators consulted approximately 1,300 ordinary Rwandans, predominantly peasants. We observed over 280 Gacaca sessions (700-plus trials) in ten communities located in different regions of the country, and resided for longer periods in the communities in order to understand the Gacaca process in the economic and socio-political context of the localities.

2.1. The Gacaca as 'traditional' dispute settlement mechanism

To fully understand the origins and purposes of the ancient practice of *gacaca*, it needs to be placed in the cosmology of the Rwandan socio-political universe of the time. The extended lineage or family (*umuryango*) was the main unit of social organization. It encompassed several households (*inzu*), the smaller lineages and units of society. Age and sex defined status within the lineage. Only aged and married men without parents were independent; all others, and especially women, were dependent upon them. The *inzu* lineage head was responsible for the observation of the ancestral cults, arranged marriages, paid or received debts and controlled the collective title on land or cattle. The lineage was the primary source of protection and security. A person had no autonomous existence; the family unit was the guarantor of security.

Political structures were superimposed over the lineages. Around the 17th century, Rwanda consisted of several smaller territories governed by kings. The king *(mwami)* at one and the same time governed things profane and the link with the supernatural. He embodied power, justice and knowledge: judicial and political powers were not separated. The *mwami* was the ultimate arbitrator, assisted by the *abiru*, the guardians of tradition. However, a popular saying goes: 'Before something is heard by the *mwami*, it needs to be brought before the wise men'. This refers to the fact that problems were addressed first at the lowest units of society, by the lineage heads. In practice this happened in what came to be known as *gacaca* gatherings.

It has become common wisdom that the word '*gacaca*' means 'justice on the grass'. In fact, the name Gacaca is derived from the word '*umugaca*', the Kinyarwandan word referring to a plant that is so soft to sit on that people preferred to gather on it. These gatherings were meant to restore order and harmony. The primary aim of the settlement was the restoration of social harmony, and to a lesser extent the establishment of the truth about what had happened, the punishment of the perpetrator, or even compensation through a gift. Although the latter elements could be part of the resolution, they were subsidiary to the return to harmony between the lineages and a purification of the social order.

Colonialism had a decisive impact on Rwandan society as a whole, and thus on the Gacaca as well. During the colonial period, a Western-style legal system was introduced in Rwanda but the Gacaca tradition kept its function as a customary conflict resolution mechanism at the local level. The colonial powers' stance towards Rwandan society was marked by indirect rule: indigenous institutions maintained their functions. However, despite the policy of indirect rule, the presence of the colonial administrators altered and weakened that which existed before their advent. At the judicial level, this is most obviously visible through the introduction of written law and a 'Western' court system imposed over the 'traditional' institutions. The latter continued to function but were hierarchically inferior to the new system. Serious cases such as manslaughter were now to be handled in the Western-style courts. Similarly, the king lost his unique position as cornerstone of the traditional institutions, and hence he and his chiefs gradually lost authority and legitimacy in the execution of judicial powers. This also implied that the legitimacy of the Gacaca courts waned.

> Colonialism had a decisive impact on Rwandan society as a whole, and thus on the Gacaca as well. A Western-style legal system was introduced but the Gacaca tradition kept its function as a customary conflict resolution mechanism at the local level. It represented both the justice of proximity and a handy mechanism to relieve the pressure on the ordinary court system.

After independence, Gacaca gradually evolved into an institution associated with state power as local authorities were supervising (or taking on the role of) *inyangamugayo* (local judges). As the modern state became more powerful, it gradually absorbed the informal and traditional. In that way the institution of Gacaca evolved towards a semi-traditional or semi-administrative body. Some new elements came to the fore: certain fixed procedures were followed, notes were taken, meetings were held on fixed days and so on. The institution functioned as a barrier so that quarrelling parties would not immediately (have to) resort to the formal court system at the provincial level (*court de canton*). If possible a dispute was settled at this lowest unit of society, as happened with the majority of cases. If necessary the case was forwarded to the higher court. Gacaca represented both the justice of proximity and a handy mechanism to relieve the pressure on the ordinary court system. Despite the introduction of some formal elements and its instrumental relation with the overarching judicial structures, the conciliatory and informal character of the Gacaca remained the cornerstone of the institution since decisions were to a great extent not in conformity with written state law (Reyntjens 1990: 36).

It is interesting that the Gacaca as it existed after independence still exists today, although it is no longer called the Gacaca. It can be said still to exist in two senses. First, on several occasions during the fieldwork we observed local authorities trying to solve the problems of the inhabitants in their locality. In fact, it is one of the most important tasks of the local administrators. Some referred to their activities as a sort of Gacaca. But even the role local authorities play in the resolution of these local disputes had greatly diminished with the installation of the Abunzi, a committee of mediators, by the end of 2004. From observation of the type of disputes it settles, the sort of penalties it can impose and the style of mediating, in its features and scope this activity resembles the Gacaca as it existed before the genocide. However, this mediation committee has been almost totally formalized and incorporated into the machinery of state power as well. As with the modern Gacaca courts, the Abunzi function according to codified laws and established procedures; but their decisions are still often inspired by custom.

2.2. (Re-)Inventing Gacaca

The possibility of using the Gacaca emerged in the immediate wake of the genocide, as a United Nations High Commissioner for Human Rights (UNHCHR) report reveals (UNHCHR 1996). These reports are the result of the research and reflection of a number of Rwandan researchers and professors working at different institutions. Not only did they investigate the nature of the ancient Gacaca, but fieldwork also established that the Gacaca was already functioning in its semi-traditional way in some areas immediately after the end of the genocide. This was initiated either by the population or by the administrative authorities. A letter from the prefect of the province of Kibuye dated November 1995, appended to the UNHCHR 1996 report, reveals that in some areas the administrative authorities took the initiative to support and widely instigate the functioning of the Gacaca practice they found in some localities. The minutes of a meeting between the population of a community and a representative of the Interior Ministry in March 1996 is proof of the fact that the government condoned the informal or semi-traditional functioning of the Gacaca. This support was informal, since it was not part of official policy, and it had no legal and institutional framework. It seems clear that the Gacaca mostly functioned as it did before the genocide, meaning that it dealt with minor disputes within the population.

The spontaneous emergence of the Gacaca activities and the gradual support for Gacaca by the authorities was clearly motivated by the fact that the ordinary justice system was virtually non-existent after the genocide. The Gacaca had to do what it did before—relieve the pressure on

> After the Rwanda genocide, the Gacaca was already functioning in its semi-traditional way in some areas, condoned by the government. The ordinary justice system was virtually non-existent.

the ordinary courts. These were now not working slowly, as they did before, but not working at all. Once they started to work, they were quickly overloaded with the cases of genocide suspects who were filling the prisons.

A new element came into play in the practice of *gacaca* in the post-genocide era—genocide-related offences and the consequences of the genocide. Crimes related to property, the main focus of the 'ancient Gacaca' but now committed during the genocide—the destruction of houses, the theft of cows and household utensils, the appropriation of land and so on—were brought before the *inyagamugayo* and the local authorities. Observation of current Gacaca court activities reveals that in cases of accusations of looting, offenders might dig up documents dating back to the years immediately after the genocide to prove that they had already restored the property they looted or reimbursed the damage they had done. The initial settlement was often struck in the context of such a (semi-)informal Gacaca meeting with the authorities often initiating the action, supervising it and providing proof (the documents used in the cases brought for the current Gacaca courts) that compensation had been paid.

> A new element came into play in the Gacaca practice in the post-genocide era—genocide-related offences and the consequences of the genocide.

The 1996 UNHCHR report states that it was an absolute taboo to talk about killings during the Gacaca sessions in those initial years after the genocide. People found tackling these crimes too sensitive a matter. Neighbours and family members seem to have covered up for those who might have taken part in the killing. However, the letter of the prefect of Kibuye mentions that the Gacaca meetings should collect the names of those implicated in the violence. Consultations in other communities where the Gacaca functioned at that time also established that people thought it should function as a mechanism to restore order and harmony in society, and reconcile families and neighbours.

In the light of the observations made of the practice of *gacaca* they found existing in the years 1995–6, reflection on the origins and nature of the ancient Gacaca and the nature of the genocidal violence, the authors of the UNHCHR report concluded that the Gacaca institution could play a role in dealing with the genocide-related crimes. They made a number of recommendations (see box 2).

Box 2: The role of the Gacaca in Rwanda: recommendations of the UNHCHR

• The violence experienced during the genocide and massacres was of such a gravity that it simply cannot and should not be handled in the Gacaca.
• Gacaca could function as a sort of truth commission with two aims. On the other hand, collecting facts about the atrocities experienced in local communities. Information would be forwarded to the classical tribunals. On the other hand, as a space to reunite Rwandans and to debate the common values they share, a mechanism that helps people to live together and be reconciled.
• Caution should be exercised against too much government intrusion, and the institution should not be subverted into becoming a formal tribunal.

Source: United Nations High Commissioner for Human Rights (UNHCHR), *Gacaca: Le Droit Coutumier au Rwanda* (Kigali, 1996), *passim*.

It is clear that the recommendations of the UNHCHR report were never seriously considered, let alone followed. In 1999, after a period of reflection and a round of consultation, a commission established by the (then) Rwandan President Pasteur Bizimungu proposed to modernize and formalize the 'traditional' dispute resolution mechanism in order to deal with the approximately 130,000 persons imprisoned for offences related to the genocide at that time—a task the 'ordinary' justice system could not accomplish in a satisfactory way. This commission was the result of and worked in the context of the so-called Urugwiro meetings which took place between May 1998 and March 1999. Every Saturday, a meeting was held at the president's office with 'representatives of Rwandan society' to discuss serious problems facing the Rwandan people. Proposals for solutions were debated. The question of justice and dealing with the genocide was given a prominent place on the agenda. The possible use of Gacaca was discussed. Serious reservations were expressed by some of the participants, but countered by arguments in favour by the proponents. Box 3 summarizes the main arguments of both sides found in the resulting report (Rwanda 1999).

Box 3: The arguments for and against the use of Gacaca made during the reflection meetings with the President, 1998–9

Arguments against
• Trying crimes of genocide and massacres in Gacaca would minimize the seriousness of these crimes.
• Can ordinary people who are not educated and acquainted with judicial procedures take care of these serious offences themselves?
• Family relations and friendships would render the trials partial. It would be very difficult to make people tell the truth, and in some parts of the country there would be nobody left to testify.
• It would be better if the Gacaca were used as an investigative mechanism, providing the classical courts with information.
• Trials by the Gacaca of accusations of genocide and massacres would create new conflicts and tensions in the local population.
• Would the Gacaca be in accordance with international laws?

Arguments in favour
• Letting Gacaca courts deal with genocide crimes does not imply a trivialization. On the contrary, it would make people deal with the crimes of genocide and other crimes against humanity at the level where they happened. The building of a new Rwanda needs to be done by every Rwandan.
• People are not so uneducated that they cannot be educated. The Gacaca system should be explained to the population and those responsible trained and assisted by lawyers.
• The danger that the truth might not surface and that partiality might prevail is real, but other participants can give contradictory evidence. This will make it possible to counter these tendencies.
• Gacaca would not only investigate but also punish. A truly participatory form of justice would give power to the population to deal with the violence experienced in their midst. After its use for genocide-related offences, it would be turned into a system dealing with common crime.
• Gacaca would accelerate the process of dealing with the backlog of genocide-related cases; it would stop the culture of impunity by singling out those who actively participated in the killings.
• The crime of genocide is an exceptional crime and needs an exceptional solution to deal with it.

Source: Rwanda, *Report on the Reflection Meetings Held in the Office of the President of the Republic from May 1998 to March 1999* (Kigali: Office of the President of the Republic, 1999).

The report makes clear that the idea of unity was being widely debated and propagated, and the focus lies on the need to rebuild the country. However, a common theme underlying the discussions in those years, as the report also makes clear, is the objective of eradicating the culture of impunity—a quest for accountability. The word 'reconciliation' is hardly mentioned, especially not in the section on justice. The notion of reconciliation or restorative justice that is currently attached to the Gacaca court system only surfaced in the years that followed, and the Urugwiro meetings may have been the breeding ground for its introduction in public discourse. But the Gacaca court system was initially conceptualized in an atmosphere where the objective of accountability dominated. The report notes that the use of community service as an alternative penalty should be examined but in such a way as to avoid 'disturbing the government's policy of eradicating the culture of impunity' (Rwanda 1999: 57). It mentions that the name 'Gacaca jurisdictions' should be used to suggest that the Rwandan heritage is a source of inspiration for the new court system which nevertheless has the same competence as the classical courts ('jurisdiction'). The blueprint of that type of Gacaca can be found in the report of the Urugwiro meetings. It is the embryo of what was later codified in law, implemented and constantly adapted.

> The Gacaca court system was initially conceptualized in an atmosphere where the objective of accountability dominated. The notion of reconciliation or restorative justice that is currently attached to the Gacaca court system only surfaced in the years that followed.

2.3. The design and practice of the Gacaca court system

The actual experience, functioning and outcome of the Gacaca courts—their scope and limitations—are in the first place defined by the way they were conceived before implementation. As is explained above, the court system was conceived during the Urugwiro meetings and has undergone several modifications in the course of time based to a certain extent on the findings from the pilots in 751 localities which started in 2002. Here we focus on the features of the system since its nationwide implementation in 2005.

> The Gacaca courts are Rwanda's main transitional justice instrument. They fit into the underlying stated objective of accountability with overtones referring to reconciliation.

The Gacaca courts were installed to prosecute and try the perpetrators of the crime of genocide and other crimes against humanity, committed between 1 October 1990 and 31 December 1994. The Gacaca process has five goals—to:

- establish the truth about what happened;
- accelerate the legal proceedings for those accused of genocide crimes;
- eradicate the culture of impunity;
- reconcile Rwandans and reinforce their unity; and
- use the capacities of Rwandan society to deal with its problems through a justice based on Rwandan custom.

To facilitate the process, three fundamental principles, or cornerstones, were incorporated into the genocide and Gacaca legislation. On the one hand, there is a popularization or decentralization of justice by installing numerous courts in every administrative unit of society. This procedure is modelled on the traditional Gacaca with lay persons presiding as judges and the active involvement—not only the physical presence—of the entire population as a 'General Assembly'. On the other hand, there is the principle of plea bargaining to increase the amount of evidence and available information. Plea bargaining was instituted to facilitate the collection of evidence. A defendant must give as much detail as possible of the offence (how, where, when, victims, accomplices, damage, etc.) and apologize in public in order to have his confession accepted and his sentence reduced. Through a presidential decree of 2003 one could, in principle, have one's sentence reduced by revealing information about crimes committed. A confession considered as complete and sincere, accompanied by a request for pardon, was the prerequisite for provisional release from prison. This fuelled the confessions in the prison Gacaca which started as early as 1998.

Motivation to confess originates in the pressure of the state through awareness campaigns, but it also has a strong religious undertone. Although a significant number of detainees have made 'total' confessions, there is a general perception that these testimonies are only partial, admitting minor crimes, and blaming some people for complicity—mostly those already deceased or 'disappeared' after the genocide—while keeping silent on the involvement of others.

These two cornerstones facilitate the surfacing of the truth, which subsequently functions as the basis of the entire transitional justice framework in post-genocide Rwanda. The truth is the information needed to identify the nature of guilt or innocence, to conduct trials of accused persons, to disclose locations in order to exhume victims, to identify the modalities of reparation, to generate knowledge of the past in general and to reconfigure and re-establish social relations.

> The surfacing of the truth is the basis of the entire transitional justice framework in post-genocide Rwanda.

A third crucial feature is the principle of categorization by type of offence. Suspects of genocide crimes and crimes against humanity are prosecuted in a system of parallel courts. Those identified as the persons most responsible and the orchestrators of the violence are tried by the ordinary courts, while others are judged by the Gacaca courts. Suspects are therefore categorized in three categories according to the crime(s) they have committed. The category determines which court should prosecute and the range of penalties applicable. The penalty varies not only according to the seriousness of the offence but also according to whether the perpetrator has confessed the crime(s) and when he made a confession. A new organic law came into effect in March 2007, modifying the 2004 law (see table 1). The changes cannot be applied retroactively.

Three fundamental principles, or cornerstones, were incorporated into the genocide and *gacaca* legislation—the popularization or decentralization of justice by installing numerous courts in every administrative unit of society; the principle of plea bargaining to increase the amount of evidence and available information; and the principle of categorization by type of offence.

Table 1: The Gacaca court system in Rwanda: categorization and sentencing

(a) June 2004–March 2007

	Cat. 1	Cat. 2, 1st & 2nd	Cat. 2, 3rd	Cat. 3
Crime	1. Planners, organizers, supervisors, ringleaders 2. Persons who occupied positions of leadership 3. Well-known murderers 4. Torturers 5. Rapists 6. Persons who committed dehuminazing acts on a dead body	1. 'Ordinary killers' in serious attacks 2. Those who committed attacks in order to kill but without attaining this goal	3. Those who committed attacks against others, without the intention to kill	Those who committed property offences
Court	Ordinary court	Sector Gacaca	Sector Gacaca	Cell Gacaca
Sentence *Without confession*	Death penalty or life imprisonment	25–30 years	5–7 years	Civil reparation
Confession before appearence on the list of suspects	25–30 years	7–12 years*	1–3 years*	Civil reparation
Confession after appearence on the list of suspects	25–30 years	12–15 years*	3–5 years*	Civil reparation
Accessory sentence	Perpetual and total loss of civil rights	Permanent loss of a listed number of civil rights	/	/

* Commutation of half of sentence to community service on probation.

(b) March 2007 onwards

	Cat. 1	Cat. 2, 1st, 2nd & 3rd	Cat. 2. 4th & 5th	Cat. 2, 6th	Cat. 3
Crime	1. Persons who occupied positions of leadership 2. Rapists	1. Well-known murderers 2. Torturers 3. Persons who committed dehumanizing acts on a dead body	1. 'Ordinary killers' in serious attacks 2. Those who committed attacks in order to kill but without attaining this goal	Those who committed attacks against others, without the intention to kill	Those who committed property offences
Court	Ordinary court	Sector Gacaca	Sector Gacaca	Sector Gacaca	Cell Gacaca
Sentence *Without confession*	Death penalty or life imprisonment	30 years or life imprisonment	15–19 years	5–7 years*	Civil reparation

	Cat. 1	Cat. 2, 1st, 2nd & 3rd	Cat. 2. 4th & 5th	Cat. 2, 6th	Cat. 3
Confession before appearance on the list of suspects	20–24 years	20–24 years*	8–11 years*	1–2 years*	Civil reparation
Confession after appearance on the list of suspects	25–30 years	25–29 years*	12–14 years*	3–4 years*	Civil reparation
Accessory sentence	Permanent loss of a listed number of civil rights	No confession: permanent loss - Confession: temporary loss of a listed number of civil rights	No confession: permanent loss - Confession: temporary loss of a listed number of civil rights	/	/

* Commutation of half of sentence to community service on probation; one-sixth of the sentence is suspended and one-third of the sentence is served in custody.
Source: *Official Gazette of the Republic of Rwanda*: Organic Law no. 16/2004 of 19 June 2004, and Organic Law no. 10/2007 of 1 March 2007.

Since 2005, Gacaca meetings have been held in each of Rwanda's 9,013 cells and 1,545 sectors. A cell in Rwandan society coincides with a small face-to-face community, comparable to a neighbourhood in an urban setting. This is the lowest administrative level. A sector is like a small village and groups together several cells. In total there are 12,103 Gacaca courts established nationwide, presided over by 169,442 *inyangamugayo*, the local judges. These judges are elected among the populace and no legal training, experience or other education is required. The defining characteristic is that they must be 'persons of integrity'. Most of the Gacaca courts are situated in rural face-to-face communities, but they are installed in every administrative unit nationwide, and thus also in the cities. It is in an urban environment that the Gacaca process encounters the most problems regarding its most basic operational functioning. Migration, urban anonymity and individuality undermine the prerequisites of the Gacaca process—shared knowledge about the past and the fact of daily living together.

There have been two phases in the Gacaca process. During the first phase, which took place at the administrative level of the cell between January 2005 and July 2006, information was collected in every cell through confessions and accusations. In practice, four tendencies were observed. First, this phase was characterized by the extensive involvement of state authorities executing and supervising a task normally allocated to the judges. Second, it was only possible to collect testimonies *à charge*, or accusations. The population could only validate the information already collected or add some more incriminating testimonies. Testimonies *à décharge* (in defence of the accused) were not recorded and needed to be reserved for the trial phase, it was explained. Third, there was the possibility of idiosyncratic interpretation and application of the guidelines set out by the National Service of the Gacaca Jurisdictions (Service National des Juridictions Gacaca, SNJG) depending on the locality. This created an element of arbitrariness in a process that was supposedly applied uniformly. Fourth, according to estimates based on the pilot proceedings, only 5 per cent of the pending cases were the result of confessions.

There was therefore a shift from confessions—the plea-bargaining procedure installed to encourage the exposure of the truth about the past—to accusatory practices. This created a particular and unexpected atmosphere in the local communities and greatly increased the number of people accused.

At the end of the information collection phase, the categorization was done by the lay judges presiding over the Gacaca court of the cell. Their decision to place a person in a certain category is based on information gathered during the initial phase of the Gacaca process, which takes place at this lowest unit of society. Although the elected judges take the decision to categorize a person, the information and evidence on the basis of which this is done come from a confession of a perpetrator and/or through accusations from members of the 'General Assembly' of the court at this level, being the entire population of the cell. Statistics provided by the SNJG indicated that by the end of the information collection phase 818,564 persons would be prosecuted for genocide-related crimes nationwide. Of those persons, 44,204 are not in the country and 87,063 are dead. Estimates in 2004 based on the results during the pilot phase already indicated that approximately 750,000 people would stand accused. Table 2 shows the shares of each category.

Table 2: Genocide-related prosecutions in Rwanda: number of suspects in July 2006

Category 1	77,269
Category 2	432,557
Category 3	308,738
Total	**818,564**

Source: Rwanda, *Report on Collecting Data in* Gacaca *Courts* (Kigali: National Service of the Gacaca Courts, 2006).

In July 2006 the second phase (the trial phase) started. Trials for those placed in the second category take place at the sector level. The information collected in the previous phase is used to conduct the trials of the accused and those who have confessed. It should be noted that in several localities information collection had not been completed and continued while trials were being held. During the trial phase the elected judges at the Gacaca court of the sector summon the parties in the case—the accused or the person who has confessed, and the accuser or victim (often the accuser is the victim, but not always). Often the accused are living free in the community. Sometimes those accused during the information collection phase have been put in preventive detention on the orders of the *inyagamugayo* in order to prevent them from fleeing. They, together with those put in detention in the immediate aftermath of the genocide, are transported to their home villages. The judges read the compiled case files—the collected testimonies—aloud, and hear the parties and possible witnesses or other persons who wish to intervene. When the case has been sufficiently examined, they deliberate among themselves and pronounce the verdict in public.

The person convicted has the possibility to appeal. His /her case can be reviewed by the Gacaca appeal court of the sector, which is composed of another group of elected judges, residents of the same locality. If a person receives a prison sentence, he or she is immediately taken into custody; if they have already served the sentence decided upon while in detention awaiting trial, they are set free. Since mid-2007, with an overload of new prisoners congesting the prisons since the start of the Gacaca process, convicts have first had to serve a period of community service. This happens in work camps, but is envisioned to be decentralized to the level of the respective communities.

Monthly progress reports indicate that in this period (July 2006–February 2007) an average of approximately 10,000 persons a month were tried. Table 3 gives an overview of the trial activities between 15 July 2006 and the end of February 2007. After March 2007, the trial procedures were modified again.

Table 3: Activities during the Gacaca trials in Rwanda, July 2006–February 2007

No. of cases tried	No. of sentences pronounced	Prison sentence	Community service	Acquittals	Appeals	Changes of category
71,405	64,800	33,233	16,348	15,219	7,200	2,889

Source: SNJG Monthly Progress Reports (on file with author).

In theory, the trials phase would last until all cases had been dealt with. However, since early 2007, the government has started increasingly pressuring the judges to speed up their work. The end of 2007 was the (ambitious) deadline, and has already been postponed. In some places, however, Gacaca activities came to an end during the course of 2007. The new law makes it possible to install numerous courts in one locality instead of the single court that existed before. As 432,557 persons needed to be tried at a pace of 10,000 a month, it would take another three and a half years to complete the exercise. Since March 2007, therefore, approximately 3,000 courts have been added to the 12,103 already existing. Some sectors have up to 12 courts functioning at the same time. Initially, there was a fixed day in the week when Gacaca meetings were held but, to speed up the trials, many localities with a great number of cases were obliged to hold two a week. A Gacaca court examines between one and more than ten cases a day. Moreover, almost 80,000 persons were placed in the first category. These people need to be tried through the classical court system. This is almost as many as the number initially incarcerated and it would be a sheer impossibility for the ordinary courts to process them.

Property offences are handled in the Gacaca courts at the level of the cell. There are two possibilities at this level. First, the parties to the dispute, victim and offender, can arrive at an amicable settlement related to the type and amount of restitution. The judges then only supervise and ratify the agreement. Second, if there is no mutual understanding, a trial takes place with the same procedures as identified above. Finally, the judges come to a decision on the nature of the restitution. It is important to note that for these offences restitution is not individualized; it is a family affair. This has no legal basis, only a customary basis.

The Gacaca process is very complex in the perception and experience of the ordinary Rwandans. Older people in particular can compare with the past since they may have had first-hand experience of the 'old' institution. They often refer to the Gacaca courts as 'an instrument of the state'. The current Gacaca is installed by the state with rules and people taking notes, while the traditional version was much more straightforward in its functioning and objective. The idea was to bring people together, talk about the problem or conflict in order to restore harmonious relations, and prevent hatred lingering on between families. Before, measures taken were mostly symbolic and restorative in nature through punishments that took the form of reparation for the harm inflicted, while the current courts aim at the punishment of individuals through prison sentences.

> The difference between the old and the new Gacaca is not one of degree but a difference in kind. The current Gacaca is installed by the state with rules and people taking notes. The traditional version was much more straightforward in its functioning and objective. The idea was to bring people together, talk about the problem or conflict in order to restore harmonious relations, and prevent hatred lingering on between families. Measures taken were mostly symbolic and restorative in nature through punishments that took the form of reparation, while the current courts aim at the punishment of individuals through prison sentences.
>
> Only when amicable settlements are made in property cases and when the judges thus function as a sort of supervising committee for the reconciliation attempt can the spirit of the older Gacaca be discerned.

The old Gacaca was mostly used for minor offences, although apparently it could also be used for cases of manslaughter. The arrival of colonialism may have had a modifying influence on the functioning of the Gacaca in that regard, by prohibiting its use for serious crimes. The current Gacaca has problems in establishing the truth, but an equally unaltered and traditional use of the Gacaca would have been inadequate to deal with the numerous problems related to the genocide. In the current Gacaca, the element of reconciliation between families (and individuals) is no longer at the centre of the institution or is even not present.

We have already mentioned that the difference between the old and the new Gacaca is not one of degree but in kind. The biggest resemblances between the current and the ancient Gacaca can be found on the level of the cell, where the Gacaca courts are dealing with property offences. There are two possibilities—a settlement or a trial. Only when amicable settlements are made and when the judges thus function as a sort of supervising committee for the reconciliation attempt can the spirit of the older Gacaca be discerned.

2.4. Other transitional justice mechanisms and objectives

The Gacaca courts are Rwanda's main transitional justice instrument. They fit into the underlying stated objective of accountability with overtones referring to reconciliation, as we have argued above. Apart from the Gacaca courts, although in the background and at a much slower rate, other transitional justice strategies have been adopted, and different mechanisms have been installed. The main responsibility for achieving accountability had originally been placed on the ordinary Rwandan justice system. But the tribunals of first instance simply could not handle the vast number of cases. The classical justice system dealt with 10,026 cases between 1997 and 2004.

In November 1994, UN Security Council Resolution 955 established the International Criminal Tribunal for Rwanda (ICTR) to prosecute individuals responsible for crimes of genocide and other violations of international law in order to ensure that these kinds of gross violations of human rights would not go unpunished. The relation between the ICTR and the Rwandan Government has always been difficult, mostly because of the possibility that the tribunal might also investigate war crimes committed by RPF soldiers and their commanders. But the track record of the tribunal is also flawed. Its outreach towards ordinary Rwandans is virtually nil. On Rwandan soil the tribunal is portrayed and (thus) perceived as an instance of the Western way of doing justice—highly inefficient, time-consuming, expensive, and not adapted to Rwandan custom. As with the ICTR proceedings held outside Rwanda in Arusha, in neighbouring Tanzania, there have been other trials held in third countries. Based on universal jurisdiction laws, trials in Switzerland in 1999 and in Belgium in 2001, 2005 and 2007 have contributed to the quest for accountability.

> On Rwandan soil the International Criminal Tribunal for Rwanda is portrayed and perceived as an instance of the Western way of doing justice—highly inefficient, time-consuming, expensive and not adapted to Rwandan custom.

Alongside this dominant 'punitive' approach, a more restorative component has been added by the establishment of the fund for the assistance of the survivors of the genocide (FARG). A fund especially preserved for the compensation of victims (Fonds d'Indemnisation, FIND) was also conceived but never became operational. Community service, which is closely connected with the Gacaca courts, also contributes to a more restorative and compensatory approach to the past.

A National Unity and Reconciliation Commission (NURC) was set up in 1999 with a mandate that can be summarized as 'promoting unity and reconciliation', most visible through the organization of the Ingando solidarity camps for reintegration and re-education. More important seems to be that the establishment of the NURC marked a shift away from an exclusively retributive approach to an additional reconciliatory element. Only in recent years has a discourse of reconciliation started to surface. Now every socio-political initiative, from poverty alleviation programmes to resettlement schemes to political decentralization, is framed in the language of 'reconciliation', 'strengthening unity', 'empowerment' and the 'rebuilding of social relations'. Despite this change in atmosphere, the Gacaca courts have difficulty shedding the retributive approach to justice which lies at their core. As is indicated above, they were conceived in a time when the objective of (or the payment of lip-service to) reconciliation was not as prominent as it is today.

2.5. The main stakeholders and actors

A closer look at the list of participants in the Urugwiro meetings where the Gacaca court system was conceived reveals the involvement of members of the government, members of important state institutions, representatives of the army and the police, and representatives of the (tolerated) political parties. For the discussion on justice, members of the judiciary and some lawyers were also invited. Considering the final modality of the political transition—military overthrow—and the subsequent balance of power, with the RPF dominant in all domains of social and political life, it is no wonder that the discussion on the nature of justice in the aftermath of genocide and war was carried without many 'alternative' ideas and other projects for Rwandan post-genocide society. It was a discussion among peers, all the more so because of the absence of 'civil society'.

There was no trace of members of civil society during the discussions, nor were they involved in the process whereby the Gacaca courts were conceived. This is hardly a surprise. Civil society was almost non-existent during the Habyarimana regime. What existed only added up in quantity, not in quality. A healthy civil society normally has a history to rely on and a socio-political environment in which it can thrive. The former is lacking in Rwanda because of the historical precedents of dictatorship, and the latter is lacking because of the deliberate choice of a new political elite. The minister of local governance, social affairs and development in the post-genocide regime, Protais Musoni, describes the Rwandan regime's position on civil society succinctly: 'There are two debates on the role of civil society organizations in developing countries by international scholars. On one side civil society is seen as a counter power to government, and on the other civil society is seen as an effective partner in service delivery and the development process. Rwanda favours the latter approach' (Musoni 2003: 14–15).

Victims' associations such as Ibuka, the umbrella association for genocide survivors, are the rare domestic voices to be heard. Their position is in general supportive of the Gacaca process but with critical interventions when problems arise, especially when genocide survivors are harassed as a result of their participation in the Gacaca process. Ibuka is also able to organize at the local level. We frequently observed meetings held by members of Ibuka to discuss the Gacaca proceedings in their localities. Ibuka representatives coming from outside the communities often advise or caution villagers who survived the genocide on their behaviour towards released prisoners or strategies to be adopted during the Gacaca sessions. These instructions do not always correspond with the government line on the Gacaca courts—which are also forwarded to the local level during numerous sensitization campaigns—but they do not fundamentally question the framework within which the government policy is laid out.

The churches, long the sole possible environment in which counter-hegemony to the government could develop, are solicited to spread a positive image of the Gacaca process. The Catholic Church, the biggest religious institution, accepts the submissive part it has to play, most probably also because of the role some of its members played in the massacres.

> Ibuka, the umbrella association for genocide survivors, is in general supportive of the Gacaca process but with critical interventions when problems arise, especially when genocide survivors are harassed as a result of their participation in the Gacaca process.

Foreign donor countries also have a high stake in the judicial activities in post-genocide Rwanda and the Gacaca court system in particular. Some even call the phenomenon in Rwanda 'donor-driven justice' (Oomen 2005). After an initial period of reluctance, most donors came to support the newly created Gacaca court system out of an awareness that it was the less bad of two possible options for tackling the past—on the one hand classical (retributive) justice which would not be able to manage and resolve that past, and, on the other hand, imperfect, unknown and revolutionary justice.

At the local level, we can identify several social groups that play a role in the Gacaca process. These groups are identity-based and often have different stakes in the Gacaca proceedings, and therefore also portray divergent stances towards the institution. The group formation on the periphery of the Gacaca arena is not simply ethnic. Since 1994, new identities have come into play. They are subcategories of the main cleavage dominating Rwandan society—the Hutu–Tutsi bipolarity.

The Batutsi can be divided into genocide survivors and 'old caseload returnees'. The former lived in Rwanda before the genocide and survived the mayhem. The latter are either former refugees or descendants of the refugees who left Rwanda after the Hutu revolution. They often settled in cities after their return to Rwanda following the genocide. Others, ordinary peasants, mostly returned to their region of (family) origin. They only play a minor role in the Gacaca proceedings. They were not affected by the genocide in the locality where they currently live. Often they are among the Gacaca judges in their community or they might intervene in the proceedings by making some general comments.

The survivors, on the other hand, are the main stakeholders in the Gacaca process at the local level. They are almost always of Tutsi identity, with only a few exceptions. Fieldwork observations make it clear that there are, in general, three defining parameters necessary to be able to make a legitimate claim as a victim seeking justice for 'wrong done' in the Gacaca courts: one needs to have suffered persecution—not simply to 'have lost'—between October 1990 and December 1994; persecution because of having a certain

> The survivors often see the results of their testimonies in the Gacaca—imprisonment or community service in work camps—as being to the sole benefit of the state.

identity; or 'identity-based' persecution because of belonging to the Tutsi ethnic group, which currently makes one an officially recognized survivor. Survivors are the catalysts of the Gacaca proceedings in that they testify, make accusations and provide information on the past. But, although they are knowledgeable about the events during the genocide in general, and more specifically about what happened to them personally, they survived because they were in hiding and thus their knowledge is limited. Their evaluation of the Gacaca courts is mixed. They see them as an opportunity to find more information on the locations where the bodies of deceased family members were thrown, or as a way to find some compensation in kind for the losses or to see those responsible for past crimes punished for their actions. However, they are also aware that their testimonies incriminating others cause 'bad relationships' with the families of the accused and imprisoned. They often see the results of their testimonies in Gacaca—imprisonment or community service in work camps—as being to the sole benefit of the state.

Among the Bahutu, four groups can be distinguished in a local community. First, there are the prisoners who are absent from daily village life and are only transported to the village when their own trial takes place. Their families are present, however, and approach the Gacaca courts as a means to get their loved ones set free. Second, a community also contains liberated prisoners who have confessed in prison and therefore been released. They are closely monitored by the authorities. Often they play an important role in the Gacaca proceedings by accusing fellow villagers, Bahutu who have never been imprisoned but were somehow implicated in the genocide. If their own confession is sincere and if they are personally convinced that revealing the truth about the past is a necessity, they function as expert witnesses and are often consulted by the *inyagamugayo*. However, their sincerity creates serious conflicts between them and those they accuse. Outright intimidation or more subtle means are employed to silence or to forge an alliance with them. The same tactics are used to influence the behaviour of the genocide survivors. Sometimes killings take place to get rid of witnesses. In general, the perception is that these released prisoners only made partial confessions in order to get out of prison, admitting minor crimes, accusing others of complicity—the deceased or disappeared—and keeping silent on the involvement of yet others. Two Hutu subgroups remain—those accused in the Gacaca and others who are not accused. The first subgroup live in fear of an upcoming trial with an unpredictable outcome. Those in the second group are relieved that they are not accused, but are very careful not to get into conflict with anyone since they are aware that current conflicts can be dragged into the Gacaca arena to be settled under the guise of an alleged genocide crime.

Initially, the *inyagamugayo* were, as tradition prescribes, 'old and wise men'. After several months, however, a significant number of them had to be replaced because they were accused in the Gacaca themselves. By November 2005, 26,752 or 15.7 per cent of the judges had to be replaced because they were suspected. They were replaced by women, younger people and genocide survivors. The Gacaca bench often contains a mixture of survivors (Batutsi) and 'non-survivors' (Bahutu). Sometimes the judges are only Hutu or only Tutsi. The ethnic composition of the bench is seen as a means to get a viewpoint passed. The judges received short training on the law and procedures. Every district (that is, approximately every ten sectors) has a coordinator to supervise the Gacaca activities. This is the person who can be consulted by the judges.

The local authorities generally do not play an overtly active role in the Gacaca proceedings but they are always present, together with some security forces, and they have received instructions from higher authorities that they need to monitor the Gacaca's activities closely and write reports. Some strictly judicial tasks such as information collection have been assigned to the local authorities, with the population and the judges only playing a secondary role. They mobilize the population in sensitization campaigns and take notes on the attendance of the people living in their administrative area. Failure to participate in the Gacaca means either being fined or refusal of service delivery when contacting the local administration. In that sense the Gacaca is, paradoxically, a form of unpopular participatory justice, with large crowds of uninterested people physically present but psychologically absent or unsupportive of the activities. Those who speak are predominantly the judges, the survivors and a small group of liberated prisoners.

> The Gacaca is, paradoxically, a form of unpopular participatory justice. Attendance is compulsory. The large crowds that attend are physically present but psychologically absent or unsupportive of the activities.

2.6. Life in the post-genocide era and the advent of the Gacaca courts

In the ten years between the genocide and the start of the Gacaca trials, victims and those who were involved in the violence but had no leading role during the genocide lived together again on their respective hills—not always as neighbours now, since survivors have often been grouped into resettlement sites, but still in the same vicinity. They therefore had to develop a way of life and ways in which to interact with each other. It is important to understand these strategies and tactics employed in daily life in the decade before the state-sanctioned installation of the Gacaca courts. It allows us to verify whether their arrival facilitated or disturbed a natural process of 'dealing with the past'. Living together was not so much a personal choice, but a simple necessity.

This cohabitation was initially marked by mutual fear, diminishing progressively with the passing of time. After 2003, this fear intensified from time to time with every wave of liberation of detainees who had confessed in prison. Until 2005—the start of the Gacaca—the consequences of the genocide were mostly phrased in terms of material and human losses. Distrust between the different ethnic groups was present, but lingered under the surface of social life. Out of necessity, life returned to a form of normality and cohabitation. Life in the hills is highly pragmatic. Tensions and conflicts are kept in the dark because neighbours and villagers depend upon each other in their daily activities and their fight for survival in conditions of shared impoverishment.

'Thin' reconciliation differs from the 'thick' version, in Rwanda as elsewhere. Cohabitation—*kubana*—is a matter of necessity, which may become less fearful for those directly involved as time passes, but interpersonal reconciliation—*ubwiyunge*—is a matter of the heart and a state of feeling in a social relation. Rwandans, and especially survivors, often refer to the 'heart' when talking about the events of the past and expressing the nature and level of trust and confidence they have in their neighbours, fellow villagers or members of the other ethnic group. In the Rwandan context, the heart is the force unifying the human being. It is the centre of reception of outward impulses and the locus of interior movement. Emotions, thoughts and will are interconnected and unified in the heart. The heart is inaccessible to others but is where the truth lies. Due to the violence experienced in their midst, 'the hearts have changed'.

> In the Rwandan context, the heart is the force unifying the human being. Emotions, thoughts and will are interconnected and unified in the heart. The heart is inaccessible to others but it is the locus where the truth lies. Due to the violence experienced in their midst, 'the hearts have changed'.

The heart has changed because of the crimes committed, the violence experienced or the dehumanizing acts observed. Living conditions, the social universe and daily interactions have changed to a form of normality again, but this outward appearance of normality does not reveal a great deal about the interior of someone. Outward appearances are deceptive, as popular expressions acknowledge: 'the mouth is not always saying what resides in the heart' or 'the rancorous stomach, you give it milk and it vomits blood'. Daily actions and interactions had become a way of dealing with the past, in a positive or negative sense: the crossing on the pathway to the fields, the offer and sharing of banana beer in the local cabaret (pub), the invitation to a wedding or the helping hand when transporting a sick person to the hospital might have been catalysts in the restructuring of emotions and relationships. Meanwhile accusations of witchcraft, threats or suspicions of poisoning, the (interpretation of) the blink of an eye or the failure to invite someone to a ceremony are enough to increase distrust. Sometimes alliances have been struck between victims and perpetrators, out of necessity, but sometimes also out of choice. Exploring and engaging in these practices was a means of inspecting the humanity of the other, crystallized in the heart.

> The general perception that the Gacaca courts did not reveal the truth about the past implies not only that factual knowledge remains absent, but that a re-humanization and re-socialization of the other—the healing dimension of truth-telling—is not easily forthcoming.

Engaging the past in these daily practices and encounters had developed over the years. What we call truth telling, rendering justice, fostering reconciliation or providing compensation (or the reverse emotions, such as vengefulness or distrust) had taken root in the ambiguities of local life. Engaging the past became enmeshed in the web of a tightly knit face-to-face community, difficult to understand from the perspective of an outsider who is used to different preconceived categories of what is taken for granted.

In any case, silence about the past was the order of the day. Things 'from before' were known or suspected but not spoken about aloud. The heart of the other person was only tacitly explored. The arrival of the Gacaca courts changed this situation significantly. They did not come as catalysts of a natural, if very difficult, process of cohabitation that had already started. They came to alter it in substance: as we have argued above, speaking, revealing or hearing the truth is the cornerstone of the court system. The (nature of) participation in the Gacaca sessions has become the activity to probe the (nature of the) heart of the other. From its installation, the truth had to be spoken in a state-sanctioned manner. The general perception on the part of the Rwandan people that the Gacaca sessions did not reveal the real truth about the past and therefore the truth of the heart for the 'other' is one of the most problematic aspects of the Gacaca court system. It implies not only that factual knowledge remains absent, but that a re-humanization and re-socialization of self and the other—the healing dimension of truth-telling—is not easily forthcoming. What Gacaca facilitated for some it disturbed or destroyed for others.

> In the decade before the state-sanctioned installation of the Gacaca courts, the survivors of the genocide had to develop ways of living together and interacting with each other. Engaging the past became enmeshed in the web of a tightly knit face-to-face community, difficult to understand from the perspective of an outsider. Silence about the past was the order of the day. The arrival of the Gacaca courts changed the natural but difficult process of cohabitation that had already started.

3. Evaluation: strengths and weaknesses

Most of the features of the Gacaca have a strong and a weak side, either because there are two dimensions to the feature or because it is perceived from a different angle. An overview of the most striking characteristics follows. We present them along a continuum from the strongest (points 1–3) to absolute weakness (points 5–7). Point 4 at the centre of this spectrum embodies as many strengths as weaknesses.

1. *Ordinary Rwandans prefer the Gacaca courts over the national courts and the ICTR* for dealing with the genocide crimes. For the ordinary peasant the classical tribunals are both physically and psychologically remote institutions. Although their thoughts on the ICTR may be partly mediated by the media reports and sensitization campaigns, they sincerely prefer the justice of proximity, despite its problems.

> Ordinary Rwandans prefer the Gacaca courts over the national courts and the ICTR for dealing with the genocide crimes.

2. *Women have taken up an important role in the Gacaca proceedings.* This is in line with developments in other domains of Rwandan society. The old Gacaca, like society as a whole, was dominated by men. While the genocide was equally mainly a male thing, women have come to play a key role in the reconstruction efforts. The Gacaca nevertheless remains biased against women because of its inadequacy for fully addressing sexual crimes. Provisions have been made to allow women to testify on sexual crimes, for example, through in camera sessions. But the embedding of the Gacaca in a local face-to-face community makes it difficult to tackle these crimes.

3. *The Gacaca proceedings are speeding up the backlog of genocide-related cases.* The Gacaca trials are breaking all records in quantitative terms. They will not only effectively deal with the approximately 130,000 persons incarcerated after the genocide, but also handle the thousands more who were unexpectedly accused when the Gacaca courts started operating on the hills in the countryside. There will be mass justice for mass atrocity, in quantitative terms. There is less certainty about their performance in a qualitative sense.

> The Gacaca trials will not only effectively deal with the approximately 130,000 persons incarcerated after the genocide, but also handle the thousands more who were unexpectedly accused when the Gacaca started operating on the hills in the countryside. There will be mass justice for mass atrocity, in quantitative terms. There is less certainty about their performance in a qualitative sense.

4. *The Gacaca court system is contradictory.* Contradiction is ingrained in the Gacaca court system and the reconciliation process in Rwanda. The post-genocide political regime has adopted a discourse of reconciliation over the course of time but it does not want to give it the chance to succeed. It obstructs that which it facilitates at the same time. It has conceived and implemented the Gacaca court system in the name of unity and reconciliation, but the legal and social engineering within an ancient institution and the behavioural attributes—the practice of governing—of the post-genocide regime are the biggest stumbling blocks to a genuine form of reconciliation. The domains in which these contradictions are manifest include the following.

> The post-genocide political regime has adopted a discourse of reconciliation over the course of time but it does not want to give it the chance to succeed. It obstructs that which it facilitates at the same time. The legal and social engineering within an ancient institution and the behavioural attributes— the practice of governing—of the post-genocide regime are the biggest stumbling blocks to a genuine form of reconciliation.

(a) *Fine-tuning or disaster management?* The Rwandan Government has shown its openness to adjustment of the process over the course of time. Several changes have made the system more effective and efficient. The gradual changes have altered the system by incorporating more restorative components—the reduction of sentence after a sincere confession and the prominent place of community service. All in all, however, the modifications have come about rather slowly and are relatively minor, as can be seen from table 1 comparing the 2004 and 2007 laws. And what looks like fine-tuning from one angle seems to be disaster management from another.

(b) *The court system is at once everything and nothing*. The changes and modifications have altered the Gacaca courts into a hybrid institution with elements of the original informal conflict resolution mechanism but now fully incorporated into the formal judicial system. This makes the court system innovative, with different traditions and objectives possibly reinforcing each other, but it also makes it fragile when the heterogeneous sources of inspiration and intended outcomes tend to be irreconcilable or might neutralize each other. The Gacaca courts are at one and the same time a centralized and a decentralized justice system: they embody the installation and completion of a process at the local level, while controlled and guided from above. It is also a formal and an informal way of doing justice. The courts are also a blend of retributive and restorative justice with 'confessions *and* accusations, plea-bargains *and* trials, forgiveness *and* punishment, community service *and* incarceration' (Waldorf 2006: 52–3). But, as is argued above, at their core lies retributive justice. They are, further, claimed to be home-grown, inspired by customary justice but in accordance with international human rights standards. Based on numerous observations of the practical functioning of the courts, we conclude that the Gacaca courts are a novelty, on the one hand, mimicking a traditional conflict resolution mechanism but with the reduced potential for reconciliation, while, on the other hand, they mimic the modern legal system, with a reduced guarantee of due process.

> The Gacaca courts are a hybrid of the original informal conflict resolution mechanism fully incorporated into the formal judicial system—at one and the same time a centralized and a decentralized justice system—a formal and an informal way of doing justice and a blend of retributive and restorative justice. On the one hand, they mimic a traditional conflict resolution mechanism but with a reduced potential for reconciliation, while, on the other hand, they mimic the modern legal system, with a reduced guarantee of due process.

(c) *Peasants or judicial technicians: can the subaltern speak?* In Rwanda the real non-state administration of justice is taking place outside the Gacaca activities, in line with what is described in section 2.5. A thorough assessment and understanding of the social practices of the population in question is necessary to verify whether an adaptation or implementation of a traditional justice and reconciliation mechanism will be productive. The strength of traditional justice mechanisms probably lies in the fact that they function in line with the socio-cultural habitat of the population in their daily activities. This may not be seen as an effective way of dealing with the past from the perspective of a human rights body, but it is *the way of the local population*, partly out of necessity, partly out of choice. Paradoxically, the activities of the Gacaca to a certain extent go against the practices already developed over time to deal with the past. They do not fit into the pragmatism of the peasant's lifestyle and are not adapted to the realpolitik of the micro-cosmos. This confirms their status as an 'invented tradition' and a rupture with the past. Moreover, there is a severe deficiency in the historical and cultural understanding of the ancient Gacaca, and the conception and implementation process of the modern Gacaca does not take into account the socio-political dimensions and consequences of the process. 'We only apply the law' has been the dominant response of the regime in general and the lawyers, and the majority of the non-governmental organizations, implementing and assisting the Gacaca process. A narrow legalistic approach can be a safeguard in the interactions with government officials in a closely monitored and tightly closed-off socio-political environment, but it also implies self-imposed partial blindness to a number of the elements at stake. A customary-inspired mechanism needs a culturally sensitive approach.

(d) *It is both too decentralized and not decentralized enough.* As is mentioned above, the ordinary Rwandan prefers the justice of proximity over national or international courts or other judicial bodies.

The fact that the Gacaca courts are operating in the natural living environment of those involved lives up to this desire. However, the Gacaca and the reconciliation process in Rwanda in general are an extremely state-driven, state-owned and top–down process with people abiding by the principles, mechanisms and discourses laid out for them. To give some examples: state officials became involved in a judicial procedure and circumvented the 'ownership' of the population when they started filtering out 'real' category 1 suspects in order to reduce the number of accused in that category. Part of the truth cannot be spoken, as we will see again below: the state controls what can be aired, creating self-censorship within the population. At the same time, the Gacaca courts, with their harsh retributive powers, are too decentralized. They operate in the social constellation of local communities all of which are characterized by their particular demographic make-up, power structure and existing conflicts. This creates the possibility for people to forge alliances or the need to follow a certain strategy in the practice of 'accusing' or 'conspiring in silence', not necessarily reflecting the procedure envisioned. This is linked first and foremost to the capacities and capabilities of individuals. The power of authority, money or the gun allows some to influence the proceedings. But it is also a result of the power of sheer numbers, the (ethnic) composition of the collective. When survivors are few and isolated they tend to keep quiet in order not to be (physically or socially) eliminated from the community or their testimonies are partially ignored. When survivors are numerous, part of the (administrative) power structure and represented on the bench of the Gacaca courts, they have more leverage—a situation that can then create the feeling of powerlessness and arbitrariness on the part of released prisoners and the accused.

(e) *Revenge, retribution or reconciliation?* We observed that the ritualistic coming together in the context of the weekly Gacaca sessions alters the strained relations, especially between the released prisoners and survivors. The importance of ritual in general, whether or not in the context of the use of a traditional conflict resolution mechanism in the aftermath of violent conflict, has often been observed, especially in an African context. But we need to distinguish between a ritual *sensu strictu* and the ritualistic dimension of a process to fully understand the effect of the Gacaca sessions. The traditional Gacaca was not a ritual, nor is its modern version. It is the repeated act of coming together in the Gacaca sessions, irrespective of what is done there in the sense of content, that seems to have a transformative influence on social relations with those encountered in those meetings. But the substance of the encounters is handled according to the purely prosecutorial logic which limits the discursive aspects normally connected with ritual doings or the dialogical and healing dimension of truth-telling processes. The ongoing Gacaca activities demonstrate only a limited potential to evolve towards trust between ethnic groups, empathy for each other's position and losses in the conflict, and a culture of democratic deliberation and dialogue. This results from the fact that the Gacaca courts function according to the logic of criminal trials and not as small truth and reconciliation commissions. In that way, the Gacaca process perpetuates the cleavages it is supposed to eradicate.

(f) *Contextual factors hinder and facilitate the Gacaca proceedings.* The Gacaca trials are not taking place in isolation. Extreme poverty has made people resort to questionable tactics and strategies in the Gacaca proceedings. Survivors lack an adequate reparation policy. Families of convicted perpetrators lose the most important source of income when the head of the household is taken away to serve his sentence. Moreover, the rule of law has not yet taken root in Rwanda. Extrajudicial killings on the periphery of the Gacaca activities are seriously hampering the stated objectives. They instil fear within the population. Moreover, Rwanda is no democracy (yet). Freedom of choice and opinion are not easily forthcoming. People are guided in their

The ritualistic coming together in the context of the weekly Gacaca sessions alters strained relations, especially between the released prisoners and survivors. It is the repeated act of coming together in the Gacaca sessions, irrespective of what is done there in the sense of content, that seems to have a transformative influence on social relations. But the substance of the encounters is handled according to the purely prosecutorial logic. The Gacaca courts function according to the logic of criminal trials and not as small truth and reconciliation commissions.

choice during elections and the local administrative structures are conceived with a balance between appointed and elected positions. Authorities occupying appointed positions at the local level form a shadow government to the 'elected' administrative authorities. Accountability goes upwards to authorities higher up, not downwards to the population. All the key figures in the (local) administration are members of the RPF and most of them belong to the minority ethnic group. This usurpation of power by one ethnic group is noticed by the Bahutu population. Although they find it to a certain extent the natural consequence of a military overthrow, resentment spills over into the Gacaca activities. Although local authorities are not overtly active in the Gacaca process, they form the framework within which the Gacaca functions. In Hutu perceptions this often means that the combination of the Gacaca, with its reference to the pre-colonial past, and a power structure that is occupied by a politico-military movement dominated by members of the Tutsi minority is perceived as a return to the feudal period when Hutu servants were subordinate to Tutsi lords in all domains of life. The government installed and supports the Gacaca process. As a stated objective, the Gacaca tribunals need to arrive at the truth, reconciliation and accountability. The court system further needs to eradicate the culture of impunity. From this perspective the Gacaca courts are a legitimate and laudable policy initiative in their own right. But the practice of governing in other policy domains, the overarching institutional build-up and the perceived nature of power undermine the functioning and legitimacy of the court system.

5. *Unpopular participatory justice.* The Gacaca courts derive their legitimacy from popular participation, but people are not very willing to participate. After initial interest, fatigue has set in. Fines and coercion have come to replace voluntary participation. This is not only because the process takes too long, but also because a majority of the Bahutu now experience the courts as a form of victor's justice through which they are unable to make their own claims.

6. *No truth in the Gacaca process.* One overarching and omnipresent opinion accompanies the Gacaca process: the truth is absent. This has serious consequences for the system in its essence and hampers its ultimate objectives. The surfacing of the truth functions as the cornerstone of the entire transitional justice architecture in post-genocide Rwanda, as we have argued. The reasons why there is no truth are multiple and complex (Ingelaere 2007). The 'truth' is, in the first place, curtailed by the a priori defining parameters of

55

what the 'truth' can be, methodologically and ideologically, but also by the features of Rwandan culture. The 'truth' is mostly 'forensic' because it is derived from a criminal procedure. It varies according to locality since it surfaces through the dynamic of local constellations idiosyncratically subverting and interpreting the truth-generating procedures. The 'truth', furthermore, has a high degree of instrumentality as it is sought through confrontation along group-based (mostly ethnic) lines, not deliberation or dialogue. It has a certain degree of arbitrariness resulting from the principle of 'confession and denunciation without verification'. As a result the 'truth' is 'partial' in the sense of 'incomplete' and 'deformed', but also 'one-sided' and 'one-dimensional', lacking a broadly based contextual anchoring.

> The general perception on the part of the Rwandan people that the truth is not emerging is one of the most problematic aspects of the Gacaca court system.

7. *Reconciliation in jeopardy and a Hutu subculture in the making?* The Gacaca courts are unable to deal with RPF crimes and revenge killings by Tutsi civilians. The genocide against the Tutsi minority cannot be equated with the civil war crimes against the Hutu population. The first was violence to exterminate, the second violence to avenge, subjugate and control. Nevertheless, the fact that the first is being dealt with and the second is eclipsed from view establishes a moral hierarchy of right and wrong, pain and suffering. The dissonance between popular embodied experiences and understandings of the conflict on the one hand and the government-controlled and government-produced way of dealing with the past, at the practical and interpretative levels, is one of the main obstacles to legitimizing the current socio-political order. It creates a mass of unexpressed grievances under the surface of daily life and the assiduous Gacaca activities, fermenting in the 'hidden transcript'. These are opinions and experiences that are not forgotten but simply not aired because *they are not expressible* through the transitional justice architecture that has been installed. Rumours—for example, the idea of a machine accompanying the Gacaca courts to destroy all Bahutu, or the idea of a double genocide—can be seen as a mere existential window on that popular social imagination. Claims by Bahutu that they suffered in the past are not a basis for a legal defence, and are certainly illegal when they are a part of genocide ideology, but they reflect genuine perceptions. A report on 'genocide ideology' reveals the extremely wide and unclear definition of what genocide ideology is (Rwanda 2006a). Its broad scope allows for a zealous, uninhibited and arbitrary use of force to eradicate not only genocidal tendencies but every slightest sign of non-conformity. As a self-fulfilling prophecy it creates, perpetuates or even enhances that which it is supposedly eradicating—a Hutu subculture. Breaking the cycle of violence—one of the objectives of the Gacaca process—needs to be based on a shared understanding of the origins of Rwandan society incorporating its innate and

> The fact that genocide against the Tutsi minority is being dealt with while the crimes against the Hutu population during the civil war period are eclipsed from view establishes a moral hierarchy of right and wrong, pain and suffering, and creates a mass of unexpressed grievance under the surface of daily life and the assiduous Gacaca activities.

complex Hutu–Tutsi bipolarity grafted on the struggle for power over time, while first recognizing its culmination point in the 1990s with *both* genocide and civil war(s) (Mamdani 2002: 266–70).

4. Conclusion

Since their inception, the idea of using the Gacaca courts to deal with crimes related to the 1994 genocide in Rwanda has circulated widely across the globe. Their existence is very well known, but knowledge of their nature and, most importantly, their actual functioning only started to surface after they were implemented nationwide in 2005. A comparison between the 'ancient' and the 'new' Gacaca has made it clear that the Gacaca courts are not a fully blown traditional justice and reconciliation mechanism. They are not the result of a gradual evolution but a novelty mimicking both an ancient dispute settlement practice and classical justice. Moreover, the in-depth insight in the micro-administration of justice in local communities, an overview of its outcome in terms of numbers of people accused and tried at the macro level and an anatomy of the nature of the societal process it has initiated (or, better, enhanced) temper the initial enthusiasm. The Gacaca courts are not a straightforward success. At the macro level we have seen that the system has strengths but that the process is overshadowed by its weaknesses. On the individual level, the Gacaca courts came to facilitate for some what they destroyed or disturbed for others, be it at the level of truth telling, seeking redress, holding accountable or creating reconciliation.

Could these weakneses have been better foreseen and could they/can they still be adequately addressed? What are the prospects for the future, the cautionary lessons learned? An answer is not straightforward and not easily forthcoming. The summing up of strengths and weaknesses above gives hints about the do's and don'ts.

The fact that the Gacaca courts suffer from a too extensive social and legal engineering campaign seems to be important. Moreover, the task that burdens the institution is extremely ambitious. Ambitions should be tempered and intrusion limited, after considering the Rwandan way of doing justice. It is important that the mechanism is built upon established and existing locally owned and socio-culturally inspired practices of 'dealing with the past', be it in the domain of healing, accountability, truth speaking or coexistence/reconciliation. This is only so to a limited extent in the case of the Gacaca. Its core is retributive, while the essence of the ancient institution was restorative. Observation indicates that the restorative aspect, for example, restitution at the level of the cell-level courts, works better than classical justice taking place among peers at the level of the sector-level Gacaca courts. Community service remains an important alternative and restorative penalty emanating from the Gacaca trials.

In addition, a thorough understanding of the dynamics and the unfolding of the violence on the periphery, the genocide (and war) out on the hills, would have made it possible to design the system in such a way as to differentiate better between those at the top of the chain of command (even at the local level) and the rank and file. Changes in the system have to bring this about ex post facto. As is said above, all this can be seen as either fine-tuning or disaster management. It is in any case an operation to bring the system more into line with what is already existing in the population and feasible for the future.

Living together again is a practice that is forged locally. The state and its policies can facilitate or obstruct these practices. In Rwanda, both facilitation and obstruction are taking place—on the one hand through the contradictory nature of the design of the Gacaca courts, and on the other hand through the policies and practice of governing surrounding the court system. It seems important not to enhance the cleavages one is supposedly eradicating and to install and support inclusive policies that are not creating an 'us vs them' dynamic within the population, enhancing identities one intends to reconfigure (unless that which one says is not that which one wants, of course). It will be difficult to adjust the Gacaca process further in that regard. Time is lacking, and the process is well under way. However, the future leaves room for an inclusive development for all in one of the poorest nations in the world. Inclusion will be paramount in the transitional justice policies possibly upcoming, for example, the possible installation of a reparation fund. The Gacaca experience has shown the elements at stake and the avenues (not) to take.

References and further reading

des Forges, Alison, *Leave None to Tell the Story: Genocide in Rwanda* (New York: Human Rights Watch, 1999)

Ingelaere, Bert, 'Changing Lenses and Contextualizing the Rwandan (Post-)Genocide', in F. Reyntjens and S. Marysse (eds), *L'Afrique des Grands Lacs: Dix Ans de Transitions Conflictuelles. Annuaire 2005–2006* [Africa of the Great Lakes: ten years of conflictual transitions. Yearbook, 2005–2006] (Paris: L'Harmattan, 2006), pp. 389–414

— 'Does the Truth Pass Across the Fire? Transitional Justice and its Discontents in Rwanda's Gacaca Courts', Discussion Paper, Institute of Development Policy and Management, Antwerp, 2007

de Lame, Danielle, *A Hill Among a Thousand: Transformations and Ruptures in Rural Rwanda* (Madison, Wis.: University of Wisconsin Press, 2005)

Mamdani, Mahmood, *When Victims Become Killers: Colonialism, Nativism, and the Genocide in Rwanda* (Princeton, N.J.: Princeton University Press, 2001)

Musoni, Protais, 'Building a Democratic Culture: Rwanda's Experience and Perspectives', Paper presented at the conference on Elections and Accountability in Africa, Wilton Park, Sussex, UK, 21–25 July 2003

Ntampaka, Charles, 'Le Gacaca: Une Juridiction Pénale Populaire' [The Gacaca:

a penal jurisdiction of the people], in Charles de Lespinay and Emile Mworoha (eds), *Construire L'Etat de Droit: Le Burundi et la Région des Grands Lacs* [Building a state of law: Burundi and the Great Lakes region] (Paris: L'Harmattan, 2003), pp. 219–36

Oomen, Barbara, 'Donor Driven Justice and its Discontents: The Case of Rwanda', *Development and Change*, vol. 36, no. 5 (2005), pp. 887–910

Pottier, Johan, *Re-Imagining Rwanda: Conflict, Survival and Disinformation in the Late Twentieth Century* (Cambridge: Cambridge University Press, 2002)

Prunier, Gerard, *The Rwandan Crisis: History of a Genocide* (New York: Columbia University Press, 1995)

Reyntjens, Filip, 'Le *Gacaca* ou la Justice du Gazon au Rwanda' [*Gacaca*, or justice on the grass in Rwanda], *Politique Africaine*, no. 40 (1990)

Rwanda, *Report on the Reflection Meetings Held in the Office of the President of the Republic from May 1998 to March 1999* (Kigali: Office of the President of the Republic, 1999)

Rwanda, *Genocide and Strategies for its Eradication* (Kigali, 2006) (2006a)

Rwanda, *Report on Collecting Data in* Gacaca *Courts* (Kigali: National Service of the Gacaca Courts, 2006) (2006b)

United Nations High Commissioner for Human Rights (UNHCHR), *Gacaca: Le Droit Coutumier au Rwanda* [Gacaca: customary justice in Rwanda] (Rwanda: UNHCHR, 1996)

Uvin, Peter, *Aiding Violence: The Development Enterprise in Rwanda* (Bloomfield, Ct: Kumarian Press Inc., 1998)

— 'Reading the Rwandan Genocide', *International Studies Review* vol. 3, no. 3 (2001)
Waldorf, Lars, 'Mass Justice for Mass Atrocity: Rethinking Local Justice as Transitional Justice', *Temple Law Review*, vol. 79, no. 1 (2006)

Websites

Avocats Sans Frontières, <http://www.asf.be/index.php?module=publicaties&lang=en&id=177>

Institute of Research and Dialogue for Peace (IRDP), <http://www.irdp.rw>

National Service of the Gacaca Courts, <http://www.inkiko-gacaca.gov.rw>

National Unity and Reconciliation Commission, <http://www.nurc.gov.rw>

Penal Reform International, <http://www.penalreform.org/transitional.html>

CHAPTER 3

CHAPTER 3

Restorative justice and the role of magamba spirits in post-civil war Gorongosa, central Mozambique

Victor Igreja and Beatrice Dias-Lambranca

1. Introduction

This chapter addresses the strategies for restorative justice at the community level that developed in the aftermath of the 1976–92 civil war in Mozambique. The General Peace Agreement, signed in Rome, Italy, on 4 October 1992 between the Mozambican Government, represented by the Front for the Liberation of Mozambique (Frente de Libertação de Moçambique, Frelimo), and the former rebel movement the Mozambican National Resistance (Resistência Nacional Moçambicana, Renamo), brought an end to almost two decades of very bloody civil war. The negotiations for peace which unfolded between 1990 and 1992 were preceded and accompanied by a comprehensive set of political changes to the post-colonial Marxist–Leninist regime, and replaced that regime with the pluralistic constitution of 1990 which established a multiparty democratic system and a market-oriented economy. Alongside the peace negotiations, these socio-political and economic changes were determining factors in the resolution of the civil war.

Although the peace agreement brought immense relief to the victims, from a transitional justice perspective the Mozambican authorities did not develop any specific policy to deal with the abuses and crimes that had been perpetrated during the civil war. After having been used and greatly abused, the victims were urged to forgive and forget the grisly past as a supposed part of peace building and national reconciliation.

Within this context of war abuses and crimes, followed by the post-war practices of denial and abandonment, the war victims and survivors in Gorongosa district in central Mozambique were not without hope. By making use of available and accessible endogenous resources, war survivors were able to begin the paramount task of repairing their individual and collective lives. We focus here on the socio-cultural practices that take the form of restorative justice and reconciliation in the aftermath of the civil war. This is the case with the *gamba* (*magamba* in the plural) spirit. *Magamba* are generally the

After the 1992 General Peace Agreement, the Mozambican authorities did not develop any specific policy to deal with the abuses and crimes that had been perpetrated during the short-lived Marxist–Leninist dictatorship and protracted civil war. Instead, socio-cultural practices have developed which take the form of restorative justice, reconciliation and healing in the aftermath of the civil war.

spirits of dead soldiers who return to the realm of the living to fight for justice. In their varied meanings and manifestations, *magamba* both heal war-related wounds and play a pivotal role in the attainment of restorative justice among the survivors of war.

2. The context of conflicts in colonial and post-colonial Mozambique

The Mozambican people have been exposed to social and political upheavals for many decades. Although the Portuguese were present in Mozambique for around five centuries, effective colonization started around the 1930s. The colonial violence took the form of forced labour. The refusal to concede socio-political, economic and cultural rights to the indigenous population was also part of the colonial political system. The Portuguese who settled in the country, on the other hand, were granted full rights of citizenship. In the early 1960s Frelimo initiated an armed struggle for independence in the north of the country. This marked the beginning of the war and violent conflict that would continue for almost three decades.

The anti-colonial war lasted for ten long years (1964–74). Rural areas were the main battlefields and their populations were by far the most exposed and worst affected. The Lusaka Peace Agreement between Frelimo and the Portuguese authorities led to independence at the end of June 1975. Peace, however, was short-lived. Initially, the post-independence violence was provoked by external forces. The Ian Smith regime of the former Rhodesia invaded Mozambique under the pretext that soldiers from the Zimbabwe African National Liberation Army (ZANLA) had found a safe haven there. The Rhodesian Army wreaked havoc in Mozambique, in 1977 perpetrating the well-known massacre at Inhazonia in Barue district (Manica Province). The civil war, initiated by Renamo, started at the same time. There are major disagreements between the adherents of Frelimo and Renamo, and some academics, over the real origins of this internal conflict. Different opinions on the respective roles of external and internal factors dominate the debate. The Frelimo authorities see the civil war as an extension of the external war of aggression, first led by the Rhodesians and later continued by the South African apartheid regime. Renamo for its part emphasizes the internal component, triggered by Frelimo's post-colonial dictatorship and repressive policies. Others prefer to speak of a combination of both internal and external factors.

The debates on the origin of the post-colonial violence are not explored here. What is crucial in this chapter is that both conflicts caused overwhelming disruption and destruction in Mozambique. Survivors of both wars agree, however, that the civil war was incomparably worse in terms of the extent of the ruthlessness and the human and physical devastation. Numerous villages were burned to ashes and many innocent civilians were severely abused, tortured and killed. The war zones were usually divided between government-controlled and Renamo-controlled areas, and many civilians shifted continuously between these two areas in search of minimal security. However, extreme traumatic events and subjugation of the people occurred in both.

Gorongosa district was at the epicentre of the civil war. Between 1981 and mid-1985, Renamo troops had their main headquarters in the area and exercised almost hegemonic control of the war zones. This meant that the majority of the inhabitants had much more direct (forced or unforced) contact with Renamo forces than with the Frelimo-led army. Since the civil war was fought mainly through guerrilla tactics, the polarization of the war zones meant that the Frelimo troops considered the people under Renamo control as enemies, and vice versa. The consequences were devastating for all those who lived in the area. Many civilians living in Renamo territory were killed by the Frelimo air force. Renamo, on the other hand, caused tremendous pain and suffering through its policy of so-called *gandira*—a system of forced labour aimed at providing logistical support for its war effort. *Gandira* also involved the use of women as sexual slaves. In this regard *gandira* was profoundly humiliating: people were compulsorily separated from their families, and others were tortured and murdered.

The number of people killed during the civil war is a matter of dispute. Some observers speak of 100,000 civilian deaths; others place the figure at 1 million (Hanlon 1991); still others suggest that 'A more realistic guess would be that some 50 000 victims lost their lives directly as a result of rebel military action throughout the entire war' (Thomashausen 2001: 98). Both Renamo and government troops compulsorily recruited young men to fight in the war. They were forced to destroy their own villages and murder their own kin. Family members were subjugated and forced to spy on one another, leading to the torture and murder of many relatives. A culture of peace was totally replaced by a culture of war. Social capital in the form of relations of trust, reciprocity, mutual support, cooperation and solidarity, and respect for taboos was severely eroded.

3. The transition from war to peace and the cultures of denial in Mozambique

Two different types of transition and two different strategies for dealing with its legacies feature in the recent history of Mozambique. The first transition took place in June 1975 when the country gained its independence from Portugal. As a result of direct negotiations with the Portuguese transitional government in 1974, Frelimo managed to negotiate, through the Lusaka Accords of 25 September 1974, the transfer of total sovereignty and power into the hands of the Frelimo authorities. The second transition, in the 1990s, encompassed a multiplicity of processes. It meant the transformation of the political regime from a Marxist–Leninist ideology to a multiparty democracy and market-oriented economy, and from civil war to peace and democracy. It was the transition from civil war to peace that most captured the attention of the local populations and of international observers.

The post-colonial era and the post-civil war period led to different transitional justice strategies.

Three years after independence, around the end of 1978, the Frelimo party, via the political speeches of then President Samora Machel, aired a political plan or strategy to deal with some of the intricate legacies of the colonial past. (Machel was the first president of post-colonial Mozambique, ruling the country from independence in 1975 until his death in 1986.) The target of this strategy was a selected group of individuals, called *comprometidos* (the compromised), who had allegedly collaborated in various ways with the ancien régime (the Portuguese colonial administration). This strategy for dealing with those allegedly compromised by the colonial past unfolded between the end of 1978 and 1982, and involved various initiatives that culminated with a general meeting known as the Reunião dos Comprometidos (the Meeting of the Compromised).

In his inaugural speech to the Reunião dos Comprometidos, Machel explained the need for a reckoning with the terrible colonial past by stating that 'Only by reviewing the past will we know the present. Only by knowing the present will we make a perspective for the future. These are the three fundamental elements in a society—the past, the present and the future. Its pages are marked by history; we cannot go against them; history is history' (Machel 1982a). He reiterated this at the end of the meeting: 'We feel the necessity to always deepen the knowledge of the past so that permanently we increase our capacity to understand and resolve the problems of the present and correctly make perspectives about the future that we desire' (Machel 1982b: author's translation).

The Frelimo party politics of memory was founded upon the idea of 'Não vamos esquecer o tempo que passou' ('Let us not forget the time that passed'). This overall strategy was conceptually articulated in various ways—as 'acts of revolutionary justice', 'reintegration strategy', 'self-liberation from the compromise with the colonial-fascism', 'self-liberation from the loaded consciousness', 'mental de-colonization', 'rehabilitation of the compromised' or 'the inner combat to liberate the consciousness'. Despite these conceptual variations, the key features of the strategy aimed 'to transform the compromised based on presumption of guilt, repentance, punishment and re-education' (Coelho 2003: 191). This strategy involved grave breaches of the Mozambican constitution of 1978. President Machel worked hard during the Meeting of the Compromised to demonstrate to everyone that above him there was no law; he was the law. On one occasion, when one alleged *comprometido* dared to challenge Machel by demanding more solid or convincing evidence that he had been involved with the colonial administration to hinder Mozambique's achieving independence, the president became furious. Ignoring the 1978 constitution, he ordered the immediate arrest of that *comprometido* and his transfer to the far fields of Niassa Province. None of Machel's subordinates who were present at the meeting, carefully witnessing this act, dared to advise the president that he had no legal right to order someone's arrest. Everyone kept silent and witnessed Machel violating the same constitution that he had struggled so hard to bring to his country. In addition, during this meeting the importance of this strategy for the victims of colonial repression was never clearly articulated.

The post-colonial transition in the early 1980s therefore attempted to tackle the problems of the violent colonial past. By contrast, during the transition from the civil war to peace and democracy in the early 1990s no attempts were made to the dig into the grisly past and no concern over the plight of the victims seems to have captured the imagination of the Mozambican political elites responsible for the transitional processes.

From a transitional justice perspective there was no public debate in Mozambique spurred, for instance, by the local intellectual elites, journalists and human rights lawyers about the best ways to address the legacies of the civil war and the short-lived Marxist–Leninist dictatorship. In fact, ten days after the signing of the General Peace Agreement of 4 October 1992, the Mozambican Popular Assembly—wholly controlled by the Frelimo party at the time—promulgated Law no. 15/92, which provided for an amnesty for crimes committed between 1979 and 1992. Again, on the occasion of the promulgation of this law, there was no public debate about its moral implications, no statements were made about the potential for truth and justice to right the wrongs of the past, and no official public demands for apology were enacted to acknowledge the suffering of the victims.

An analysis of the official discourse of the representatives of the two main antagonistic parties, (Frelimo, the party in government, and Renamo) at the time of the signing of the General Peace Agreement demonstrates in differing degrees the importance of the victims in their public addresses. Joaquim Chissano, the then president of the country, was completely inattentive to the suffering of the victims in his public speeches. The only political message he uttered was that the signing of the General Peace Agreement was an act of great significance and a victory for the Mozambican people. Not a single sentence acknowledged the suffering the people had gone through during the protracted civil war; not a single word to demonstrate compassion and respect for the memories of the victims came out of the president's mouth.

It was the leader of Renamo, Afonso Dhlakama, who early on dedicated some words of acknowledgement of the suffering of the victims. He stated: 'We recall in the first place our brothers who died; all Mozambicans, combatants and non-combatants, from one or the other side who fell in this fratricidal fight... their blood was not shed in vain and on top of their sacrifice a renewed and reconciled nation is now being built. We recall as well all our suffering people who

The peace agreement was founded upon a culture of denial. The accepted, although largely unstated, belief was that 'the less we dwell on the past, the more likely reconciliation will be'.

have waited so anxiously for this day in the cities, in the bush. It is to them, and above all to the young people, that we address our message of hope. Let's start anew, let's work to reconstruct the country' (Mozambique Radio; author's translation).

As Priscilla Hayner has noted, 'In Mozambique the accepted, though largely unstated, belief was "the less we dwell on the past, the more likely reconciliation will be". There has been almost no focus in Mozambique on accountability for past crimes… there have been virtually no calls at the national level for justice, accountability, punishment, or banishment from public office' (Hayner 2001: 187). Other observers of the transitional process have confined themselves to acknowledging that the Mozambican peace process 'opened social spaces' (Baptista-Lundin 2002) which allowed 'a more open attention to the historical and ritual ceremonies that had allowed for healing of fractured communities in the past' (Jacobson 2005: 142). Still other observers have pointed out that 'In the FRELIMO political program, in the new constitution [1990] and in the new government policy there is a clear and neat willingness of reconciliation with the different social forces. This is related to the private entrepreneurs, the religious community and other groups that before were opposed to the FRELIMO policies. This process of reconciliation is unfolding in a limited sphere of people and especially at the central level' (Abrahamsson and Nilsson 1994: 325). In relation to the rural people who were the direct targets of war, Hans Abrahamsson and Anders Nilsson add that 'At this moment it is not possible yet to glimpse any sign of real reconciliation with this group of population, through a consequent politics of support of the rural areas' (Abrahamsson and Nilsson 1994: 326). This reality has not changed much, although there is one exception—the approval of Decree Law no. 15/2000 of 20 June 2000, which establishes the relationships between the state local organs and the community authorities (*Boletim da República* 24, June 2000). It formalized the recognition of some community authorities, particularly the traditional chiefs, who had been stripped of their leadership positions and alienated by the post-colonial policies of the Frelimo-led governments.

Unquestionably, the end of the civil war brought relief from the horrors and the appalling forms of human disruption and degradation. But the peace agreement was founded upon *cultures of denial*: the political authorities 'encourage turning a collective blind eye, leaving horrors unexamined or normalized as being part of the rhythms of everyday life' (Cohen 2001: 101). As a result of the post-war cultures of denial in Mozambique, the plight of the victims and survivors was completely disavowed. The immediate consequence of the post-civil war official strategy of denial was that the victims and former perpetrators and their associates had to share and to live in the same villages where the most appalling abuses and egregious crimes had taken place.

The debates on transitional justice suggest that this type of post-war settlement gives rise not only to feelings of revenge but also to actual physical violence as a form of reckoning with war-related abuses and crimes. However, as is demonstrated below, in Gorongosa such acts of physical violence largely did not take place at family and community level.

One of the most important ways of addressing the abuses and injustices of the civil war, without setting in motion new cycles of physical violence, can be observed through the *life situations* in which the survivors of war actively make use of the community resources that are available to them to deal with the multiple wartime legacies. This is the process of healing and the dispensation of restorative justice by *magamba* spirits and *magamba* healers.

The debates on transitional justice suggest that this type of post-war settlement gives rise not only to feelings of revenge but also to actual physical violence as a form of reckoning with war-related abuses and crimes. In Gorongosa, such acts of physical violence largely did not take place.

4. The legacies of the civil war and the socio-cultural landscape of Gorongosa

The people of Gorongosa inhabit a pluralistic environment in terms of the sources of power and legal order, and traditional and Christian religious beliefs and practices. All these resources have interesting histories in the light of the Portuguese colonial policies and the post-independence Marxist–Leninist ideologies promoted by Frelimo. In spite of the historical metamorphosis that some of these resources have gone through, particularly traditional power, justice, and medicine, all of them, including the Christian religious groups, have played a role in dealing with different aspects of the legacies of civil war.

For instance, in the aftermath of the 1992 peace agreement and in the months immediately following, traditional chiefs and judges assumed increased importance. The whole process of population resettlement and relief operations required a major coordination effort, to which the local chiefs were indispensable. Also of key importance was the immediate peaceful resolution of conflicts among people who had been bitterly divided because of the war. The chiefs' overall message to their fellow war victims was to insist upon reconciliation and to rule out *ku hirindzira* (revenge). The chiefs advised the people to do *ku lekerera* (to forgive) and *ku lekererana* (to forgive one another) as the best strategy to end the cycles of violence brought about by the civil war. Traditional healers in particular played a key role in the reintegration of the ex-soldiers not only in Gorongosa but also in different regions of the country. They conducted reception and reintegration rituals for former soldiers as a way of reconnecting to their former alienated communities in the post-civil war Mozambique (Dolan and Schafer 1997).

Christian religious groups also participated in the post-war reconciliation processes. The majority of the churches in Gorongosa engaged in spreading a clear and strong message of peace and reconciliation without any type of *justiça terrena* (earthly justice). Ideas about obtaining formal justice and *ku hirindzira* were totally discouraged. The responsibility for enacting justice against those individuals who had abused and killed innocent people during the war was left to God. In parallel to preaching reconciliation through forgiveness, religious groups engaged energetically in healing the sick.

In Gorongosa, the war-related magamba spirits and gamba healers are the only post-civil war phenomenon that relates closely to transitional justice in a broader sense. They engage with the grisly past discursively, bodily and by means of a performance to create post-war healing of war-related wounds. They also create public spaces where restorative justice is attained in a context of the transition from a civil war to peace.

These agents and the resources at their disposal play an important role, but they do not actively engage with the violent past. They instead promote reconciliation through forgiveness, and a unilateral forgiveness, as it were, which requires no acknowledgement of responsibility from the perpetrators. For this reason, we have opted here to examine only the war-related *magamba* spirits and *gamba* healers. They are the only post-civil war phenomenon that relates closely to transitional justice in a broader sense. *Magamba* engage with the grisly past in a profound way—that is discursively, bodily and by means of a performance—to create post-war healing of war-related wounds. In their multiple meanings and manifestations, *magamba* also create public spaces where restorative justice is practised and attained in a context of the transition from a civil war to peace.

5. The role of *magamba* spirits in post-war Gorongosa

The *magamba* spirits emerged into the socio-cultural world of Gorongosa, which historically was already inhabited by a plethora of spirits and healers, in the context of the Mozambican civil war, and are particularly prominent in the Gorongosa region. They play different roles in society. The various spirits initially cause suffering, but then the suffering is transformed into a healing power. Particularly with *magamba* spirits, the procedures followed to transform affliction into healing disclose the existence of social spaces and momentum for the enactment of restorative justice.

The magamba spirits initially cause suffering, but then the suffering is transformed into a healing power.

People in Gorongosa, as in many other parts of Africa, live in a social world that traditionally practises the belief that the death of individuals through traumatic acts, or the breaking of taboos such as the killing of human beings without metaphysical and/or social legitimization, is an offence that requires immediate redress through atonement rituals. If wrongdoing is not acknowledged, the spirit of the innocent victim will return to the realm of the living to struggle for justice.

Historically, *madzoca* healers have controlled the world of the spirits in Gorongosa. These healers worked under the guidance of ancestral spirits. They were specialized in divination and had the monopoly of states of possession or trance. This monopoly had three implications. First, only individuals who belonged to families with a history of ancestral healing spirits could work as healers. Second, during the healing of any affliction the patient did not have a voice. There was a socio-cultural expectation that by using the very powerful ancestral spirits the *madzoca* healer would disclose the aetiology of the health or social problem. Through a technique called *ku fema* (to sniff), which was enacted in a state of possession by the spirit or trance, the *madzoca* healer was capable of transferring the problem from the body of the patient or client to his or her own body. Thereafter the healer would disclose all the invisible dimensions of the problem at hand and define an intervention strategy to be followed. Finally, these healing procedures concentrated a great deal of power in the hands of the *madzoca* healers and their ancestral spirits, and the patient was expected to take a submissive role.

Perhaps because the Gorongosa communities were functioning under conditions of relatively bearable stresses, the role played by the *madzoca* healers was never greatly contested.

In addition, in the 19th century, as a result of the migration of Nguni ethnic groups from the south to subjugate the populations in the centre of Mozambique, many acts of generalized violence and killings of members of local groups are reported to have taken place. As a corollary of this generalized violence, without any metaphysical or social legitimization, a new spirit was introduced in the centre of Mozambique, called *n'fukua*. This spirit, which returns to the realm of the living to seek justice by afflicting the culprits and their social group, signalled the presence of human-made mass pollution in the Gorongosa communities. The *n'fukua* phenomenon was also seen in the south of the country (Honwana 1996). However, the *n'fukua* spirits never managed to establish themselves to the extent of creating a solid institution among the Gorongosa people. According to testimonies of older people in Gorongosa, *n'fukua* spirits remained a concealed phenomenon and there are very few material traces of them now left. Perhaps one important aspect to consider is that *n'fukua* spirits can be considered the predecessors of the *magamba* spirits in terms of the logic of their operation—revenge for an alleged unjust death. Yet, unlike the *n'fukua* spirits, the *magamba* spirits went further by establishing themselves as a local institution of healing activity alongside the existing ancestral *madzoca* healers.

6. *Magamba* spirits: a new era, serious afflictions and social spaces for healing

Against the background of the *madzoca* healers, who embodied the ancestral spirits, *magamba* spirits ushered in a new era in Gorongosa. This new era featured rejuvenation, the strength and 'voice' of young people, and an attempt to achieve a balance between individual and collective responsibility. *Magamba* spirits also ushered in a new period in that reformed rules and procedures were introduced in the healing activity. In order to understand the restorative justice embodied by the *magamba* spirits, we need to examine the ethnographic facts and contrast them with the procedures of the institution of *madzoca*.

A key feature of the *gamba* spirit is its randomized dimension, that is, the spirits broke with the conservative rule which maintained that only individuals belonging to families with healing histories could become possessed by spirits and work as healers. *Magamba* spirits can possess anyone in Gorongosa so long as the individual or his/her family has a history of abuse, abandonment, trauma and victimization through murder. Since the protracted civil war was a fertile period in which extreme human-on-human abuses, humiliation and suffering of all kinds took place, the *magamba* spirits rapidly gained prominence. Many people, particularly young women, started to become possessed by them. Possession by a *gamba* spirit brings severe health and social afflictions in the life of the victim/host and his or her close kin. However, the spirits also create the possibility for healing to take place.

Magamba spirits bear witness in multiple forms to the violent events that occurred during the civil war. For instance, unlike the *madzoca* healers who have as their main working instrument a *mutchira* (the tail of an animal), which is the indication of the interconnections between the ancestral spirits and nature, the *magamba* healers have as their main instrument a bayonet, which represents the violent past. These bayonets are said to be those found attached to the Kalashnikovs (AK-47s) that were used many times to stab and kill people. *Magamba* healers suggest that if these spirits are to be dealt with successfully the violence of the past cannot be ignored. There is a need to engage with the past, to find out what injustices were done, to acknowledge the wrongdoing and to repair the damage.

> Magamba spirits bear witness to the violent events that occurred during the civil war. If these spirits are to be dealt with successfully, the violence of the past cannot be ignored. There is a need to engage with the past, to find out what injustices were done, to acknowledge the wrongdoing and to repair the damage.

This process is illustrated here with two related case studies—of Cenoria and her mother Amelia—which epitomize the healing and restorative justice dimension of the *magamba* spirits.

6.1. Cenoria: the background to the case

Cenoria is a young woman of 27. She was born amid the civil war in very traumatic circumstances. Her parents were living in a Renamo-controlled area, and one day three Renamo troops arrived at their house to take them to do *gandira*. At the time, Cenoria's mother, Amelia, was in a very late stage of pregnancy, carrying Cenoria. Cenoria's father intervened to ask the soldiers not to take his pregnant wife to do *gandira*. The soldiers became very annoyed, beat Cenoria's father severely and forced Amelia to go on the *gandira* mission. On the way they were ambushed by Frelimo-led government troops, and everyone ran away. The shock and fear led to Cenoria's mother giving birth to Cenoria alone and in the middle of the bush. Miraculously, both mother and baby survived and the whole family decided to move away from Renamo area to the government-controlled area.

However, the elder brother of Cenoria's father—Zeca—refused to move to the government-controlled area and remained living under Renamo control. Strangely, three weeks after Cenoria's parents moved to the government-controlled area, Renamo soldiers invaded the area, forced the door of Cenoria's parents' house, kidnapped her father and took him back to the Renamo-controlled area. He was severely tortured and accused of treason. The fact that Renamo soldiers were able to find Cenoria's parents raised rumours that Zeca had betrayed his brother by leaking information to the soldiers about his whereabouts, and this denunciation almost cost him his life. Cenoria's father permanently severed relations with Zeca.

When the war was over in October 1992, amid advice from the political authorities to forgive, forget and be reconciled, Cenoria's father and Zeca remained alienated from one another and never attempted to get together or restore their relations. In the meantime, Cenoria grew up, reached the age of marriage and married a young man from the neighbourhood. She became pregnant, and some weeks before giving birth began to be seized by a spirit. They went to a healer and the presence of a *gamba* spirit was diagnosed. Since the date for the birth was coming closer, the *gamba* healer decided to perform an ad hoc ceremony to placate the *gamba* spirit so that the baby could be saved. Indeed, Cenoria managed to deliver the baby safely.

The *gamba* healer had indicated that a more comprehensive ceremony was needed to call up the *gamba* spirit lodged in the body of Cenoria so that the problem could be solved definitively. However, as Cenoria gained strength and the baby was growing up healthy, she and her family did not follow the healer's instructions. Two years passed, she continued to live with her husband, and she became pregnant again. This time the baby died some weeks after it was born. They mourned, buried the dead baby and moved on, living their own lives. Two years later, Cenoria and her husband began to realize that she was failing to get pregnant. They decided to continue trying for another baby for one more year, but failed. In the meantime, Cenoria started having very frightening nightmares and sometimes experienced dreams as if she were releasing spirits. According to the local interpretation, this indicates the presence of a bad spirit.

Cenoria and her parents decided to consult a *gamba* healer again. During the initial consultation, Cenoria became possessed and the spirit came out. The spirit disclosed that he was revenging a wrongdoing perpetrated by Zeca during the civil war, and that unless Zeca acknowledged and made restitution for the damage done Cenoria was doomed to suffer even more.

As already mentioned, Cenoria's parents had had no contact at all with Zeca since the days of the civil war. Since they had accused Zeca of betrayal, how could they approach him and convince him to go to a *gamba* healer with them to respond to the accusations of the spirit lodged in Cenoria's body? On the one hand, accusing Zeca could trigger another cycle of bitterness and even violence between Cenoria's father and his elder brother. On the other hand, if Cenoria's father failed to comply with the *gamba* spirit's request, that is, to bring Zeca for the healing session, Cenoria would not survive and would certainly fail in life. There was no other way out because *magamba* spirits cannot be definitively healed unless the person who is accused and his/her relatives come forward, acknowledge wrongdoing in front of everyone present at the healing session, and accept making restitution for the war-related havoc (when *magamba* spirits manifest themselves their voices target not individuals but entire collectives).

Under these circumstances, Cenoria's father decided to tell his brother Zeca about the problem. There was no violence, but Zeca denied any wrongdoing during the civil war and adamantly refused to take part in any ceremony related to his younger brother. Since Cenoria's father could not force his elder brother, he decided to report the case in the community court. Zeca was called before the court, and the judges enjoined him to attend the healing session for Cenoria's sake and referred the case to the headquarters of AMETRAMO (the Mozambican Association of Traditional Medical Practitioners). In this way the entire family of Cenoria and the two brothers were eventually reunited for the first time after many years. The presence of the *gamba* claiming justice broke the silence and enjoined the alienated people to come together and address their war-related conflicts.

6.2. Amelia: the background to the case

Amelia is aged 40. Part of her traumatic experience has already been described in the context of the birth of her daughter, Cenoria. What can be added is that during the war Amelia was separated from her kin—her father, mother, brothers and sisters. In the very early stages of the civil war, Amelia's parents decided to abandon their *madembe* (place of origin) to live in an area controlled by the government authorities. They remained under government control until the end of the civil war. Amelia stayed behind in the *madembe* with her husband and under Renamo control until the very late stages of the war when they also decided to escape to a government-controlled zone.

Amelia's problems started during the civil war. After the dangerous but successful birth of Cenoria, Amelia started to have reproductive health problems. Sometimes she would become pregnant, but after some months she would have unplanned miscarriages. On other occasions she gave birth, but the baby did not survive the first six months of life. On still other occasions she simply failed to get pregnant.

To seek a treatment for Amelia, she and her husband joined a Christian religious group. They remained loyal to the Christian life for many years, to the extent that Amelia's husband even became a pastor, but Amelia was not healed. Amelia asked for help from her father and he advised her not to give up praying, since he is also a Christian. After many years without a resolution Amelia and her husband gave up the Christian religious life and her plight almost fell into oblivion. It was the case of their daughter Cenoria that resurrected Amelia's case.

6.3. Transmutation of voices and truths about the past: Cenoria and Amelia

Within the context of political impunity and silence that characterized the Mozambican post-civil war period, the emergent *magamba* spirits create social spaces where alienated people can get together to address their war-related conflicts. In order for the *gamba* spirit to create healing and restorative justice, a ceremony has to be performed resulting from a collective endeavour under the closer monitoring of a *gamba* healer. At this level, the role of the *gamba* healer is to ensure that the performance unfolds adequately in order to convince the *gamba* spirit, lodged in the body of the afflicted patient or the patient's kin, to manifest itself to the public.

Usually when any healer (*madzoca* or *gamba*) receives a patient in his/her house who is in need of *ku socera* (a diagnosis ceremony), the healer beats a drum to tell the neighbours about the forthcoming ceremony. In the night, the neighbours appear at the healer's house to help perform *ku socera*. In a diagnosis and healing session, the *gamba* healer and the participants sing songs that evoke the events of the war, suffering and death. While they sing, the patient is placed sitting in the middle of the participants. The *gamba* healer enters a trance, takes hold of his/her bayonet and starts re-enacting events from the civil war. He or she begins to crawl, shoot, fight, make strange movements, run, smoke *nbanje* (cannabis) and drink alcohol. The principal objective of this performance is to trigger a combination of fear and empathy in the patient in order to induce the state of possession. As a result, the patient begins to be hyper-aroused, making uncontrolled body movements, and the participants—no longer singing—start screaming loudly to call upon the spirit to manifest itself. This is a moment of suspense in the ritual since it is unclear to the participants at this point whether the patient will be able to let the spirit assume full control of his/her body. Just before the spirit manifests itself, the patient gives a loud scream as if s/he is being hurt. The patients acquire extraordinary physical strength; they become violent in their body movements and speech, and glare fixedly. The Gorongosa theory is that the spirit is returning to take revenge for past misdeeds, and for this reason the *gamba*'s presence is marked by very violent acts.

The *gamba* healer, in a state of trance, manages to appease the patient's *gamba* spirit by empathically asking the spirit to disclose what happened during the war. When the *gamba* spirit subsides, the healer then returns to his or her normal state and a transmutation of voices and roles takes place. The focus is now solely on the patient who is possessed by the spirit. The spirit starts disclosing what happened to him so that every participant can hear.

The *performance* by the *gamba* healer and the other participants is extremely important because the spirit who is afflicting the patient has to manifest itself to the public through the patient's body. This is greatly in contrast to the procedures practised by *madzoca* healers. As is stated above, these *madzoca* healers were believed to have extraordinary powers, to the extent that during the diagnosis process the patients were not expected to have a voice; it was the voice of the ancestral spirit that disclosed the whole truth. *Magamba* spirits transmuted this logic by giving a central position to the patients' bodies instead of the healer. When the *gamba* spirit is ready to make the indictments, the role of the *gamba* healer is then to mediate the public deliberations in order to reach a settlement.

It was with these expectations—a public ceremony to disclose the truth about the violent past and determine individual responsibilities—that Cenoria, her parents and Zeca and his family went to AMETRAMO. The *magamba* healers affiliated to this organization performed *ku socera* and the *gamba* spirit came out through Cenoria's body. His name was Fernando. He said that he was a former Renamo soldier and that he had died in a battle. After his death, Zeca had secretly taken parts of his body to make a spell in order to cope with the extreme famine of the time by increasing his agricultural production.

Initially, Zeca adamantly denied this. He said that he had seen many corpses during the war, but he had never touched the dead body of a soldier. There were very heated arguments; the *gamba* healer in charge was mediating the discussions and the entire audience was listening carefully. The spirit further disclosed that after the civil war Zeca had decided to 'launch' (*ku tussira*) or to take him to the house of his young brother in order to live in the body of Cenoria. The other *gamba* healers present at the session urged Zeca to confess the truth surrounding these allegations so that the spirit could be appeased. After many hours of deliberation Zeca stated that someone during the war had advised him to seek out such spells in order to cope with the famine. Zeca also said that after the war, since his younger brother did not try to meet him to count the number of their dead and worship them, he decided to launch that spirit to dwell in the body of Cenoria.

Zeca acknowledged wrongdoing and the *magamba* healers asked the spirit to determine how he should make reparation. The *gamba* ordered that Zeca should bring back the scattered parts of his body and build him a house in the nearby forest close to a tree called *mussequessa* (often found in cemeteries) where he would live. In turn, the healers ordered both Zeca and Cenoria's father to look for the parts of the body in the bush, and the healers tried to identify a location with the *mussequessa* tree. After that Zeca and his brother built the house for the *gamba* spirit.

The following day, very early in the morning, the *magamba* healers together with Cenoria, both her parents and Zeca went to the bush to perform the reparation and closure ceremony. The few participants sang the calling songs and the same *gamba* spirit came out again through the body of Cenoria. The healers showed the house to the spirit and Zeca and his brother were urged to utter some reconciliatory words for the spirit. Zeca in particular respectfully apologized to the spirit and asked him to leave Cenoria's body. The *gamba* spirit ordered Cenoria's entire family to stop *ku dungunha* (murmuring) in private, to remove the grudges harboured within their hearts and to live in peace (*mutendere*) and with understanding (*ku verana*).

While the *magamba* healers were performing *ku socera* for Cenoria, something strange happened to Amelia, who was also helping to sing and clap her hands. She suddenly started doing *ku tekemuka* (shaking), which is an indication of the presence of a spirit. The *magamba* healers and the whole audience noticed her plight and indeed Amelia became possessed. The name of this spirit was Alberto. He disclosed that Amelia's paternal grandfather had killed him at the beginning of the civil war and had secretly offered Amelia to the spirit as compensation for the damage. However, the grandfather was already dead. In such cases, where the indicted person is dead, the only person who could do *ku himirira* (the senior member of the kin group who assumes responsibility for the kin group) was Amelia's father. Since he was not present that night, the *magamba* healers terminated the session. They ordered Amelia and her husband to request Amelia's father to come to AMETRAMO to deal with their past estrangement.

The case of Amelia was very complicated because, as stated above, her father was a Christian. Usually, Christian believers refuse to assemble with what they call *wanu wa dzico* (people of this world)—people who do not follow the lifestyle prescribed by the Christian canon. Amelia and her husband spoke to Amelia's father about the need to take part in a healing session at AMETRAMO, but he refused. Worse, he stated that he would rather die than step into the house of a traditional healer. Despite many attempts to convince him, he never changed from his very inflexible position, but made it clear that any attempt to force him to enter the house of a healer would end in tragedy since he would kill himself. In these circumstances, neither Amelia and her husband nor the *magamba* healers could go any further. No public ceremony, and no voices and collective truths about the past were discovered that could pave the way to addressing Amelia's condition. She would have to live with the spirit of someone her grandfather had murdered; and, worse, this spirit was blocking her reproductive wellbeing and that of her husband.

> Traditional healing practices are holistic, and magamba embody this tradition. They are as much about healing as about restorative justice and reconciliation.

6.4. The efficacy of a gamba *healer's interventions*

The lives of Cenoria and her mother were followed for three years. One year after the intervention Cenoria managed to conceive and gave birth to a baby. In the third year, once again she managed to conceive and delivered another baby. Currently, she lives a peaceful life with her husband and three children. The side effects of the intervention were that Cenoria's father and Zeca re-established their family relations (Zeca was imprisoned, accused of cultivating cannabis in his fields, but released some months later because of lack of solid proof).

For Amelia, Cenoria's mother, the situation had not changed at all. She did not manage to become pregnant and her relationship with her husband experienced difficulties. He was convinced that the failure to conceive children was the fault of his wife and her paternal kin. The relationship between Amelia and her father deteriorated since he was apparently blocking the possibility for his daughter to procreate and consequently to have a dignified and happier life. In turn, Amelia's father believed that he was not blocking anything; he argued that he preferred his daughter to continue in the church and seek a solution via the Christian God. However, the problem of the Christian religious groups is that they neither encourage discourse and practices that revisit the violent past nor demand any form of responsibility of people involved in war-related conflict. Christian religious groups in Gorongosa rely entirely on unilateral forgiveness since God is considered to be the most important figure in the resolution of conflicts. This is not to suggest that this is a bad strategy. The dilemma is that when a conflict persists, and as a result people experience profound agonies and serious afflictions, the Christian approach is lacking in terms of providing sensitive interventions that respond to the real needs of war survivors. For people like Amelia the Christian religious approach represents a serious limitation since the source for the resolution of their problems lies precisely in the capacity of living people to engage with the violent past. It is through the re-enactment of the violent past by the *gamba* spirit that the aetiology of current problems can be unveiled, healing, justice and reconciliation attained and communal stability restored.

> For people like Amelia the source for the resolution of their problems lies in the capacity of living people to engage with the violent past.

7. Legacies of the civil war, *magamba* spirits and practices of restorative justice

The cases of Cenoria and her mother Amelia are not unique. They mirror the plight of many survivors in the post-civil war period in Gorongosa. Although the two cases described here concern mainly women, there are also men who become possessed by *magamba* spirits and undergo similar resolution procedures. The procedures followed by the *gamba* healer demonstrate powerfully that healing and war-related justice cannot be conceived as two separate phenomena. Traditional healing practices are holistic, and the *magamba* spirits embody this tradition. They are as much about healing as about restorative justice.

As is stated above, the civil war seriously weakened various features of the social capital that for many years had contributed to trustful relations among family members and social stability in the communities. Many families were divided and family members were sometimes forced to spy on one another, which resulted in the killing of their kin. When the war was over, very few families decided to reunite to count their dead and worship their angry spirits. Family members wanted to forget the horror. They tried to take refuge in silence and avoided getting together in order to look back seriously and thereby move forward. However, the Gorongosa people live in a socio-cultural milieu in which histories of abuse, humiliation and (particularly) innocent killings do not easily vanish away. In fact, unless a crime is properly addressed, it will always come back to haunt the culprits, their relatives and society as a whole.

The *gamba* spirit embodies this value—extreme suffering and violent killings will never end unless they are properly addressed. Within this context, the *magamba* spirits broke down the walls of silence that the official authorities of the nation state, including many survivors of the war, had built in order to deny and to forget the past. The *gamba* spirit challenges the prevailing politics of denial and compels war survivors to deal with some of their unsettled war-related disputes.

The cases of Cenoria and her mother Amelia demonstrate that *magamba* spirits create the social space where the past can be worked through. In these post-war social spaces, the anger of the *gamba* spirit is dealt with by bringing together the plaintiff, the defendants and their respective families. Most of these families were torn apart during the civil war and remained divided in the post-war period. *Magamba* spirits force them to come together and address aspects of their amoral and shameful past. Above all, they allow many people to feel that they are victims and to reassert that they were wronged during the civil war. They also serve as an agency for the war survivors that permits them to redress the legacies of the civil war at the family and community level.

In the past (before the civil war), *madzoca* healers were the most important figures in the healing procedures and patients hardly had any agency. *Magamba* spirits re-formed this logic. Now, it is the aggrieved survivor who has a voice and has to take responsibility. The voice acquires a compelling power and authority through the presence of the *gamba* spirit. It is this power and authority that allow war survivors to deal with certain truths of their violent past.

Yet several questions can be asked.

First, whose truth do the *magamba* spirits evoke?

Magamba spirits do not primarily evoke individual factual truths. What counts in the scenes of *gamba* spirit possession are testimonies of *collective* truths of victimization and post-war responsibility and accountability. This is because, according to this African logic, responsibility and guilt are collective (Amadiume 2000: 52). This is not to suggest that testimonies portraying the factual truths of individual agents are not evoked during the *gamba* healing sessions. They are. It is perhaps appropriate to mention what Annette Wieviorka writes in relation to processes of cultural production of testimonies. She states that 'testimonies, particularly when they are produced as part of a larger cultural movement, express the discourse or discourses valued by society at the moment the witnesses tell their stories as much as they render an individual experience' (Wieviorka 2006: xii).

In this sense it is possible to explain how the presence of the *gamba* spirit in the case of Cenoria paved the way for the traumatic history of Amelia to be told. Although the

> Magamba spirits do not primarily evoke individual factual truths. What counts in the scenes of gamba spirit possession are testimonies of collective truths of victimization and post-war responsibility and accountability.

testimony of her life history was not the key factor that allowed the healing ceremony to take place, there were moments during the deliberations when Amelia brought up aspects of her past to argue that the suffering they were going through had to stop. In one of these moments Amelia said in an disenchanted way: 'I suffered a lot with this child [Cenoria] (…) this child was born in the middle of the bush and we were both about to die because of the war. Now the war is over but the suffering is continuing, how is this possible? How can someone build a house [family] in this way?' The *gamba* healer gazed at her and responded, 'That is why we are here tonight. The spirit is a person; he is seeing that we are very concerned with his complaints. When the family of your husband follows what the spirit is saying, when they pay what the spirit wants, your problem will be resolved and this case will end'.

One very important aspect of the answer of this *gamba* healer is that it is not devoid of meaning. It carries a profound message of hope since it acknowledges the suffering of the patient and promises to restore their dignity so long as the violent collective history is not avoided, the discursive practices of confession are enacted and the reparation is performed. These types of narrative, evoking personal experiences of suffering, are often disclosed in the middle of the highly agitated sessions of *gamba* healing. Yet the most significant narratives are the ones that evoke the *collective* truths and it is the responsibility of the *gamba* spirit to air this collective truth.

A second important aspect to consider vis-à-vis the voice of the victim heard through the presence of the *gamba* spirit is the following: in general, a *gamba* is the spirit of a dead soldier, that is, a former perpetrator. How is it possible for a former perpetrator to return to the realm of the living to fight for justice? Whose victimization and whose justice are at stake in cases of possession by a *gamba* spirit? It may seem paradoxical that the former perpetrator does not return to apologise and ask for forgiveness, as Christian religious practices would expect. Instead, the former perpetrator comes back as a victim. Looking at the dynamics of the civil war in Mozambique, it could be argued that many of the young men who actively took part in the fighting could indeed claim that they are victims. Those on the side of Renamo were usually abducted and those on the side of the Frelimo-led government army participated as part of compulsory military service, which was sanctioned by the law. Should we not therefore be struggling for justice vis-à-vis those who were directly responsible for the abductions and forced military recruitment?

> How is it possible for a former perpetrator to return to the realm of the living to fight for justice? Magamba spirits reflect the profound contradictions of surviving a civil war.

Although it is very reasonable to raise such a question, this is not the main issue among the *magamba* spirits and the people who believe in the inner logic of the way they operate. The heart of the matter is that *magamba* spirits reflect the profound *contradictions of surviving* a civil war at the very epicentre of where the war was fought. These contradictions bespeak that actions for post-war reparation cannot be driven by fixed categories—'perpetrator', 'victim', 'bystander', 'coward' and so on. Surviving a protracted war compels the survivors to acknowledge the extreme plasticity of personal identities at the time of the war and the consequent recognition of the need for flexibility in post-war conceptualizations. It is the capacity to conceive of and to accept the malleability of identities and categories that permits war survivors in Gorongosa to achieve resolutions to their war-related conflicts.

Within this context of acknowledgement of malleability or plasticity—that is, from the socio-cultural perspective of the Gorongosa people—it is precisely the impossibility of a spirit asking for forgiveness that creates the possibility for those living to achieve reconciliation and healing through mechanisms of restorative justice. The perpetrators of extreme abuses and crimes during the war come back as *magamba* spirits and as victims. The struggle of the spirits creates the social spaces where the war survivors who were the victims of abuses and those who have perpetrated abuses, as well as their families and the entire community, get together. In the social spaces that are thus created, the violence of the past is re-enacted: the grudges, bitterness and discontent in the hearts of the survivors can be conveyed without the risk of starting fresh cycles of abuse and violence.

To generalize, ethnographically, *magamba* spirits present (a) the violent history of the region and of the living and dead collective: *gamba* is about the *manhadzo* (shameful) acts of the past war; (b) the possibility for negative feelings and bad memories among the war survivors to be channelled in a positive way: when *magamba* spirits come out they disclose what happened; (c) a safe and social space for a communal dialogue and transformation of communal war legacies: *magamba* spirits insult people because they are very annoyed with what happened; and (d) restorative justice by repairing the dignity of individual war survivors and their families who until then were living with deep divisions and afflictions: 'your problem will be resolved'.

> In the social spaces that are created in the magamba healing ceremonies, the violence of the past is re-enacted: the grudges, bitterness and discontentment in the hearts of the survivors can be conveyed without the risk of starting fresh cycles of abuse and violence. They channel negative feelings and restore the dignity of individual war survivors and their families.

The idea and the practice of restorative justice are reinforced since, during the procedures to deal with *magamba* spirits, the ethnographic facts demonstrate that *gamba* healers do not use, for example, the communal concepts of healing or curing (*ku lapa* or *ku londziwa*). Instead they apply legal concepts such as *ku tongwa* (to judge), *ku vundzissana* (to interrogate one another), *ku bueca* (to confess), *ku lipa* (to pay), *ku lekerera* (to forgive) and *ku verana* (understanding).

When the momentum created by the *magamba* spirits is socio-culturally explored, the individual victims and their families are able to achieve reconciliation and to move on in life with dignity and social stability. This is well demonstrated by the case of Cenoria. On the other hand, when denial persists among the war survivors, the outcome is sadness and continuous suffering. This is illustrated by the case of Amelia.

Finally, despite these very positive aspects, we should also take a critical approach to the content of *gamba*. It carries a gender bias. That is, the women killed during the Mozambican civil war are unable to return as spirits to the realm of the living to claim justice. Only the spirits of men can do this. In this sense, although *magamba* spirits break with the silence of the past, structurally the justice they offer helps to reinforce patriarchical power in a country that is struggling for gender equality. Within this context, there is a need to establish a political agenda that is informed by well-established socio-cultural knowledge to address the gender bias imposed by *magamba* spirits. Female war survivors and women in general in Gorongosa need complementary (outside) interventions that can give them voice and agency not only in the domain of healing and through the language of spirits but also in other domains of the social, legal and economic organization of their communities, so that they can more effectively transform their present predicament.

8. Conclusion

The Mozambican peace agreement put an end to the violence of the civil war and brought relief from the horrors and appalling forms of human suffering. However, from a transitional justice perspective the peace agreement rests on very unjust foundations. Through a culture of denial, the Mozambican political elites precluded any legal or political process for a reckoning with the gross violations of human rights and the crimes perpetrated during the civil war.

In the aftermath of a protracted civil war, to reconcile deeply divided families and communities is a very complicated task. The challenge is more difficult and overwhelming when those who bear direct responsibility for the violence abandon the war survivors (the victims and former perpetrators) to resolve their profound war-related conflicts by themselves. Yet, in spite of this deliberate official neglect and abandonment, the war survivors living in the former epicentres of the civil war in Gorongosa have neither resorted to violent revenge (as Richard Wilson (2001) describes in relation to the townships in post-apartheid South Africa) nor gone along with the official authorities, who urged survivors to 'forgive and forget'. Instead, inspired by their own cultural wisdom, the survivors in Gorongosa managed to develop their own socio-cultural mechanisms to create healing and attain justice and reconciliation in the aftermath of the civil war.

Through the emergence of the *magamba* spirits, social spaces were created in which the grisly past is rescued from silence and individuals, families and members of the community are forced to come together to address the legacies of violence. These performance-based practices and the procedures they involve heal war-related wounds and create a local form of restorative justice, which gives dignity to the survivors. From a political perspective, *gamba* is not a response to the failure of the state institutions to provide accountability measures as part of a transitional justice process in the aftermath of the civil war. *Gamba* is part of the development of a well-established local tradition of settling accounts with histories of individual and collective violence. When an innocent person dies unjustly, no matter whether or how the secular justice system intervenes, the spirit of the dead person returns to the realm of the living to haunt the culprits, their families and their communities. Unless the appropriate rituals are performed the culprits and the collective are doomed to suffer. In this regard, *magamba* spirits evoke socio-cultural forms of justice and reconciliation in the aftermath of a horrific past which allows war-torn communities to contain violence, re-establish social order and foster a sense of continuity and communal identity.

In the process of determining the general impact of *magamba* spirits in Mozambique, it is clear that these spirits and the practices they evoke are making a decisive contribution to everyday forms of post-war reconstruction of the Mozambican state institutions through the provision of health care and access to certain types of truth and justice. Moreover, *magamba* spirits and healers reinforce the idea of the plurality of the African institutions of justice, reconciliation and healing.

Socio-cultural processes such as those enacted by *magamba* spirits and healers belong to what we term *entangled truths*. That is, *magamba* spirits and healers allow war survivors to attain justice, and this is creating healing and reconciliation in central Mozambique.

Yet in spelling out these important local achievements, *magamba* and other similar post-war phenomena run the risk of being wrongly used by the national political elites. For instance, political elites can use the success of *magamba* spirits and healers as arguments to justify their option for post-war amnesties, impunity and silence. The argument revolves around the idea that 'Mozambicans have their own way' and it is therefore not necessary to unleash formal justice processes to reckon with the abuses and crimes perpetrated during the civil war and the Marxist–Leninist dictatorship. This position is confirmed by what former President Joaquim Chissano told journalists on the occasion of the 12th anniversary of the General Peace Agreement, on 4 October 2004. Mozambican journalists quoted him inveighing against any investigation of the crimes of the past: 'We do not need to know who killed more between one and the other' (*Diário de Moçambique* 2004). The newspaper indicated that 'Chissano reiterated that he was against the creation of a truth and reconciliation commission, as it happened in the "post-apartheid" South Africa, to investigate anything related to the armed conflict in Mozambique (…) Chissano said that reconciliation in Mozambique is being made in a Mozambican way, with daily actions, and this is being applauded worldwide' (*Diário de Moçambique* 2004; author's translation). Chissano is right in his assertion, since socio-cultural phenomena such as the one presented by *magamba* spirits both bear witness to the experiences of extreme war violence and bespeak everyday forms of engaging in post-civil war justice, reconciliation and healing. However, on two counts Chissano is not so correct. First, he confuses community and state responsibilities, and, second, he fails to develop a critical approach to the 'Mozambican way' and to the actions of the national political elites over the past.

In the end, the fact that war survivors are engaged in everyday forms of attaining justice, reconciliation and healing should not be used as an excuse for state inaction vis-à-vis the violent past. The responsibility of individuals and families that survived the war within the former war zones is one thing; the accountability of those who were directly responsible for the indiscriminate violence that killed thousands of people and destroyed large parts of the country over a period of 16 years is another. In relation to post-war accountability, the former statesman Chissano remained mute. So far, no organized groups have emerged in Mozambican society to systematically chivvy the political authorities to investigate the crimes perpetrated during the civil war. The result is that politicians from both Frelimo and Renamo use the memories of the civil war as weapons for political gain.

References and further reading

Abrahamsson, Hans and Nilsson, Anders, *Moçambique em transição* [Mozambique in transition], transl. Dulce Leiria (Gothenburg: PDRI and Maputo: CEEI-ISRI, 1994)

Amadiume, Ifi, 'The Politics of Memory: Biafra and the Intellectual Responsibility', in Ifi Amadiume and Abdullahi An-Na'im (eds), *The Politics of Memory: Truth, Healing and Social Justice* (London: Zed Books, 2001), pp. 38–55

Baptista-Lundin, Irae, 'Uma leitura analítica sobre os espaços sociais que Moçambique abriu para colher e cultivar a paz' [A reading of the social spaces that Mozambique opened to receive and cultivate the peace], in Brazão Mazula (ed.), *Moçambique: 10 anos de paz* [Mozambique: ten years of peace], Vol. I (Maputo: CEDE, 2002), pp. 96–139

Boletim da República, series I, no. 42, Quarta Feira, 14 October 1992. Supplement

Cohen, Stanley, *States of Denial: Knowing about Atrocities and Suffering* (Cambridge: Polity Press, 2001)

Coelho, João Paulo, 'Da violência colonial ordenada à ordem pós-colonial violenta: Sobre um legado das guerras coloniais nas ex-colónias Portuguesas' [From ordered colonial violence to the violent post-colonial order: a legacy of the colonial wars in the ex-Portuguese colonies], *Lusotopie*, 2003, pp. 175–93

Diário de Moçambique (Maputo), 5 October 2004

Dolan, Chris and Schafer, Jessica, *The Reintegration of Ex-combattants in Mozambique: Manica and Zambezia Provinces*, Final Report to USAID Mozambique (Oxford: Refugee Studies Programme, 1997)

Hanlon, Joseph, *Who Calls the Shots?* (Bloomington, Ind.: Indiana University Press, 1991)

Hayner, Priscilla, *Unspeakable Truths: Confronting State Terror and Atrocity* (New York: Routledge, 2001)

Honwana, Alcinda, 'Spiritual Agency and Self-renewal in Southern Mozambique', PhD thesis, School of Oriental and African Studies (SOAS), London University, 1996

Igreja, Victor, 'Why Are There So Many Drums Playing until Dawn? Exploring the Role of *Gamba* Spirits and Healers in the Post-war Recovery Period in Gorongosa, Central Mozambique', *Transcultural Psychiatry*, vol. 40, no. 4 (2003), pp. 459–87

Igreja, Victor and Dias-Lambranca, Beatrice, 'The Social World of Dreams and Nightmares in a Post-conflict Setting', *Intervention*, vol. 4, no. 2 (2006), pp. 145–7

Igreja, Victor, Kleijn, Wim and Richters, Annemiek, 'Women's Posttraumatic Suffering after the War in Mozambique', *Journal of Nervous and Mental Disease*, no. 194 (2006), pp. 502–9

Jacobson, Ruth, 'Gender, War, and Peace in Mozambique and Angola: Advances and Absences', in Dyan Mazurana, Angela Raven-Roberts and Jane Parpart (eds), *Gender, Conflict, and Peacekeeping* (Lanham, Md: Rowman & Littlefield, 2005), pp. 134–49

Machel, Samora (President), Inaugural speech for the Reunião dos Comprometidos, Maputo, 2 July 1982 (1982a) (author's translation)

— Concluding speech for the Reunião dos Comprometidos, Maputo, 7 July 1982 (1982b) (author's translation)

Thomashausen, André, 'Mozambique: A Case Study', Paper presented at the Conference on Politics of Identity and Exclusion in Africa, University of Pretoria, 2001, available at <http://www.kas.de/db_files/dokumente/7_dokument_dok_pdf_5094_2.pdf>

Wieviorka, Annette, *The Era of the Witness*, transl. Jared Stark (Ithaca, N.Y.: Cornell University Press, 2006)

Wilson, Richard, *The Politics of Truth and Reconciliation in South Africa* (Cambridge: Cambridge University Press, 2001)

CHAPTER 4

CHAPTER 4

Northern Uganda: tradition-based practices in the Acholi region

James Ojera Latigo*

Cultural norms and values which are often at the core of human development and informed coexistence are founded and bonded on specific sets of principles that guide human behaviour in favourable ways. Resort to culture should therefore not be seen through lenses that depict primitive undertones but rather in such a way as to identify the values that will be useful to humanity.

1. The conflict

1.1. Descriptive chronology

Since independence in 1962, Uganda has been plagued by ethnically driven, politically manipulated violence referred to by some as a history of 'cycles of revenge and mistrust'. Deep-rooted divisions and polarization remain between different ethnic groups, and these have been greatly exacerbated by the way in which the country's leadership has developed since independence. The current National Resistance Movement (NRM) leadership has been in power for the past 21 years and only recently opened up the political space after 19 years of monolithic rule. The dominance of the NRM generated the rise of ethnically based fighting groups or militias and the creation of some unique, non-institutionalized and personalized military structures. In the recent past all these have brought ethnicity to the fore in order to claim an ideological shape as a way of laying claim to a constituency of support. Accusations of ethno-regional power grabs and confrontations have been rife, and are reflected in successive armed conflicts, the most devastating and enduring of which is the ongoing conflict in northern Uganda.

In order to anchor the problems which beset the country, and particularly northern Uganda, we need first to highlight some of the historical and political context.

*For an extended version of this chapter see www.idea.int/rrn

1.1.1. Historical roots: perceived military clout of the northerners

The British colonialists saw the northern part of Uganda as a 'problem' area. It was described at the time as 'a disturbed, hostile territory, in which there were some tribes powerful enough to offer stiff and prolonged resistance' to their occupation (Barber 1968, chapters 10–11). When the British decided to take control of the north, it was because of security concerns, in order to secure the south and west of the country, which the British had effectively occupied and where it wanted to install an administration. Until 1921, therefore, the area called the north was under military occupation by the Northern Garrison—an assumption of power and authority over the area 'in which the tribes had no say' (Barber 1968: 121). After World War I, the Acholi were used as part of the British 'divide and rule' policy when the British were seeking to 'pacify' the north by pitting the Nubians (an ethnic tribe in southern Sudan which had been employed to carry out punitive expeditions against the Lango, an ethnic group close to the Acholi) and the Baganda (an established kingdom in the south of Uganda) against the Banyoro (a strong Luo dynasty organically linked to the Acholi). The unsubstantiated myth created by the British of the Acholi people in the north as being a 'martial tribe' dates from that time. It was based entirely on prejudice and misrepresentation of facts and was used for political reasons. Previously, the Acholi had been considered as enemies and not 'martial' enough to fight British wars. Now, however, they began to feature in British military recruitment, although only by offering inducements to the chiefs, who were paid 3 rupees for each Acholi recruit for the war. When they were recruited into the army in large numbers, this was linked more to economic conditions in Acholi than for cultural reasons. Their numbers in the army dropped markedly in the 1950s when large numbers of recruits came from the Lango and the Iteso (a Nilo-Hermitic ethnic group in the east of Uganda).

1.1.2. The post-colonial experience

The continuation of the British-created myth of the Acholi as a 'martial tribe' and the perceived 'divide and rule' policy of the British colonialists are partly responsible for setting the stage for the turmoil that later engulfed the region. The post-colonial political elites took advantage of the arguments used to support these myths and the ethnic divisions based on them, and cynically started using them as a means of political manipulation for their own ends. The result of this political game plan was the upsurge of the many armed conflicts the country has experienced.

From independence in 1962 to date, 45 years down the road, Uganda has had nine different heads of state with varying tenures. Dr Milton Obote, who received the instruments of power from the British at independence, became the first president with executive powers and set the trend for the future leaderships. In a sense he became the mentor of the presidents who succeeded him, including Idi Amin and Yoweri Museveni. Obote, Idi Amin and Tito Okello Lutwa, who all hailed from northern Uganda, served as heads of state for a total of 21 years between them—a length of time that has only been surpassed by Museveni's rule, for which no end seems to be envisaged. The significant turning point in the development of the leadership in Uganda, into a manipulative one, came in 1967, when Obote abrogated the independence constitution and introduced the republican constitution (commonly referred to as the 'pigeon-hole constitution') which granted the president the means to exercise his executive powers according to his whim. He could promote, transfer, dismiss and deploy army officers/commanders at will.

The advent of manipulative politics paved the way for the rise of militarization and armed conflicts in the country. Box 4 gives a chronology of selected important episodes.

Box 4: The background to the conflicts in Uganda since independence

1966: The first internal armed conflict occurs. General Idi Amin Dada, then an army commander during Milton Obote's first term as president, led a military operation on Lubiri Palace, the seat of the Kingdom of Buganda, sending King Frederick Edward Mutesa II fleeing into exile. This leads to the desecration of the Kingdom of Buganda and the subsequent dismantling of all the cultural institutions in the country.

1971: A military coup is staged by General Amin to topple the Uganda People's Congress (UPC) government of Milton Obote, thus ushering in nine years of brutal military dictatorship, in which an estimated 500,000 people, mainly Acholi, were murdered.

1979: After Amin invades the Kagera region of neighbouring Tanzania in 1978, the Tanzanian People's Defence Forces (TPDF) together with Ugandans in exile (many of them, significantly, from northern Uganda) mount a liberation war which ousts the military regime of the self-proclaimed life president— then Field Marshal Dr Idi Amin Dada VC DSO MC, conqueror of the British Empire.

1979–80: Administrative wrangles, contests over power and power shifts ensue after the fall of Amin, culminating finally in a general election in 1980, which was 'won' by Obote's UPC party, ushering in his second term as president. The Democratic Party (DP) is alleged to have won, amid claims of massive vote-rigging which prompt other groups, led by Yoweri Museveni, to take up arms in the bush of Luwero to wage a protracted war on the elected UPC government.

1980–6: Several uprisings (not of a significant scale) emerge involving various armed groups, until 1985 when mutinying soldiers of the national army overthrow Obote's second (UPC) government and constitute a Military Commission, headed by General Tito Okello Lutwa (another northerner) to govern the country. The new de facto head of state immediately initiates comprehensive negotiations with the various conflicting groups in what become known as the Nairobi peace talks, and in December 1985 an agreement is reached and signed by all parties except Museveni's rebel National Resistance Army (NRA). The NRA tears up the agreement and breaches it with impunity. In January 1986 the NRA overthrows the government by force of arms, thus ushering in the National Resistance Movement (NRM), which has remained in power to this day.

The new establishment initially introduces an ideology dogmatically referred to as the Ten Points Programme, ostensibly geared to bringing about a 'fundamental change' in the governance of the country. A new era seems to open for the people of Uganda. However, seeming optimism hides increasing authoritarianism on the part of the NRM leadership. The situation is far from ideal today. From 1987 to date, a series of rebellions and insurgencies (22 in number) have been waged against the NRM government by various actors.

Since it began in 1986, the conflict in northern Uganda has gone through various stages and transformations, with several groups emerging to fight the government of Lieutenant-General Yoweri Kaguta Museveni. They have included the soldiers of the former Uganda National Liberation Army (UNLA) (the army formed to oust the Idi Amin regime); the Uganda People's Democratic Army (UPDA) led by the late Brigadier Odong Latek; the Holy Spirit Mobile Forces (HSMF), led by a prophetess, the late Alice Auma Lakwena (who died in February 2007 in a refugee camp in Kenya); the Holy Spirit Movement II (HSM II) led by Alice's father, Severino Lukoya; and the Uganda Christian Democratic Army (UCDA), led by Joseph Kony, which changed its name in 1991 to the Lord's Resistance Army (LRA) and is still active, with devastating consequences, including across the national borders.

Since a peace agreement was signed between the UPDA and the NRM/National Resistance Army (NRA) government at Pece Stadium in 1988, there have been successive transformations in the conflict—from the earlier UNLA/UPDA rebellion to the later rebellions. It is neither 'scientific' nor even consistent in a 'political' sense to generalize the war in Acholiland as emanating from the remnants of the Amin and Obote regimes, as many authors have done. Apart from the factual inaccuracies, such a generalization does not take into account the numerous political and spiritual transformations of the conflict. It is this lack of a nuanced understanding of the conflict in northern Uganda that may partly explain its persistence and duration. There have been three main phases in the conflict: first, the war waged by the UNLA/UPDA generals in 1986–8; second, a spiritually inspired peasant rebellion led by Alice Auma; and third, the transformation of both the HSMF and the UCDA into the Kony-led LRA. Each of these phases has had its import and impact and, although there have been some continuities in these conflicts, there have also been discontinuities, which have to be considered analytically. Internal factors and deep frustration arising out of the dynamics of the conflict cast light on a number of developments in Uganda. The early, isolated rebellions which were a reaction to the NRA harassment and killings were abandoned, crushed or transformed into new ones. These transformations cast light on the internal causes of the conflict.

> The primary source of evil in Uganda has been and remains untrammelled and absolute power.

1.2. The causes of the conflict

There is no consensus on any one theoretical and factual account of the cause of the conflict in northern Uganda, which is still largely unresolved. The sheer duration and dynamics of the conflict have generated intervening factors which have tended to blur the primary causes and perpetuate it. Consequently, there has been no general agreement as to whether the conflict should be resolved militarily or by way of dialogue. If we are to arrive at an amicable, consensus strategy for resolving it, we have to identify and understand the structural causes of the conflict, the triggers of conflict and the factors that have perpetuated it.

By and large, the causes of the civil strife in Uganda, and particularly in northern Uganda, can be assumed to include the interplay of major factors which include ethnic dominance (or polarization), which produces stereotyping and hate and enemy images; economic disparities (marginalization) and/or underdevelopment, exacerbating poverty; inconsistent pseudo-democratic and autocratic regimes; and other complicating factors. These are summarized below. However, the primary source of evil in Uganda has been (and remains) untrammelled and absolute power.

1.2.1. Ethnicity, stereotypes, and hate and enemy images

Most commentators have sought to portray the conflict as reflecting the north–south divide, explained in terms of the notorious colonial policy of 'divide and rule', ably applied with impunity by both the colonial and the post-colonial regimes. The colonial entity called Uganda was forged out of diverse nationalities and ethnic groups. To manage this diversity in a way that suited imperial interests, mechanisms were put in place to lead the different ethnic groups and nationalities to see each other as manifestly distinct and at times as enemies. Part of the structural causes of the conflict in Uganda has been explained as rooted in the 'diversity of ethnic groups which were at different levels of socio-economic development and political organisation' (Ugandan Parliamentary Committee on Defence and Internal Affairs 1997).

The perceived colonial policy of divide and rule fed stereotypical prejudices and the misrepresentation of facts for political reasons. This has been the main reason why since independence the political elites have politicized ethnicity as a means by which they can acquire and maintain political power in the country. The stereotypical labels of 'backwardness', 'primitiveness' and 'ignorance' and the enemy images and stigmatization that are often applied to the northerners arise from the unprincipled political tribalism with which groups compete for public resources. Even government officials have tended to legitimize oppression in ethnic terms. According to the local press, President Museveni himself spoke of the Acholi as being like grasshoppers in a bottle 'in which they will eat each other before they find their way out'. This unfortunate remark generated a great deal of emotion among the Acholi people, adding to the feeling that the war in northern Uganda has been designed as an instrument of vindictive governance.

Enemy images have instilled insensitivity to the extent that people perceived as enemies can be construed and ignored as not mattering. A former Cabinet minister who was a key figure in a Presidential Peace Team (PPT) constituted in 2002, addressing elders in Lango on the atrocities committed by the NRA in the northern districts of Gulu, Kitgum, Lira, Apac and Teso, was reported by the local media to have warned them that 'they did not matter as long as the south was stable'. The northerners' sense of betrayal has produced a groundswell of mistrust of virtually any overtures from the government to the rebels.

Some arguments locate the use of this strategy by the NRM/A rebels to the 'Luwero triangle' in central Uganda, which was the theatre of the rebel war from 1980 to early

1986, in order to garner popular support. In reality, their underlying drive was essentially 'unique greed for absolute political power' in total contempt of democratic means (Odongo 2003).

1.2.2. Economic disparities, marginalization, underdevelopment and poverty

Although the top leadership in Uganda from 1962 to 1985 hailed from northern Uganda, the region has continued to be marginalized economically. This is reflected in the great imbalance between the level of development and investment in eastern and northern Uganda and that in central and western Uganda, which is perceived as a land of milk and honey. This marginalization, deliberate or otherwise, has resulted in worse poverty in the north.

Although at times poverty may be treated as an escalating factor that creates resentment in society, its role in the conflict in northern Uganda is part and parcel of the structural factors underlying the conflict. The *Poverty Status Report, 2003* indicates that 'one third of the chronically poor (30.1%) and a disproportionate percentage [of those] moving into poverty are from northern Uganda' (Ugandan Ministry of Finance, Planning and Economic Development 2003: 102). This represents 7 per cent of the total population of Uganda.

Among young people, unemployment alone drives them to violence for economic gain. Any development intervention in the north should be geared towards providing alternative means of livelihood in order to increase the opportunity cost of resorting to violence, because people would have a living that enhances their stake in a stable society.

1.2.3. A weakening state?

The unstable and weak nature of the state is a major factor and a source of grievance in the conflict in northern Uganda. The simultaneous uprisings in the Teso sub-region in eastern Uganda and the Acholi sub-region in 1987 took place at a time when political and economic conditions had rendered the Ugandan state 'thin on the ground'. This was further aggravated by the atrocities committed against the population by the NRA. The legitimacy of the NRM/A government was dented as it failed in its responsibility to protect the population. The issue of political legitimacy was raised in a parliamentary report of 1997: 'The question, which perturbs many, is whether there is a legitimate authority in place whose task is to protect lives and properties of its citizens. One also wonders if the government forces have a sense of direction in quelling the rebellions given their poor record of human rights abuses' (Ugandan Parliamentary Committee on Defence and Internal Affairs 1997).

The government's failure to discharge its responsibility to 'protect' created a vacuum which could be exploited by different actors who might be political opportunists, criminal gangs or armed men seeking political power or opportunities for plunder.

Joseph Kony and the LRA emerged after the 1988 Addis Ababa Agreement between the Museveni government and the political wing of the UPDA, and the subsequent Pece Stadium Accord, also of 1988, which enabled most of the fighters to be integrated into the NRA. Their emergence was a manifestation of the government's loss of legitimacy. It had failed to protect its citizens against the atrocities committed by the rebels and by government forces and the LRA began to challenge and contest that tenuous authority. When the establishment in Sudan took advantage of the LRA and began to give it support in 1994, government authority was further undermined, producing a governance nightmare in the areas of conflict.

1.2.4. Complicating factors and concluding notes on the causes

Consequent to these developments, further complicating factors were introduced into the war in Acholiland in the form of resort to invisible spiritual forces to cleanse the evils. This became an 'extension of politics by other means', since 'normal' politics did not provide any avenue or mechanism for dealing with the increasingly complex problems in Acholiland in particular and Uganda in general. Spiritual actors were brought into play through metaphysical means to explain events and provide a moral basis for new forms of action in order to bring a semblance of moral order.

The autocratic actions of the political leadership in Uganda further created the preconditions for mistrust and suspicion among the different communities in the country. Such mistrust provided (and still provides) the foundation for a revenge syndrome in the psychology of many people in Uganda. Social–psychological studies of collective behaviour do argue forcefully that feelings of deprivation and frustration can tip over into and amplify a violent course of events, especially when small arms and light weapons are easily available.

> Resort to spiritual forces became an 'extension of politics by other means', since 'normal' politics did not exist. Spiritual actors were brought into play to explain events, provide a moral basis for new forms of action, and bring a semblance of moral order.

The government of Uganda sought to dismiss the conflict in the north as a minor problem of insecurity caused by criminals and terrorists, and supported by opportunists in neighbouring countries. Government propaganda became the ammunition for shooting down or pre-empting understanding and explanations of the rebels' viewpoints, political agenda and programmes.

The LRA has published at least three manifestos dated 4 April 1996, 1998 and 1999. The latter built on the previous two but added a number of issues. The 1996 manifesto had ten objectives: the restoration of multiparty politics; the introduction of constitutional federalism; the promotion of human rights; nationwide economic balance; the establishment of nationwide peace and security; an end to corruption; free and fair elections; good relations with neighbouring countries; the separation of the military from the judicial and executive arms of government; and the reform of parliament to empower it to deal with the critical political and economic issues in the country. On 28 December 2003, Brigadier Sam Kolo, chief political commissar of the Lord's Resistance Movement (LRM)/LRA, in an interview on a local FM radio station called Radio Rhino in the town of Lira in northern Uganda, alluded to the fact that the LRM/A perceives the conflict in northern Uganda as part of a protracted 'people's war' to remove 'the dictatorial government of Lt-General Museveni from power' to 'restore the rule of law'. He pointed out that the 'LRA is not a terrorist organization. It is a liberation movement. The word terrorist just came because anybody who opposes the government of Lt-General Museveni is deemed to be a terrorist. This is NRM propaganda which some friends of Museveni in the international community want to believe'.

The issues/arguments presented by the LRA, which I believe have been digested over time, are significant reflections of the turbulent political history that Uganda has gone through for the greater part of the post-independence era. The LRA, being a product of this troubled history, could not have preconceived these grievances at the start. However, having remained an outstanding opposition force which the government has to reckon with, it naturally became the torch-bearer for all the contentious issues and grievances that other 'opposition' political groups identify in the governance of the country.

The government of Uganda, for its part, was aggressive in propragating the view that the rebels were criminal gangs, and considered the option of using military force to crush them, or at best, due to local leaders' demands, 'amnestying' them. It was only after considerable pressure from elsewhere (particularly the government of South Sudan, which offered to mediate) that the government reluctantly agreed to another round of peace talks. More of the rebel demands have thus emerged and been heard with the advent of the Juba peace talks, which started in July 2006.

Thus, in terms of understanding, predicting or even controlling the risk factors responsible for causing, perpetuating and transforming the conflict, the international community ended up with a one-sided propagandist, statist–militarist and legalist perspective. This was candidly reflected by the US Administration in a statement that the 'armed conflict is supported by an extremely small minority of the population and does not pose a threat to the current government, but does compromise security, rule of law and economic growth' ('Executive Summary of the Proposed USAID/Uganda Integrated Strategic Plan 2002–2007'). The stage was then set for the Ugandan Government and some of its international allies to push for a military solution, because Kony, leader of the LRA, supposedly had no justification for going to war, his motives being perceived as merely a continuation of plunder and savagery by extremists. In the event, however, military stalemate ensued, with grave consequences for and devastating effects on the poor population.

The option chosen in resolving this conflict will either save lives and end the long suffering of the people or merely prolong their silent persecution.

1.3. Degree of internationalization of the conflict

The conflict in northern Uganda has been shown to be part of the chronic 'conflict corridor' traversing the Horn and Great Lakes Region of Africa, and is a manifestation of the 'new wars' that have tormented Sub-Saharan Africa. (Conflict research has generated the concept of 'new wars', based on examination of the mode of warfare, the goals and the resource bases of the conflicts encountered in Angola, the Democratic Republic of the Congo (DRC), Liberia, Sierra Leone, Somalia, Sudan, Uganda and elsewhere. Africa is seen to be witnessing wars which thrive on primordial social–ethnic identities and metaphysical belief systems and seemingly, by implication, lack clear-cut ideological agendas. The goals are characterized as bizarre, irrational and even crazy. Often the same characterization is extended to the leaderships themselves.)

The external element to the conflict in northern Uganda was of immediate relevance from August 1986, when some of the former UNLA officers who had lost the power struggle in Kampala withdrew to southern Sudan and sought refuge there. The attack on their refugee camp by the forces of the Sudanese People's Liberation Movement/Sudanese People's Liberation Army (SPLM/A) took the conflict across the national borders, in addition to the internal rebellion. This led to the UNLA officers seeking support from Sudan to launch their first resistance against the NRM government. The LRA later received both political and military support from the Sudanese Government, which allegedly supported it in retaliation for the Ugandan Government's political and military support for the SPLM/SPLA. This included deployment of the Uganda People's Defence Force (UPDF) inside Sudan. In many ways the Khartoum government gave the LRA considerable military support since it had an interest in using the LRA to weaken the military activities of the SPLA and the Ugandan Government's support for it.

This dual support scenario meant that the two conflicts, in southern Sudan and northern Uganda, increasingly became combined into one complex conflict across international borders.

In a desperate attempt to reach a settlement, the US Administration pressured Khartoum to allow the Ugandan Army to enter Sudan to 'flush out' the LRA in what was codenamed Operation Iron Fist. This attempt failed to end the rebellion and instead permitted the LRA to cross into the DRC and the Central African Republic, encountering and killing eight members of the United Nations (UN) peacekeeping personnel deployed in the DRC.

1.4. The legacies of the war in northern Uganda

In the northern Uganda conflict, the coalition Civil Society Organizations for Peace in Northern Uganda (CSOPNU) put the net cost of the conflict (by November 2002) at 'at least US$ 1.33 billion over the last 16 years—representing about 3% of GDP or US$ 1000 million annually' (CSOPNU 2002). The bulk of these costs relate to military expenditure (29 per cent), loss of livestock and crops (24 per cent) and the cost of ill health and deaths (21 per cent).

Over 1.6 million people, representing 90 per cent of the affected population in Acholiland, were forced to abandon their often self-sufficient homesteads for a life confined to the squalid internment camps commonly known as internally displaced persons (IDP) camps, dependent on food assistance—a situation described by UN Under-Secretary-General for Humanitarian Affairs Jan Egeland, in a widely reported address to the United Nations, as 'the forgotten humanitarian crisis'. The CSOPNU in a survey report released in July 2003 revealed that at least 1,000 people, mainly children, were dying in the camps every week.

The protection of IDPs remained precarious, and life became a daily struggle for survival. Chronically high levels of sexual and gender-based violence are reported for women and girls, who remain at great risk. An estimated 30,000 children, mainly from the Acholi sub-region, have been abducted and conscripted as child soldiers and rebel 'wives'. Many have suffered gross violations of their human rights, being abducted, beaten, maimed, tortured, raped and murdered on a daily basis. Up to 40,000 children were forced to become night commuters to spend their nights on verandas in town centres, churches or hospital compounds in order to avoid abduction.

The perpetrators in the northern Uganda conflict are often victims of abduction in the first place, forcibly turned into perpetrators as a means of enforcing loyalty to the rebel ranks. Moreover, the government's own UPDF, which should have offered protection to the people, was in many instances implicated in gross human rights violations, having failed to offer protection to the population. This complicates any attempts to apply a known, just system of accountability for those responsible for the atrocities, and gives a new twist to the question of whether justice should take precedence over peace in the circumstances.

1.5. Previous attempts at intervention to end the conflict and their failure

Since 1986, the government of Uganda, individuals, foreign governments, non-governmental organizations (NGOs) and the rebels themselves have initiated many processes in a bid to end the conflict in northern Uganda.

1.5.1. The government's carrot and stick

The Ugandan Government initially approached its peace initiative with a carrot and stick policy, to be achieved by a combination of military means of pressuring the rebels, enforcement of the law, an amnesty law and propaganda. However, partly owing to this approach and partly because of other complicating factors, the conflict raged on and expanded, to reach such a scale and become so devastating that sceptical voices began to doubt the government's capacity to win the war and bring about peace on its own. It seemed that the government had boxed itself into a corner because of President Museveni's repeated declarations that Kony would be defeated militarily. It became impossible for Museveni to concede that he could not. Meanwhile, military victory had not been easy to deliver because the army was riddled with command and control problems, corruption and inefficiency. It was demotivated and, as a result of its failures, unable to win the hearts and minds of the local populations.

Some of the government's failed moves are telling. In August 1986, Museveni went to Gulu to address the people of Acholiland about the rebel war, roundly condemning the former UNLA soldiers and vowing to wipe them out with guns. He swore never to talk peace with the 'criminals who have no cause to fight for', and utterly refused to listen to complaints from the Acholi elders about the iron-fisted tactics of his own soldiers. Systematic attempts then ensued to implement this vow by way of various military manoeuvres, none of which succeeded.

After these unsuccessful military episodes, the local Acholi leaders began to pressurize the government to pass an Amnesty Act. Amnesty was advocated out of two genuine concerns—the trend the conflict was taking, with no apparent viable end in sight; and the moral imperative to provide an outlet for the victims who were abducted against their will. Parliament then passed the Amnesty Act of 2000, establishing the Amnesty Commission to facilitate the return and reintegration of ex-combatants into the national army or civilian life. The rationale has been to stem the widespread fear of prosecution, borrowing largely from traditional approaches that emphasize 'forgiveness'. To date, 23,000 people have benefited from the amnesty, of whom 2,000 were from the Allied Democratic Forces (ADF) rebels but the majority engaged in activities related to the LRA.

Box 5: The Ugandan Amnesty Act, 2000, (Cap. 294, Laws of Uganda), Entry into force 21 January 2000

An Act to provide for an amnesty for Ugandans involved in acts of a warlike nature in various parts of the country and for other connected purposes.

Declaration of amnesty.
(1) An amnesty is declared in respect of any Ugandan who has at any time since the 26th day of January 1986, engaged in or is engaging in war or armed rebellion against the government of the Republic of Uganda by –
    (a) actual participation in combat;
    (b) collaborating with the perpetrators of the war or armed rebellion;
    (c) committing any other crime in the furtherance of the war or armed rebellion; or
    (d) assisting or aiding the conduct or prosecution of the war or armed rebellion.
(2) A person referred to under subsection (1) shall not be prosecuted or subjected to any form of punishment for the participation in the war or rebellion for any crime committed in the cause of the war or armed rebellion.

It would appear that the government also saw the opportunity to use the amnesty process to its own manipulative advantage. The implementation of the process has been suspect because the measures do not go far enough to reassure the rebels: a number of the returnees were subsequently arrested by the government and charged with treason. Moreover, most of those people from northern Uganda who are expected to benefit from the amnesty are victims of abduction. To give them amnesty in the legal sense is to criminalize them unjustly. That simply adds to the bitterness, of which they already have plenty, stemming from their experience of abduction.

Amnesty is often seen as favouring the winning side in a conflict irrespective of whether it is right or wrong or whether the losing side has legitimate complaints. Consequently, peace by means of an amnesty is not a principled peace. It sidesteps the truth. Painful as it is, the truth must be brought out and responsibilities must be assigned and accepted.

> Peace by means of an amnesty is not a principled peace. Painful as it is, the truth must be brought out and responsibilities must be assigned and accepted.

Amnesty is also based on the assumption of the rebels' guilt, the idea that the government is all-merciful, and the assumption that both sides will abide by the spirit of the declaration and accept the amnesty. None of these assumptions is valid. There is no question that the rebels have committed plenty of atrocities, but so has the government. There is no reason to believe that if rebels accept the amnesty they will be safe, since the president continues to threaten to kill the rebel leaders. There is also no evidence as yet that either side in the conflict has a mechanism in place to ensure that the conditions under which the amnesty is given are strictly enforced. Giving amnesty or accepting it without carefully, seriously and honestly negotiating these terms is like putting the cart before the horse.

As part of the carrot and stick approach, this amnesty programme was designed to isolate the leadership of the rebels by encouraging defections by the rank and file. As it turned out, those who defected met with disappointment because some of them fled from one difficult situation only to be recruited into the UPDF and sent off to fight the rebels they had just escaped from or to be deployed into the DRC or recruited as Local Defence Unit personnel.

However, while the amnesty has failed to meet the people's expectation for peace, it has been a very useful propaganda tool for the regime as a substitute for any real effort to engage in a peaceful resolution of the war. In the meantime, former abductees who did not need an amnesty in the first place have been paraded as examples of the resounding success of the amnesty.

The Amnesty Act has to be continuously amended to extend it, as well as giving a government minister the prerogative to declare individuals ineligible for amnesty.

Box 6: The Ugandan Amnesty (Amendment) Act, 2006
An Act to amend the Amnesty Act, Cap. 294

. . .

3. Insertion of section 2A
The Amnesty Act is amended by inserting immediately after section 2, the following new section:
"2A. Persons ineligible for amnesty
Notwithstanding the provisions of section 2 of the principal Act, a person shall not be eligible for grant of amnesty if he or she is declared not eligible by the Minister by statutory instrument made with the approval of Parliament."
4. Insertion of section 16
The principal Act is amended by replacing section 16 with the following:
"16. Duration
(1) The Principal Act will remain in force for a period of two years from the date of coming into force of this Act.
(2) The Minister may by statutory instrument extend the period referred to in subsection (1).
(3) The Minister may by statutory instrument declare the lapse of the operation of Part II of the principal Act."

1.5.2. Civil society interventions

Between 1994 and 1996, when it became increasingly apparent that no end to the conflict was in sight, many peace-loving people in the community and some Acholi in the diaspora began to explore plausible ways and means of ending the conflict peacefully. Organizations like the Kacoke Madit (an Acholi term meaning 'Big Meeting') emerged. Other initiatives included the so-called peace forums.

Traditional leaders/elders and the Acholi religious leaders' peace initiative
Traditional leaders and elders, in keeping with their cultural roles providing guidance to the community, became significant actors in the pursuit of peace in northern Uganda. Their efforts were supplemented by the crucial support of the religious leaders who have been closely associated with the dialogue process right from the beginning of the conflict. In 1997, the Catholic, Anglican, Muslim, and later the Orthodox religious leaders of Acholi formalized their increasing cooperation on peace issues by setting up the Acholi Religious Leaders' Peace Initiative (ARLPI). Established at a time when the prospects for a negotiated settlement seemed very bleak indeed, the ARLPI threw itself into the task of seeking a negotiated peaceful end to the conflict and distinguished itself as one of the most credible forces in pursuing dialogue. Its strength lies in its credibility and close links with community and global networks. For instance, it explored its links across Sudan to establish contact with Joseph Kony and his commanders, who in turn found it more agreeable to hold discussions with or call by telephone than the government side. Archbishop Odama, the chairman, led a six-person delegation to the United Nations, the USA, Canada, the United Kingdom and the European Union (EU) to lobby for support to end the war through dialogue.

Peace forums

The three districts which comprise the Acholi sub-region formed peace forums in their respective districts as a means by which peace-building messages and concerns can be voiced and deliberated. In Kitgum there was the Kitgum Joint Forum for Peace, in Pader the Pader Peace Forum, and in Gulu the District Reconciliation and Peace Team. These forums were made up of a broad spectrum of the local community, from the top district leadership down to the grass roots, and they included representation from civil society, traditional and religious leaders, local government, and women and young people. The three forums later merged to form the sub-regional Acholi Peace Forum.

These forums were originally driven by the principal aim of promoting the Amnesty Law and dialogue in general. They meet regularly to share experience and coordinate activities at the regional level. They have translated and distributed Luo versions of the Amnesty Law and held regular meetings between the peace teams to explore the alternatives for carrying forward the amnesty and dialogue process, and their efforts contributed to the establishment of the Amnesty Commission. However, they have also played a vital role in Acholi traditional reconciliation processes and in preparing the community to receive former combatants.

With the help of the Northern Uganda Peace Initiative (NUPI), funded by the United States Agency for International Development (USAID), these same structures were later replicated with expanded objectives to cover the 24 districts in northern Uganda. All of them were then united under an umbrella organization called the Northern Uganda Peace Forum with a permanent office in Gulu.

1.6. The current situation of the conflict and the justice vs peace debate

In November 2003, the Ugandan Government made a referral to the International Criminal Court (ICC) in The Hague. The ICC promptly commenced investigations, and in August 2005 issued its first-ever arrest warrants, for the LRA's five top commanders, namely Joseph Kony (the LRA leader), Vincent Otti, Okot Odhiambo, Dominic Ongwen and Raska Lukwiya (who died recently).

On 14 July 2006, dialogue commenced in the town of Juba in southern Sudan between the two belligerents with a view to reaching a comprehensive peace agreement. It was mediated by Dr Riek Marchar, vice-president of the transitional government of South Sudan. The path to a final peace agreement must of necessity pass through negotiating agendas that are long and strewn with intractable obstacles. The LRA wanted the Ugandan Government to discuss and address the underlying political, economic and social root causes of the conflict, and expressed this clearly from the start. The government side, on the other hand, baulked at entering into political discussions on what it preferred to see as primarily a military problem and hoped to negotiate a solution that it termed 'a soft landing' for the LRA. This divide was bridged by the crafting of a five-point agenda for the talks which encompassed both military and structural issues. The items on the negotiating agenda for the Juba talks were thus agreed to be the cessation of hostilities; comprehensive solutions to the conflict; reconciliation and accountability; a formal ceasefire; and disarmament, demobilization and reintegration.

On 26 August 2006, after many long hours of hard bargaining, a Cessation of Hostilities deal was signed. It covered 13 action points touching on a declaration of cessation of hostilities; hostile propaganda; the 'surfacing' of LRA forces (their coming out into the open and to assembly points); a process for assembling the LRA forces in Sudan; safe passage for the LRA forces; monitoring and protection of the LRA forces at the assembly areas; communication of the declaration of cessation of hostilities; completion of the movement of LRA forces to the assembly areas; supervision/monitoring of the implementation; the provision of basic services; renewal of the terms of the agreement; commencement of the agreement; and dispute resolution.

Meanwhile, the ICC indictment has become one of the major sticking points and threatens to derail the peace process completely. While the LRA wants the ICC to retract the indictment in order for the peace talks to proceed smoothly, the government insists that the ICC will not stand in the way of a comprehensive agreement, and that a successful peace process coupled with the working mechanism of a traditional Acholi reconciliation practice would be sufficient to persuade the ICC to back off. The ICC has as yet shown no intention of revoking the indictment.

> In August 2005 the International Criminal Court in The Hague issued its first-ever arrest warrants, for the LRA'S five top commanders. These indictments have been a stumbling block in the peace talks ever since.

With this impasse still unresolved, the LRA side came up with new demands—for a change of both venue and mediator, having lost faith in the impartiality of the Sudanese establishment. This stalled the resumption of the peace talks in January 2007. After two months of uncertainty, the parties—the Ugandan Government and the LRA—agreed in principle to meet and resume negotiations. This was after wide consultations and interventions involving UN envoy Joaqim Chissano, former president of Mozambique, and north Ugandan leaders. In the compromise that was reached, five countries (the DRC, Kenya, Mozambique, South Africa and Tanzania) agreed to send high-level observers to the government of South Sudan-initiated process.

A comprehensive agreement appears to be possible only after three contentious issues have been addressed—trust, transparency and transitional justice. On the question of transitional justice, the Ugandan Government reiterated its stand and promised to seek revocation of the ICC indictments of the LRA leaders, but only *after* a comprehensive agreement had been reached. The LRA is still demanding stronger assurances about its members' security. An alternative mechanism for accountability—such as traditional justice rituals—is essential in order to provide a viable 'third way' between the polar opposites of the ICC and impunity. The need for greater sensitivity and flexibility to local needs must be impressed on the ICC.

> An alternative mechanism for accountability—such as traditional justice rituals—is essential in order to provide a viable 'third way' between the polar opposites of the ICC and impunity.

The other face of justice involves the long-standing political exclusion of the war victims, who are mainly Uganda's northerners. Neither the Ugandan Government nor the LRA can honestly claim to represent their best interests. Ultimately, a just peace will require processes that empower the northerners to express and overcome their grievances. A start would be granting the opportunity for the indigenous people to revive their cultural beliefs, values, norms and practices and inject them into the peace process. Such a move would be a most important reminder to the parties that negotiations are not just about politics, but about people's lives.

The peace talks resumed on 26 April 2007, with the assurance from the deputy commander of the LRA, Vincent Otti, that the LRA would sign the comprehensive agreement but would not leave its positions and send its forces to the assembly areas until the ICC withdraws the indictment. If it does not do this, the continuation of war remains an option.

> Agenda item 3 of the Juba peace talks provided for the application of the traditional justice system process and the application of the traditional rite called *mato oput*.

Ruhakana Rugunda, who is the Ugandan minister of internal affairs and leader of the government negotiating team at the Juba talks, when leaving to start discussions on agenda item 3, on reconciliation and accountability, defended the traditional justice system called *mato oput*, as an alternative to the ICC trials: 'The traditional methods are both symbolic and real. They have worked. Instead of rushing for Western solutions, it is good we have revived them'. He added that the system would be upgraded to meet international standards (*New Vision* 1 June 2007).

Even if the ICC arrest warrants are just one among many other issues that need to be resolved, they have nonetheless provoked great debate about the dichotomy between peace and justice. Which should prevail first? This becomes a confrontation between the traditional justice system and the international justice system.

In trying to assess the role of the ICC in the present conflict in northern Uganda and deal with the claims made for the Acholi traditional concept of justice and reconciliation, it is necessary first to identify and analyse the relevant issues.

> Which should prevail first, peace or justice? This becomes a confrontation between the traditional justice system and the international justice system.

The first of these is the current understanding of international law on issues of intra-state conflicts and, within this focus, the role of the ICC in conflicts of this kind. I will make the provocative proposition that the present system of international relations on which current international law is based cannot be defended and maintained. Institutions such as the ICC are placing new burdens on collapsing nation states which cannot even implement the laws they make. In such circumstances, it is morally and politically wrong to create new institutions that carry forward the inequities of the past and impose them on marginalized communities such as the Acholi in complete disregard of their norms and institutions—which are, moreover, often based on sounder ethical principles than those of a positivistic, secular system.

The other, broader issue is the role of the post-colonial state in Africa and the way in which this role relates to traditional understandings of its functioning as wielder of the right to the monopoly on the use of force. Here the issue is one of its legitimacy given the Ugandan Government's alleged involvement, through its agents, in the crimes against humanity that are alleged to have been committed by non-state actors such as the LRA. The other side of the same coin is the question of whether its claim to a monopoly on the legitimate use of weapons of violence entitles it to claim power over individuals that it cannot even protect. What then is the nature of the African post-colonial states and how legitimate are they in the eyes of the people in their communities?

In an interesting turn of events, it is instructive to note that, in the ongoing peace talks in Juba, on 29 June 2007, the LRA and the Ugandan Government signed a package deal on accountability and reconciliation—a sticking point in the agenda—thus moving closer to a final peace agreement. The pact recommends alternative traditional justice: '3.1. Traditional justice mechanisms, such as *Culo Kwor*, *Mato Oput*, *Kayo Cuk*, *Ailuc* and *Tonu ci Koka* and others as practiced in the communities affected by the conflict, shall be promoted, with necessary modifications, as a central part of the framework for accountability and reconciliation' (Agreement on Accountability and Reconciliation between the Government of the Republic of Uganda and the Lord's Resistance Army/ Movement, Juba, Sudan, 29 June 2007). It further reads: 'accountability mechanisms shall be implemented through the adapted legal framework in Uganda' (article 4.4); and 'Legislation shall introduce a regime of alternative penalties and sanctions which shall apply, and replace existing penalties, with respect to serious crimes and human rights violations committed by non-state actors in the course of the conflict' (article 6.3). It excludes double justice for the same crimes. 'Where a person already has been subjected to proceedings or exempted from liability for any crime or civil acts or omissions, or has been subjected to accountability or reconciliation proceedings for any conduct in the course of the conflict, that person shall not be subjected to any other proceedings with respect to that conduct' (article 3.10).

The parties committed themselves to honour the suffering of victims by promoting lasting peace and justice, preventing impunity and promoting redress in accordance with the constitution and international obligations, especially the requirements of the Statute of Rome which set up the ICC. Reparation would include rehabilitation, restitution, compensation, guarantees of non-recurrence of acts of violence, and other symbolic measures such as apologies, memorials and commemorations. The government also committed itself to strike the LRA off the list of terrorist organizations as soon as the rebels renounce rebellion, sign a comprehensive peace agreement and submit their members to the process of disarmament, demobilization and reintegration.

By signing the 11-page document, the delegates ended a month of protracted negotiations on this contentious point on the agenda of the talks, which had been referred to as the fulcrum on which the process hinged. However, the agreement simply presents the general principles. Further consultations are continuing to work out the finer details.

2. Acholi traditional justice and reconciliation mechanisms in their 'original' form

2.1. Background and description

In order to understand the workings of the Acholi traditions in relation to conflict management, it is important to highlight the indigenous system of governance under which this tradition operated. In pre-colonial times, and before the people of Acholiland were forcibly split up and moved from their homesteads, practically all conflicts in Acholiland were settled amicably through a well developed mechanism for the prompt resolution of conflicts as soon as they arose. Prior to the formation of the state of Uganda which replaced the British colonial administration, the Acholi people maintained a traditional government that was rooted firmly in their religious beliefs, norms and customs, which demanded peace and stability in Acholiland at all times, based on their philosophy of life. This structure was maintained by the real anointed chiefs of the Acholi people, known as the *rwodi moo*.

In this society, traditional religion was the source of the principles of governance. The *rwodi*, or chiefs, who headed the Acholi traditional government, were believed to have been chosen by the supernatural powers, and were enthroned and specifically anointed with fat preserved from the carcasses of lions in solemn religious ceremonies. After these ceremonies they were believed to have been initiated into an esoteric relationship with the world of invisible deities and spirits of ancestors. They were thus held in high esteem, adored and respected by their people.

Notably, these traditional chiefs had no executive powers to rule the people single-handed, so dictatorship was not possible. They worked or governed strictly through the intercession of 'masters of ceremonies' or an aide-de-camp known as the *luted-jok* and under the guidance of the most powerful Council of Clan Elders, called the Ludito Kaka. The members who made up this council were chosen democratically by the particular clan to sit on the Grand Council known as the Gure Madit. As guardians of the society, the elders, sitting together in the Grand Council, identified the problems and urgent needs of their people and together thought out and charted appropriate solutions to the problems of the society and how to realize its urgent needs. Their principal aim was to eliminate the vast and complex social causes of unhappiness in Acholiland. The Grand

Council also doubled as a 'Supreme Court' to try cases of mass killings and land disputes between different clans, essentially handling all cases of both a criminal and a civil nature. It made laws and took decisions in the form of religious injunctions to be observed and implemented by the members of the Acholi society for their own good, akin to the functions of judiciary, parliament and executive in 'modern' government systems.

Given the religious-based system of governance, no godless citizen could become a political leader, and all public figures were devout people who governed their society strictly in accordance with their beliefs, norms and customs. This ensured that no person could commit a crime and go unpunished, although there were no formal law enforcement institutions such as police and prison services. As the governing body, the Councils of Elders at all levels dealt firmly with recalcitrant individuals and groups and ensured that everyone conformed strictly to the Acholi world view.

Unfortunately, the British colonialists stripped the chiefs of their political power, replacing them with colonial administrators. Cultural leaders were not sufficiently recognized again until a 1995 constitutional reform. Even then the re-emergence of the Ker Kwaro Acholi (KKA)—the cultural institution of the Acholi presided over by a paramount chief—was largely based on the blueprint of the inherited colonial administrative structure without the necessary anchoring in the deep traditional beliefs, culture and norms that had been practised hitherto. Thus both the status and the popular authority of this cultural institution, once considered as 'providers' and guides of their people, have been severely weakened.

2.2. The rite of reconciliation called mato oput

The negotiating teams in the ongoing Juba peace talks agreed in principle that the application of this traditional rite, among others, is one of the appropriate mechanisms to address the issues of accountability and reconciliation.

Acholi society believed firmly that man is a sacred being whose blood ought not to be spilled without just cause. The killing of human beings is strictly forbidden by their religion. The community was enjoined to observe this strictly by worshipping the same supreme deity, Nyarubanga, through an intermediary deity, known as the *jok-ker*, which meant 'the ruling deity'. Within such a community, if one person happened to kill another person(s) from the same or a different clan, the killing would provoke the anger of the deities and ancestral spirits of the victim(s). It was and still is believed that the angered deities and spirits of the ancestors would permit or even invite evil spirits to invade homesteads and harm the inhabitants. Moreover, such killings automatically create a supernatural barrier between the clan of the killer and the clan of the person(s) who has/have been killed. As soon as the killing happens, the members of the two clans immediately stop eating and drinking from the same bowl or vessel, and engaging in social interaction of any form. This supernatural barrier remains in force until the killing is atoned for and a religious rite of reconciliation has been performed, to cleanse the taint.

In the meantime, the killer is ostracized and treated as an outcast or unclean person. The taint of killing that makes the killer an evil man is called *ujabu*. A killer is therefore prohibited from entering any homestead other than his own for fear that he is a companion of the evil spirits which constituted the *ujabu* and will pollute the soil of the homestead with the evil spirits. The *ujabu* can be created or invoked by both deliberate and accidental killings.

In all cases of deliberate or accidental killing, the clan of the killer is required to pay blood money to the clan of the person killed. The Council of Elders appoints a leading man from a different clan to mediate between the two clans. The mediator, who is expected to be completely impartial, coordinates the arrangements for payment of the blood money. It is strictly unacceptable to pay for the killing by killing the killer (there is no death sentence), since it is believed that this will only mean a loss of manpower to the society, without benefiting either side. The payment of blood money is preferable since the money paid to the bereaved family can be used to marry another woman who, in turn, will produce children to replace the dead person—a form of reparation.

After the payment of the money (reparation), the elders arrange for the customary rite of reconciliation to take place in order to bring the estranged clans together to resume a normal working relationship. The reconciliation ceremony always takes place in an uncultivated field which is usually somewhere between the villages or communal settlements of the two clans, away from any footpath or any place commonly frequented by women and children.

To perform the reconciliation ceremony, the killer provides a ram and a bull (*dyang me dog bur*), while the next of kin of the person killed provides a goat. Unused new vessels are required and a large quantity of beer is brewed for the occasion. On the appointed day, the traditional masters of ceremony, conciliators and elders from both clans assemble at the chosen site and stand facing westwards in solemn silence. An invocation is then performed which sums up the entire spirit and intent of reconciliation. This always runs as shown in box 7.

Box 7: The *mato oput* reconciliation rite in northern Uganda

The master of ceremonies:
'You our ancestors and the children of the Supreme Deity! I now plead with you and ask you to realize that sin is part of man's life. It was started by those who ever lived before us. This man whose fault brought us here today has merely repeated the perennial SIN which man has hitherto failed to discard since time immemorial. He killed his own brother. But since then he has repented of his evil deed. He has paid blood money which may be used to marry a woman who will produce children who, in turn, will keep the name of his killed brother for our posterity. We now beseech you our ancestors to let the two families resume a brotherly relationship . . .'

All the assembled elders join in and chant together:

'Let a man who will be given the blood money to marry a wife be sharp and pick on a vivacious woman . . . a virgin woman who will produce many and healthy children to grow up well and take over the empty home.'

Another master of ceremonies from the clan of the killed person responds to the solemn invocation in the following terms:

'We are not the first clan to suffer premature death of this kind. The killer has repented his misdeed. He has paid for it. We now supplicate you our ancestors to bless the blood money given to the family to marry a wife to produce a replacement for our killed brother. . . .'

All the assembled elders join the invocation and chant together:

'Let us accept the blood money and wash our hearts clean, and begin to live and work together as we have been doing in the past . . . Our enemies who have heard of this reconciliation and are not happy that it will now bring peace and prosperity to our two clans. . . . Let their ill will be carried away by the sun to the west, and sink with it down, deep and deep down. . . '

In a new vessel, the masters of ceremony mix the pounded extract from the roots of the *oput* tree with an alcoholic drink, and then the killer and the next of kin of the person who has been killed kneel down and begin to drink from the same vessel simultaneously while women from both clans make shrill cries and shout the war cries of the two clans. Members of the two families join in to drink from the same vessel for the first time. Meanwhile the master of ceremonies cuts off the head of the ram brought by the killer and the head of the goat from the next of kin of the dead man. The ram's head is ceremoniously handed over to the next of kin of the dead man and the goat's head given to the killer. The bull is ritually speared to death and skinned and the meat is cooked and eaten together. Other cooked food items from both sides are served to the elders, who are allowed to mingle freely. From now on, the members of the two clans resume their normal social intercourse. In this way, the Acholi people make good the damage caused by the spilling of the sacred blood of human beings.

The USAID-funded NUPI, through the KKA, supported 54 of these ceremonies between 2004 and 2006.

2.3. The rite of 'stepping on the egg' (nyono tong gweno)

Rooted in the firm belief about preserving the sacredness and social stability of their homesteads, the Acholi cleansing ceremonies maintain this ideal. The most common and best-known ritual is *nyono tong gweno* ('stepping on the egg'), which essentially is intended to welcome home family members who have been away from the homestead for an extended period of time. It relates to the belief that away from home people could contract spirits which, if not cleansed, will adulterate and/or bring misfortune to the whole community. The ceremony helps restore confidence in the traditional approaches to justice, and is a precursor to the eventual *mato oput* rite where applicable. The practice, however, goes beyond a mere cleansing ceremony, and extends to cover even those who may have left the clan after a quarrel or an unresolved disagreement with people at home, and on some occasions sworn not to return. *Nyono tong gweno* is thus performed as a gesture to welcome them and is a commitment on the part of both the community and the returnee to begin living together in harmony again.

The 'stepping on the egg' is ideally performed at the family or clan level, but has on occasion been organized on a larger scale where many returnees collectively step on eggs in one ceremony. This has been roundly condemned by most knowledgeable elders, who argue that the ritual can only be significant and meaningful when applied on an individual basis at the respective family/clan level.

Almost all the LRA returnees (their numbers are estimated at over 12,000) have undergone this ceremony, including victims from tribes other than the Acholi in ceremonies conducted collectively by the KKA and the respective families, some of which were supported by USAID/NUPI.

2.4. Other rituals

The ritual of 'cleansing the body' (*moyo kum*) is a more complex ceremony performed with persons returning from captivity. This calls for a gathering of the elders to bless the returned person, wash away their ill-deeds, chase away evil spirits, and appeal to the ancestors for their blessing. The practice varies from clan to clan, involving in some cases the simple act of spearing a goat and dragging it across a compound to rid the clan of *cen* (the marauding evil spirit), and in some cases a ceremony lasting several days in which the person who has returned must replicate the life lost by re-enacting parts of their lives. This ritual has some precedent in other post-conflict reconciliation practices, for example, in Angola, Mozambique and Sierra Leone.

'Cleansing of an area' (*moyo piny*) is another ritual which in the context of the conflict involves a sacrifice of goats to appease the ancestors and cleanse an area of evil spirits that are believed to dwell in places where war-related massacres have occurred, such as the sites of deadly ambushes, mass murder in fields or compounds, and battle. Many indigenous people hesitate to return to their original settlement or homestead where such deaths have occurred until this ceremony is performed, out of fear of marauding spirits.

'Bending the spear' (*gomo tong*) is a vow between two conflicting parties to end hostilities. It is considered a highly sacred act, invoking the ancestors, and thus once it is completed no further blood should be shed. In 1985, *gomo tong* was used in a landmark effort to resolve the serious tensions between on the one side the Acholi, who were killed on a large scale by Idi Amin and his henchmen during his dictatorial regime, and on the other the people of West Nile (where Amin came from), who suffered severe reprisals in 1980 after Amin's fall. It is instructive to note that later on the West Nile Bank Front (WNBF) I & II, composed mainly of people from West Nile who had joined Museveni's army, refused to be deployed to fight the LRA, citing the 1985 *gomo tong* ceremony between the two communities, which remains eternally binding. ('Bending the spear' would have been the appropriate ceremony to address the perceived tensions between the Acholi and the neighbouring communities of Lango, Teso, Madi and southern Sudan caused by the LRA incursions into those areas if the LRA had been acting on behalf of the Acholi, which was clearly not the case.)

Other rites practised by neighbouring ethnic communities that are based on similar principles and usage, as cited in the Juba agreement on the principles of accountability and reconciliation, include *kayo cuk* ('biting of charcoal'), a traditional ritual performed by the Lango, a neighbouring ethic community to the Acholi, to reconcile parties formerly in conflict, after full accountability; *tonu ci koka*, the traditional rituals performed by the Madi to reconcile parties formerly in conflict, also after full accountability; and *ailuc*, traditional rituals performed by the Iteso to reconcile parties formerly in conflict, again after full accountability.

2.5. The substance of the traditional justice mechanisms

From these accounts, we can isolate some of the essential principles of the Acholi polity that were exemplified in the behaviour and practice of the people and their rulers for generations past. This is by no means the end of the story. There is still a need to continue tracing the processes which led to the development of some of the original, informed traditional practices, the decay of others and the emergence of new ones, such as various forms of psychotherapeutic healing in Acholiland and elsewhere in Africa.

The principle of conflict resolution among the Acholi is to create reconciliation which brings the two belligerent sides together through the intercession of elders, leading to the acceptance of responsibility and an indication of repentance. Terms for compensation are then determined. The precursor for all these processes of societal recovery is acknowledgement aimed at ultimately furthering both the act and the process of forgiveness through the remaking of relations of trust and the restoration of social cohesion.

Mato oput is predicated on full acceptance of one's responsibility for the crime that has been committed or the breaking of a taboo. In its practice, redemption is possible, but only through this voluntary admission of wrongdoing, the acceptance of responsibility, and the seeking of forgiveness, which then opens the way for healing.

Tolerance and forgiveness are enshrined in the principles of *mato oput* and other associated rituals. The rite embraces collective guilt as well as individual guilt. It is a process whereby the parties to a conflict resolve to deal with the consequences of the conflict and its implications for the future in a collective, mutually and democratically acceptable, manner. The process recognizes and seeks to salvage and affirm the moral worth and dignity of everyone involved—victims, perpetrators and the community at large—in the pursuit of a decent society, with the primary focus on coexistence and the restoration of relationships between former enemies as a basis for the prevention of the recurrence of gruesome crimes. The severing of relations between the conflicting societies until the cleansing ceremony is performed is an act of condemnation of evil. It allows the victims, for the period for which it lasts, to suppress their resentment and the hatred that has developed as a way of moving on in anticipation of the beginning of a new relationship. The act of slaughtering the goat and ram and exchanging the heads reminds the perpetrators and those witnessing the ceremony that there is a price to be paid for violating the agreed rules of coexistence. *Mato oput* embodies the principle that society and the perpetrator contribute to the extent possible to the emotional restoration and repair of the physical and material well-being of the victim. The embedded principles underlying it, which the Acholi uniquely have used successfully in conflict management for generations, are actually the very principles of transitional justice mechanisms now paraded in modern studies as 'models', encompassing the same principles of truth, accountability, compensation, and the restoration of relationships.

> The rich body of traditional systems of law and justice in northern Uganda reflects principles of conflict management with both retributive and restorative elements where the objective is to reintegrate the perpetrators into their communities and reconcile them with the victims, through a process of establishing the truth, confession, reparation, repentance and forgiveness.

> There should now be an attempt to reconcile the principles of retributive justice and restorative justice and on that basis a more synthesized and comprehensive approach to peace and war can be envisioned on a global basis.

The conflict in northern Uganda has revealed that there is a rich body of traditional systems of law and justice that reflect principles of conflict management with both retributive and restorative elements where the objective is to reintegrate the perpetrators into their communities and reconcile them with the victims, through a process of establishing the truth, confession, reparation, repentance and forgiveness. This body of traditional practice is based on sound theory, which emphasizes peace before justice. It is in distinct contrast to the retributive, adversarial approach, which insists on justice before peace. The differences are not just conceptual but cosmological and epistemological, as the description of the processes above shows. There should now be an attempt to reconcile the two systems of thought—retributive justice and restora-tive justice—and on that basis envision a more synthesized and comprehensive approach to peace and war on a global basis.

3. Traditional mechanisms of restorative justice today

3.1. The impact of the conflict and the resulting potential of traditional mechanisms of restorative justice

The conflict in northern Uganda has eroded the hitherto solid and rich Acholi social fabric which was the foundation upon which these traditional norms, belief systems and practices were meaningfully and effectively regulated. Certain practices and beliefs are still widespread in some areas of Acholiland but less common in others. Moreover, some rituals might not have been performed for a long time in a particular area because wartime insecurity and the resultant extreme poverty made it impossible to put together all the necessary components; but they might still be applicable and sought after by the community. The dynamism inherent in this conflict has inevitably changed the form of cultural identity among the Acholi, who are now shaped not only by tradition but also by the Christian and Muslim faiths, as well as by 'modernity'. Yet, identifiably, the pillars of the current Acholi identity are related to—and expressed through—certain beliefs, attitudes and practices on the ground such as rituals, prayers and court hearings. This complex and dynamic blend of identities and beliefs must always be kept in mind.

Even if 'traditional' approaches are still meaningful and important in Acholiland, they are less relevant to some of the people. This is especially true for young people who have grown up during a time of war with restricted opportunities to experience or participate in such practices. Some Christian believers reject traditional practices outright as being 'Satanic'. Yet in the African psyche neither Christianity nor any other 'imported' religion can replace their firm moral and spiritual beliefs; they may merely 'add them on' to their original belief system that was practised long before the 'introduction' of foreign religions. Similarly, the LRA, much as it purports to uphold Christian principles, does not divorce itself from the values enshrined in the traditional practices. These practices are, moreover, likely to be more relevant to the LRA because (in my own opinion) their real fear is not the ICC indictment but rather fear of confronting and living with the communities on which they have inflicted various forms of atrocities when they finally end the rebellion.

During the two decades of the current war, many traditional beliefs and practices have declined, while others which have remained relevant have been adjusted to current circumstances. New beliefs and practices have emerged which tend to hybridize with Christian religious practices. It will be critical for the Acholi community to engage in a thorough and open discussion of the ways in which traditional rituals and beliefs can be used to foster processes of healing and reconciliation in war-ravaged Acholiland, at whatever level this is possible among different sectors of the community.

3.2. Relationship to other transitional justice policies and instruments

In Acholi jurisprudence, there is no contradiction between accountability and reconciliation—indeed, the two are aligned. Above all, impunity is never accepted. The Acholi traditional justice and reconciliation system is a practical reflection and application of the nascent concept of transitional justice, namely counter-factual investigations into the past and the present in order to forge the future. This investigative process can bring to the fore options for a victim-centred post-conflict implementation process. It is possible through such an interrogative or probing process to identify and problematize the causative factors and the consequences of violations of human rights. In turn, this will inform the way forward, identifying ways in which to address those violations of human rights in the post-conflict period. This type of retrospective investigation into past betrayals through a concerted consultative process can, moreover, potentially lead to the implementation of a national plan.

> The Acholi traditional justice and reconciliation system is a practical reflection and application of the nascent concept of transitional justice, namely counter-factual investigations into the past and the present in order to forge the future.

Uganda has gone further than any other country in incorporating certain principles of traditional restorative justice into the amnesty law that is currently operative. One of the obstacles to the speedy advancement of the Juba peace talks is the question of the ICC indictment. To overcome this impasse, everything points to traditional mechanisms as a way out: work to codify the process in conformity with acceptable and feasible 'Western' standards is already at an advanced stage.

In the Ugandan scenario, peace building ultimately must unfold as a national programme. However, the atrocities have been concentrated in the northern region. Thus, only people to whom the 'truth' is relevant need to take part in the process of coming to terms with the past. In reality, the process would function as a silencing or 'social forgetting' process, where persons share common intimate knowledge, which is kept within the confines of trusted social groups. Trust is one of the building blocks of any social development, and the connection of such interpersonal trust with the strengthening of civic institutions and the re-establishment of social relationships can have significant implications for a society's transition from a divided, dysfunctional society. This trust, which politics has failed to nurture, can only be realized when it is anchored in the valued traditional cultures of the people affected, in which they believe. The successful reintegration of ex-combatants is a key driver of the peace process and can only be meaningfully done in the context of the lived traditions that provide the obvious 'alternative to life in the bush'.

> There is a need to see reconciliation in a context where, instead of replacing or undermining Western retributive justice, it can potentially serve as a 'bridge' from a past where such justice was denied to a present where it is not yet practically possible to a future where, hopefully, it can become an integral part of the social order.

Putting it more simply, our pursuit of national reconciliation today should include establishing an appropriate and effective African traditional system of restorative justice as an alternative option to a Western justice system.

3.3. Main actors, stakeholders and degree of inclusion

The holistic approach to dealing with the delicate challenges set out above is incredibly difficult but very necessary. This calls for concerted efforts by various actors and stakeholders who must all play a role.

The working of the Acholi traditional system during conflict—based on constant consultations, negotiating solutions to problems, consensus and respect for the authority of the chiefs/elders—must be actively revitalized. Traditional leaders and elders should play their special roles as mediators to break the deep-rooted mistrust between the parties in conflict and to bridge the gap (as peace emissaries), build confidence by encouraging talks and discouraging hostilities, initiate direct contacts with belligerents, reintegrate returnees through traditional cleansing ceremonies, and mediate and prevent fights among individuals and sub-clans as a result of the conflict. Additionally, they could undertake advocacy and lobbying roles through networking with various individuals and groups—local, national and international.

Civil society—the realm of organized social life that is voluntary, self-generating, self-supporting, autonomous from the state, and bound by a legal order or set of shared rules—has a critical role to play in the peace and reconciliation efforts through the medium of communication, institutions and social networks outside the state and the economy. The actors in civil society can be broadly categorized as including economic organizations, cultural bodies, development organizations, civic organizations, interest-based organizations, issue-oriented organizations, and the 'ideological marketplace' in the form of the independent mass media and institutions in the broad field of autonomous cultural and intellectual activities. These are private in nature but public in orientation, that is, they are outward-looking for the benefit of the entire community, and relate to the state, but keep a safe distance from formal power under the state, while at the same time they work for concessions, benefits, policy changes, relief, redress and accountability.

The area of intervention by civil society should involve the many issues that affect the full enjoyment of human rights, at which peace is the epicentre. These should embrace facilitation, arbitration, negotiation, mediation and conciliatory roles.

Other actors can be categorized as the top-level leadership, involving military, political and religious leaders such as the ARLPI leaders with high visibility; a middle-level leadership, actors who are leaders respected in sectors, ethnic/religious leaders, academics, intellectuals, NGOs and the media; and the grass-roots leadership, to include actors who are local leaders, the leaders of indigenous NGOs, community developers, local health officials or traditional healers, and IDP camp leaders.

In all these instances, women and young people are involved in playing complementary roles in a significant way to their adult male counterparts without undue discrimination.

4. An analysis of strengths, weaknesses, opportunities and threats

The various initiatives that have been attempted in the search for a solution to the northern Uganda conflict have provided useful lessons in efforts to pursue peace and reconciliation. Of late, the focus of attention and hope has become the traditional systems of conflict management to help break an apparent impasse in the peace process.

This section summarizes the author's own views on the strengths, weaknesses, opportunities and threats of the Acholi traditional justice system in relation to its applicability to resolving the two-decades long conflict in the region, and its possible adaptation to other conflict scenarios globally.

4.1. Strengths

1. The traditional justice system fosters the culture of *dialogue and inclusiveness* which is intrinsically enshrined in the processes. In any conflict situation, dialogue plays a significant role as a first step towards a peaceful resolution.

2. It is *culture-specific* and consistent with tried and tested methods that have restored relations in the past. This makes it difficult for the ever-present 'spoilers' to manipulate the process for cynical political purposes.

3. The *open nature* of the process applied is in itself a deterrent to many who would have contemplated committing similar crimes.

4. The traditional justice system fosters a greater *sense of unity* by allowing many community members to witness and/or participate in the process, as well as ironing out any doubts about whether fair justice is being dealt.

5. The traditional justice process often generates *community-focused* outcomes that impact positively on the entire community.

6. Community and human powers sanction the agreements reached. The agreement reached is normally unassailable and has to be implemented to the satisfaction of the entire community. *Compliance* is often achieved to a very high degree.

7. The *possibility of perpetrators negating or avoiding the process is limited* since it is largely an intra-community process.

These inherent strengths of the traditional justice processes represent convenient, viable options for bringing about genuine peace and reconciliation. After years of costly military activity, the conflict in northern Uganda has not yet evolved to such a state that any one approach can be said to hold the key to resolution.

> The role of traditional leaders and the community ceremonies of reconciliation which they mediate are indispensable to trust and confidence building and the enhancement of genuine reconciliation.

4.2. Weaknesses

1. The traditional justice system is *culture-specific and not flexible.* It is often difficult for people who do not belong or subscribe to the particular culture to respond positively to the traditional justice processes. There is very little leeway and no possibility of changing or bending the rules hitherto prescribed to suit particular circumstances.

2. The system relies heavily on the contribution of the *elders' knowledge and experience* in varying circumstances, as opposed to professional mediators. Currently, where elders are not readily available, the community may be tempted to postpone the traditional justice process.

3. The absence of a clear, written structure or framework for *coordinating* all the processes can complicate them, or even render them completely futile.

4. The traditional justice process has to be performed *at a convenient time* following an agreed formula, and this may delay the dispensation of justice.

5. The *agreements reached are verbal* and compliance depends on the commitment, goodwill and character of those involved.

6. The practice *may not be readily acceptable to neighbouring communities*, and this may limit its application.

7. The practices *may not be entirely consistent and uniform* among the different Acholi clan communities.

8. Being a tribal remedy, the Acholi traditional justice system is always considered to be

appropriate to reconcile the Acholi LRA captive foot soldiers with their local communities, where they had been forced to commit heinous crimes against humanity. However, the system in its original form was not conceptualized as a method for adjudicating over *war crimes and crimes against humanity*, because in pre-colonial Acholiland these never occurred. Hence it is not well suited to being applied as the sole reconciliation measure to the LRA architects of terror. Moreover, in Ugandan law, customary authorities and laws are not allowed to adjudicate in any criminal case, let alone the much more serious crimes against humanity and war crimes.

9. A fundamental weakness of the application of *mato oput* as a remedy is that, conceptually, it wrongly projects the LRA insurgency as a local Acholi affair. In reality this war had inherent *national and international* dimensions.

10. The judicial functions of the Acholi traditional mechanisms are bound up with the extensive *social education* received in the home and in the community through teachings surrounding the celebrations and everyday activities of the community. Over the years, this social space and social fabric have been desecrated by the prolonged conflict and the internment of entire communities in the camps, and thus the application of the traditional systems cannot readily be appreciated, especially by the younger generation. The revival of these core tenets among Acholi society on a massive scale is an enormous and strategically important priority as the population prepare to return to their original homesteads.

> The judicial functions of the Acholi traditional mechanisms are bound up with the extensive social education received in the home and in the community. Over the years, this social space and social fabric have been desecrated by the prolonged conflict and the internment of entire communities in the camps, and thus the application of the traditional systems cannot readily be appreciated, especially by the younger generation.

4.3. Opportunities

1. The traditional justice system offers experimental *learning opportunities*, especially to the members of the community. It is only after one has undergone the ritual that the real import of what it represents will be realized. It has the unclaimed potential of restoring sanity to the society.

2. *Community members act as witnesses* to the decisions reached. A 'My word is my honour' promise is witnessed and will serve as a standard for monitoring the subsequent behaviour of the miscreant. The community itself performs the function of correctional services while allowing the culprits to continue their usual productive activities and contributing to the welfare of the family and the community. The 'modern' or Western judicial system would sentence a culprit to prison to serve a specified sentence, thus cutting him/her off from the community until the term of the sentence is finished.

3. The actors involved in the traditional justice system are given the opportunity to demonstrate that they have learnt the lessons of inclusiveness and flexibility, and respond accordingly. This creates a *sense and spirit of collective responsibility* within the community.

4. The process is *open to anyone*, since the sessions are conducted under shade of a tree(s) and on open ground. This allows all and sundry to register the fact that justice has been done and to respond accordingly by reciprocating forgiveness.

5. The traditional justice system addresses the *restoration of social norms, values and belief systems* which offer the opportunities to correct social ills in the community.

6. Traditional justice processes are largely *free and voluntary*, and there are no fees for the mediators, in contrast to the exorbitant legal fees and remuneration paid to advocates, magistrates and judges in the Western justice system. Its application is therefore potentially inexpensive.

7. The cultural practices give the communities involved a *sense of identity* which can be built on to pursue more collective positive social and development objectives.

These opportunities can be exploited by offering the communities concerned, and by extension the entire country, the perfect benchmark to re-examine their turbulent history and design home-grown solutions to their problems. Often, our failure to appreciate that as Africans we have our own understanding of life has led us to accept everything European, without any critical analysis of the alien ways. Every culture in African societies is of value to the people concerned; this explains why cultures are preserved and transferred from generation to generation. The challenge is to improve the methods so as to reduce the pain and danger of creeping social ills.

4.4. Threats

1. The *skill and agility* of the mediators influence the outcome. If a weak or inept mediator is chosen then the desired outcome may not be speedily realized, or the real import and gravity of the entire process may be diluted.

2. Poor *coordination* of the processes may endanger the desired final outcome.

3. The assumption that underlies the traditional justice process is that the aggrieved party(ies) and the community will be willing to forgive. But *forgiveness* is an extremely delicate and personal thing which *can be influenced but not enforced*.

If forgiveness is to provide a channel for social cohesion and healing, people have to be willing and able to forgive one another, which in itself is a process of overcoming attitudes of resentment and anger that may persist when one has been injured by wrongdoing. The processes of both acknowledgement and forgiveness are very demanding and best served when unfolding at personal levels. Forgiveness, healing and reconciliation are deeply personal processes, and each person's needs and reactions to peacemaking and truth telling may be different. Indeed, we can never really tell whether genuine forgiveness has taken place. The simple utterance of the words 'I forgive you' does not have to be followed up in subsequent action, as a 'promise' does. It is not an event but rather a process, which requires working over, amending and overcoming attitudes. This essentially translates into taking ownership of conflict resolution by leaving aside all other peace-building efforts such as peace talks and the ICC issue.

The question is whether the justice 'bar' for past crimes is set too low through the application of forgiveness. From the perspective of a retributive or punitive justice system, the practice of blanket amnesty and forgiveness may be perceived as defying justice, with critical shortcomings as a result where accountability is concerned. But, again, who is responsible for what happened? Have crimes also been committed by people other than the LRA, in the name of the LRA or by the nation's armed forces? If these questions were to be answered in a court of law, a prime assumption would have to be that access to justice does exist where it is needed. That would hardly be the case in northern Uganda. Instead, local practices of restorative justice mechanisms seek alternative forms of justice, just as the government of Uganda did, when the amnesty option was enacted in 2000, as a means of offering the insurgents incentives to give up the conflict. However, the government's referral of the LRA to the ICC and the subsequent indictments run counter to the rationale of both amnesty and forgiveness. The complications lie in the simultaneous functioning of the two systems, with the one targeting punishment of the LRA leadership while rank-and-file members are offered amnesty by the government, but at the same time left to the local restorative justice systems.

> The conflict in northern Uganda has not yet evolved to such a state that any one approach can be said to hold the key to resolution.

5. Conclusions and recommendations

5.1. Summary of findings

Since independence in 1962, Uganda has witnessed an unbroken cycle of human rights abuses on one level or another or outright conflict, from the fight over power and dominance to Idi Amin's assault on the population and the atrocities carried out on the Acholi population by the mysterious LRA. Often, over this fairly short time span, the north or northerners have been at centre stage either as the dominant actors or at the victim end of the spectrum. In the violent early years after independence, the country's governments managed to militarize the public space by turning the army into a guarantor of the political prominence of those in power. But as a political instrument the army itself was subject to or the victim of ethnically based rivalry.

No single clear-cut reason can be identified to explain why the country has been plagued by this cycle of conflicts, but an understanding of the causes and drivers of the conflicts is essential if Uganda is to be able to stop or prevent violence or war. Not only does the complex nature of the causes make it difficult even to agree on the origins of the conflicts, but new dimensions and factors are likely to emerge as the longer-lasting conflicts evolve and mutate. A case in point is the fact that the LRA conflict seems to have been sustained or fuelled by increasing levels of Sudanese support, giving the conflict in northern Uganda an international dimension.

Confronted with the dire humanitarian effects of the two-decades-long conflict, interlocutors in Uganda tend to overlook the history of the conflict in the pursuit of an end to immediate suffering.

The findings of our present study suggest that the Acholi people maintain their sophisticated cultural beliefs about the spirit world and their social order which to a great extent shape the perceptions of truth, justice, forgiveness and reconciliation that they would wish to invoke and apply.

The unique importance of the Acholi traditional system is that the perpetrators of atrocities will remain in society even after a peace deal is reached. Unlike the process of the Nuremberg Tribunal, where the victor could simply walk away after accounts had been settled in 'judicial' fashion, the settlement of the LRA conflict will entail a social future where both perpetrators and victims, and their respective families, live together.

Generational and social teachings around these concepts have been severely disrupted by the uprooting of approximately 1.8 million people from their homesteads and their transfer to internment camps. The weakening of the authority and essential roles of the elders and chiefs in enforcing understanding and adherence to local standards has been obvious. It is against this background that residents in the internment camps often call for the revitalization and empowerment of the home-grown traditional structures and practices of their society as the only avenue of relief from their dire situation, as opposed to some alien and abstract justice system.

> The unique importance of the Acholi traditional system is that the perpetrators of atrocities will remain in society even after a peace deal is reached. The settlement of the conflict will entail a social future where both perpetrators and victims, and their respective families, live together.

Acholi culture and society are very complex and in a process of constant change, and this has been heightened and shaped in particular directions by the horrors and dislocation of over 20 years of war. In this context, simplifications are not useful. Neither glorifying traditional approaches as the only cure nor relegating them to the realm of the devilish is helpful to people seeking assistance in their suffering. It is only prudent to acknowledge the positive potential of traditional rituals and beliefs, not as contradictory to or competing with other approaches but as complementary to them. To ignore or discard traditional ways that have been seen to work in the past makes no sense. On the other hand, they cannot provide the cure for all ills.

An important aspect that should be recognized and promoted is the crucial role of the Acholi traditional and religious leaders. In what has been a long and fratricidal conflict, the role of traditional leaders and the community ceremonies of reconciliation and other rituals which they mediate are indispensable mechanisms for trust and confidence building and the enhancement of genuine reconciliation. The most effective persuasion should be seen as emanating from outside the formal dialogue process and involving members of the affected community and their families together with the religious and traditional leaders, who are all invaluable allies in the search for practical and more realistic options for resolution of the conflict. The negotiating teams of the belligerents brilliantly accepted this when they signed the contentious agenda item 3 of the Juba peace talks, which provided for the application of the traditional justice system process, albeit in part, thus bringing a long-standing impasse to an end.

> Neither glorifying traditional approaches as the only cure nor relegating them to the realm of the devilish are helpful to people seeking assistance in their suffering.

The poor coordination that has characterized the various initiatives and attempts provides another critical lesson. The absence of a clear structure or framework for coordinating all these attempts can at best complicate them, if it does not render them completely futile.

The challenge is to understand and use all different approaches in ways that complement each other synergistically, rather than working against each other. Thus traditional means of promoting reconciliation and healing can be drawn upon alongside the contributions of Christian and other religious beliefs, Western psychotherapeutic methods and modern courts, as well as numerous other mechanisms and tools that might come into play, such as truth and reconciliation commissions, reparations, rituals of purification, memorials and so on. This is important in the current context of an ongoing conflict and continued displacement, and even more relevant in the post-conflict scenario when issues of resettlement, reintegration and the recovery of a sustainable livelihood become key.

> The challenge is to understand and utilize all different approaches in ways that complement each other synergistically, rather than working against each other.

5.2. Recommendations

One would expect it to be very difficult to establish the 'truth' in regard to a conflict which has lasted for over two decades. The sheer intractability of the conflict implies serious disagreements that reflect fundamental differences in society. The characterization of this conflict—which depends on whom one talks to—poses its own problems in defining the methods for resolving the problem. Uncoordinated efforts have proved to be and will be futile.

Peace and justice will only be achieved in northern Uganda through an inclusive process that involves a wide range of actors embracing victims, bystanders, perpetrators and all other stakeholders. Wide and broad sensitization to the feasibility and applicability of the traditional justice system is required, while giving those most affected by the violence a voice in the process by granting them leeway to employ their unique traditional processes.

A multi-pronged political approach to the conflict is therefore desirable because only this will be able to address the political issues that were responsible for the outbreak of the conflict. Such a political approach must be inclusive of all actors and all erstwhile enemies, and should avoid a 'winner-takes-all' outcome. It will be vital to resolve the conflict on a win–win basis. This will help trust and confidence building, and the reconciliation process which Uganda now needs rather than vindictiveness based on some abstract justice. While it is understandable that impunity should not be possible, the objective of achieving justice should be tempered by considerations of healing the afflicted community.

The old men who are the last to remember the traditions of their people may die before they can pass on what they know to be written down and preserved. If this should happen, a part of the unique contribution made by many peoples to the total sum of human culture will be lost forever and we shall all be the poorer. It is important to consider just what these traditions represent in the lives of the peoples of Acholiland, Africa and the world at large. Perhaps they have not yet been recognized for what they really are. Evidently, there is an incredible wealth of knowledge inherent in the traditional practices and culture of the Acholi and other African people, which offers credible principles for conflict management and harmonious living within the wider global society.

As Professor Kwesi Kwaa Prah asserts, 'There is a sense in which the signification of Africa to knowledge is argumentatively defensible; not only defensible but also evidentially sustainable. That is recognizing that there are distinct traditions, histories, chronologies located in specific societies in which a distinct strand of knowledge production and knowledge articulation as an epistemological fund within a specific time frame can be traced' (Prah 2005).

> While impunity should not be possible, the objective of achieving justice should be tempered by considerations of healing the afflicted community.

References and further reading

Allen, Tim, *Trial Justice: The International Criminal Court and the Lord's Resistance Army* (London: Zed Books, 2006)

Baines, Erin et al., 'Roco Wat I Acholi. Restoring Relationships in Acholi-land: Traditional Approaches to Justice and Reconciliation', Vancouver and Gulu: Liu Institute for Global Issues, Gulu District NGO Forum and Ker Kwaro Acholi, September 2005, available on the Liu Institute for Global Issues website, <http://www.ligi.ubc.ca>

Barber, J., *Imperial Frontiers* (Nairobi: East African Publishing House, 1968)

Caritas Gulu Archdiocese, 'Traditional Ways of Coping in Acholi', Report written by Thomas Harlacher, Francis Xavier Okot, Caroline Aloyo Obonyo, Mychelle Balthaard and Ronald Atkinson, 2006. Copies may be obtained from <caritasgulu@iwayafrica.com>

Civil Society Organizations for Peace in Northern Uganda (CSOPNU), 'The Net Economic Cost of the Conflict on the Acholiland Sub-region of Uganda', Kampala, 2002

'Executive Summary of the Proposed USAID/Uganda Integrated Strategic Plan 2002–2007' [consultants' report]

Latigo, James, 'The Acholi Traditional Conflict Resolution in Light of Current Circumstances: National Conference on Reconciliation, Hotel Africana, Kampala', *Law Reform Journal* (Uganda Law Reform Commission), 4 (September 2006)

New Vision (newspaper) 1 June 2007

Odongo, Onyango, 'Causes of Armed Conflicts in Uganda', Historical Memory Synthetic Paper, Centre for Basic Research (CBR) Conference, Hotel Africana, 2003 (Historical Memory Project Synthetic writings)

Prah, Kwesi Kwaa, 'African Knowledge Production, Language and Identity', Keynote address at the inauguration of the Marcus Garvey Pan-African Institute (MPAI), Mbale, Uganda, 9 July 2005

Ugandan Amnesty Commission, *Amnesty Commission Report 2004/2005*, Kampala, <http://www.amnestycom.go.ug>

Ugandan Ministry of Finance, Planning and Economic Development, *Poverty Status Report, 2003*

Ugandan Parliamentary Committee on Defence and Internal Affairs, *Report on the War in Northern Uganda*, 1997

CHAPTER 5

CHAPTER 5

Reconciliation and traditional justice: tradition-based practices of the Kpaa Mende in Sierra Leone

Joe A. D. Alie

1. The conflict

1.1. Descriptive chronology

In March 1991 Sierra Leone was plunged into anarchy when an insurgency force calling itself the Revolutionary United Front (RUF) invaded the country from three directions on the Sierra Leone–Liberian border. The first group entered Bomaru (in Kailahun district) on 23 March and was led by Foday Sankoh, a cashiered officer of the Sierra Leone Army (SLA). The second group entered the same district from Koindu four days later. A third force entered from the south-east and occupied Zimmi, a strategic town in Pujehun district, on 28 March. The rebels soon overran the Kailahun district, where they maintained a strong base throughout the period of the conflict. There was little government presence in these districts, following years under an inept and over-centralized All People's Congress (APC) administration. Kailahun and Pujehun had been hotbeds of opposition to APC rule.

The rebels consisted of three distinct groups of fighters: those who had received military training in Libya; Sierra Leonean dissidents based in Liberia; and hard core National Patriotic Front of Liberia (NPFL) combatants who included Liberian and Burkinabe mercenaries. The invading force numbered about 100. Their aim was to overthrow the one-party government of President Joseph Saidu Momoh, which the rebel leadership described as corrupt, tribalistic and lacking a popular mandate. They indicated that their goal was to establish a dictatorship of the proletariat in which ordinary citizens would be actively involved in all the decision-making processes. Moreover, the RUF would vigorously promote socio-economic development including rural regeneration. Initially, some marginalized young people and the rural poor, including teachers, were attracted by the RUF rhetoric and joined the movement.

The RUF invasion took the government and the military by surprise, even though the NPFL rebel leader, Charles Taylor, had indicated months before that he would attack Sierra Leone, where the Economic Community of West African States (ECOWAS) peacekeeping force, the ECOWAS Monitoring Group (ECOMOG) deployed to Liberia, had established a base. It was from Sierra Leone that ECOMOG jets attacked rebel bases in Liberia. The SLA was ill-prepared for battle and demoralized, but it had to engage the insurgents. The officers tried to make up for what the force lacked in morale, training and equipment with massive and indiscriminate recruitment of men. The result was an influx of recruits who lacked the requisite qualifications and discipline, and some of whom were drug addicts, convicted criminals, fortune seekers and early school-leavers. This group of misfits and criminal elements was to dominate the army, with disastrous consequences.

While the APC government was trying to contain the rebel onslaught and at the same time devise dubious means to stay in power indefinitely, a group of young SLA officers from the war front in the Eastern Region stormed Freetown, the capital, in the early hours of the morning of 29 April 1992, to protest against poor conditions on the battlefield. By midday, what had started as a mutiny had developed into a fully blown coup. President Momoh was flown to Conakry, Guinea, by ECOMOG soldiers. The army officers then set up the National Provisional Ruling Council (NPRC) with Captain Valentine Strasser as chairman. The NPRC vowed to end the war quickly and return the country to constitutional rule. Initially, the NPRC was enormously popular, especially among young people.

During 1992 and 1993 the fortunes of the rebel RUF fluctuated. The new military regime in Freetown appealed to traditional hunters, some of whom had formed themselves into civil defence units at the start of the war, to help them prosecute the rebels, since they knew their terrain very well. However, the cooperation between the government soldiers and the civil defence units was short-lived, as the latter began to discern an unholy alliance between some army soldiers and the rebels. Civilians called these soldiers-cum-rebels 'sobels'. By 1994 the RUF had occupied the major diamond mining areas and the proceeds from the sale of diamonds were used to fuel the conflict.

The situation in the army was also becoming critical, with many soldiers defecting. Those who remained in the force did so for personal gain. Captain Strasser was forced to approach the United Nations (UN) for assistance. In April 1995, the RUF rebels were only miles away from Freetown. The RUF was estimated by some to have an overall strength of 3,000–4,000 with a hard core of only 500–600 fighters.

Democratic elections were held in Sierra Leone in February and March 1996. They saw the Sierra Leone People's Party (SLPP), which had ruled from 1961 to 1967 but was defeated by the opposition APC party in 1967, back at the helm of government. President Alhaji Ahmad Tejan Kabbah of the SLPP held peace talks with the rebels and a peace agreement, the Abidjan Peace Accord, was signed on 30 November 1996. It was short-lived.

Another military coup on 25 May 1997 briefly disrupted the democratic process. The government of President Kabbah and several agencies were forced to flee to Guinea. The junta, which called itself the Armed Forces Revolutionary Council (AFRC) under the leadership of a Major Johnny Paul Koroma (who was awaiting trial for an alleged coup attempt), invited the RUF rebels to help them administer the country. The period of AFRC rule (25 March 1997–February 1998) was characterized by extreme lawlessness and mayhem. It also saw unprecedented civil disobedience against the regime.

ECOMOG troops, together with the Civil Defence Forces (CDF) and loyal soldiers and police officers, successfully drove the AFRC junta out of Freetown in February 1998. President Kabbah's government was restored a month later. The rebels retreated to the countryside where they continued to wreak havoc.

The RUF and its allies again appeared at the gates of Freetown on 6 January 1999, catching both the government and ECOMOG off guard. Using women and children as human shields, some RUF and AFRC fighters were able to bypass ECOMOG troops and join comrades who had already infiltrated the city. In the fighting that ensued, an estimated 5,000 people died, including cabinet ministers, journalists and lawyers who were specifically targeted. Before the rebels were ejected from Freetown, large parts of the city were burned down and about 3,000 children abducted as the rebels retreated.

In spite of these latest atrocities—or because of them—the government, in concert with civil society groups and the international community, held peace talks with the rebels, and on 7 July 1999 the Lomé Peace Agreement was signed. Following the signing of the agreement, ECOMOG troops were gradually replaced by UN troops, who helped to keep the peace. On 18 January 2002, President Kabbah formally declared the civil conflict over.

1.2. The causes of the conflict

Sierra Leone, a small country on the West African coast measuring 27,000 square miles and with a population of roughly 5 million, has had a rather chequered history since it regained independence from the British in 1961. At independence, the country seemed to hold great promise; the educational, political, administrative, judicial and other institutions critical to the well-being of the state were functioning relatively well. There was a high degree of ethnic, political and religious tolerance and Sierra Leone was the envy of other countries in the sub-region. However, as in many other independent African countries, the euphoria that greeted the birth of the new nation, with its accompanying high hopes and great expectations, soon turned to despair and despondence largely as a result of the actions (and inaction) of the political leadership. The RUF rebel onslaught had been preceded by a long period of political, economic and social decline as well as a prolonged history of social injustice. The reasons for the country's slide into chaos and anarchy were therefore many and varied.

The first was maladministration. Under the APC (1968–92) the gains of the early years of independence were systematically eroded by bad governance and reckless economic management characterized by indiscriminate plunder of the country's resources to service patron–client relationships. The APC leadership, moreover, developed dictatorial tendencies and liberally used the language of violence as an instrument of political competition.

The state machinery was also over-centralized. This began in 1971 and reached its zenith in 1978 with the declaration of a one-party system of government. Over-centralization led to the systematic crumbling of the fabric of the state, resulting in near state collapse, which was marked by the loss of control over the political and economic space. The weakening of the state through over-centralization helped to open the way for some foreign countries, including Burkina Faso, Côte d'Ivoire, Liberia and Libya, to encroach on Sierra Leone's sovereignty by involving themselves in its politics directly and by hosting dissident groups who played politics from neighbouring sanctuaries. In addition, the concentration of power in the capital, Freetown, led to the neglect of or truncated development in the rural areas and created the conditions for the disempowerment of the rural population in particular. The system exacerbated corruption, nepotism and other ills detrimental to the well-being of the state. There was a complete absence of transparency and accountability in the public administration system. The judiciary too was compromised. An over-centralized, inefficient and bankrupt one-party system rewarded sycophancy and punished hard work, patriotism and independent thought. The effects were disastrous.

The second was poor economic policies and a declining economy. The government failed to translate the country's rich endowment of mineral and marine resources, as well as its considerable areas of arable land, into improved welfare for the majority of the population. The 1970s and 1980s were characterized by fiscal constraints and declining output. The annual inflation rate increased from about 5 per cent in 1970 to 13 per cent in 1980 to over 85 per cent in 1985. There were also frequent shortages of much-needed imported commodities, such as petroleum and rice. These problems were compounded by the oil shocks of the 1970s and 1980s, which had a telling effect on the economy. By the 1980s, Sierra Leone's human development and social indicators, including life expectancy, literacy, primary school enrolment, child mortality rates and maternal death rates, were among the worst in the world. Not surprisingly, the country was ranked 126 out of 130 in 1990 on the United Nations Development Programme (UNDP) Human Development Index, a year before the start of the civil conflict.

The third factor was weak access to justice. The corruption and politicization of important state institutions such as the judiciary and the traditional court system led to abuse of power by judges, lawyers and local court officials. In the provincial areas especially, young men suffered at the hands of corrupt and high-handed local authorities. Some of these aggrieved young men were later to return to their communities during the civil conflict to exact revenge on their former oppressors.

Fourth, young people became alienated. Over the years poor educational facilities, inadequate and inappropriate curricula and programmes, and lack of employment opportunities for young people helped to marginalize them and turn them into a rebellious group. Many became socialized in a climate of violence, drugs and criminality, and it was among this ready pool of alienated young people that many of the rebel leaders recruited their first crop of fighters. Young men were at the centre of the Sierra Leone crisis, for they sustained the rebel groups as well as the government soldiers and civilian militia forces.

Finally, there were lapses in state security. Since the 1970s there had been a continuing and dramatic decline in national security resulting from the politicization of the military and the police, the creation of security organizations with personal or political allegiances, and systemic corruption. These seriously undermined the national security apparatus.

From the above, it can be seen that there were a great many structural and other forms of violence existing in Sierra Leone before the civil conflict began. Rebel leaders capitalized on the people's suffering to pose as liberators.

1.3. Degree of internationalization

The civil crisis became heavily internationalized due to the involvement of neighbouring 'rogue states', many of whose interests were purely economic—namely, access to Sierra Leone's resources, particularly its diamonds. It has been argued, and with justification, that without the support of foreign states the war would probably not have become so protracted and bloody. Burkina Faso, Côte d'Ivoire, Liberia and Libya were notorious for fuelling the conflict. Libya provided bases and military training for the insurgents, while Burkina Faso provided many fighters to bolster the rebel ranks.

The government, in turn, used foreign troops. They included anti-Taylor fighters from Liberia, the Gurkhas from Nepal and the South African security company Executive Outcomes. Working closely with segments of the Sierra Leone Army, these foreign fighters achieved some successes. For instance, within a few months of its arrival in 1995, Executive Outcomes was able to secure Freetown and the Kono diamond fields and to retake the bauxite and rutile mines in southern Sierra Leone.

The rebel outfit that invaded Freetown on 6 January 1999 also included many mercenaries. They had, again, received logistic and other critical support from President Charles Taylor of Liberia. It is reported that the invading force comprised several nationalities, including over 3,000 Liberians of Taylor's NPFL, 300–500 Ukrainians as well as by Burkinabes, Libyans, South Africans, Israelis and Taiwanese (Abraham 2000).

Throughout the conflict ECOWAS was heavily engaged in finding a peaceful solution. With the assistance of the UN, the Organization of African Unity (now the African

Union), the Commonwealth and other bodies, it helped to broker the two peace agreements—the 1996 Abidjan Peace Accord and the July 1999 Lomé Peace Agreement.

Between May 1997 and February 1998, ECOWAS leaders made several attempts to reason with the coup plotters and their RUF allies to return the country to constitutional rule. One such effort was the Conakry Agreement, brokered by ECOWAS and the AFRC on 23 October 1997. The key provisions were an end to all hostilities, the resumption of humanitarian aid and the reinstatement of the ousted government of President Kabbah by 22 April 1998. Representatives of the Kabbah government were only observers at the talks. Despite the peace plan, fighting continued, with the civil defence forces, and particularly the Kamajor militia, making life difficult for the junta, particularly in the south-east of the country. ECOMOG troops successfully drove the rebels from Freetown following the 6 January 1999 invasion.

1.4. The nature of the transition

Several key actors were involved in the transition from war to peace. They included international agencies (governmental and non-governmental) and their local counterparts. Following the January 1999 invasion of Freetown the UN, ECOWAS and some Western countries, principally the United Kingdom (UK) and the USA, and local civil society organizations supported the Kabbah government in its efforts to make peace with the rebels. The Togolese capital, Lomé, was chosen as the venue for peace talks between the RUF and the Sierra Leonean Government as the Togolese president, Gnassingbé Eyadema, was the chairman of ECOWAS.

After long and often tortuous deliberations, President Kabbah and RUF leader Foday Sankoh, flanked by the presidents of Burkina Faso, Liberia, Nigeria and Togo, finally signed the Lomé Peace Agreement on 7 July 1999. The agreement was a significant improvement on the 1996 Abidjan accord. It dealt with issues relating to the cessation of hostilities; governance (e.g. the transformation of the RUF into a political party and enabling its members to hold public office); pardon and amnesty for former combatants; truth and reconciliation; post-conflict military and security issues (e.g. the transformation of ECOMOG and a new mandate for the United Nations Observer Mission in Sierra Leone (UNOMSIL)); security guarantees for peace monitors; disarmament, demobilization and reintegration (DDR); the restructuring of the Sierra Leone Armed Forces; and humanitarian, human rights and socio-economic issues. The general feeling was that the agreement offered the best hope for achieving peace. The rebels benefited immensely. They and their leader Foday Sankoh were pardoned for all their misdeeds committed since they took up arms in 1991. However, the UN special representative (Francis Okelo) remarked that the UN's interpretation was that the amnesty and pardon did not apply to international crimes of genocide, crimes against humanity, war crimes and other serious violations of international humanitarian law (Lord 2000: 83).

As part of the peace agreement, some RUF leaders and renegade soldiers were given ministerial and other key positions in the government. For example, RUF leader Foday Sankoh was appointed chairman of a commission for the management of strategic resources, including diamonds. The RUF was to become a political party and expected to contest national elections.

1.4.1. Keeping the peace

Following the signing of the peace agreement, in October 1999 the UN Security Council established a 6,000-member UN Mission in Sierra Leone (UNAMSIL) under chapter VII of the UN Charter, to replace ECOMOG. By December, UNAMSIL troops from Bangladesh, India, Jordan, Kenya and Zambia had begun to arrive, and in February 2000 the Security Council agreed to increase their number to 11,000. The DDR programme began but moved at a snail's pace. In May 2000, in the same week as the last ECOMOG contingents left Sierra Leone, the RUF surrounded, disarmed and abducted some 500 UNAMSIL troops, killing several in the process.

The UN Security Council then appointed a Panel of Experts to look into the connection between the illicit diamond trade and the RUF's access to weapons. A rump faction of the AFRC known as the 'West Side Boys' kidnapped a number of British soldiers, holding them for ransom. A dramatic British rescue operation on 25 August 2000 released the prisoners and put an end to the West Side Boys. The rescue mission also demonstrated British resolve to stay in Sierra Leone as a back-up force to both UNAMSIL and the new Sierra Leonean Army, which the UK now began to recruit, train and equip in earnest.

Throughout 2001 the peace process continued to make significant progress. The RUF again reaffirmed its commitment to the peace process. Nigerian President Olusegun Obasanjo promised to offer scholarships to RUF members who wanted to study, and asked the Sierra Leonean Government to help the RUF convert itself into a political party. On 18 January 2002 President Kabbah officially declared that the conflict was over, with the symbolic burning of some 3,000 weapons at Freetown International Airport in Lungi. At the ceremony, the special representative of the UN secretary general, Ambassador Oluyemi Adeniji, said that the day marked a new beginning in the lives of over 46,000 ex-combatants. A few months later, presidential and parliamentary elections were held throughout the country. The RUF, which had now converted itself into a political party under the new name Revolutionary United Front Party (RUFP), did badly, getting only 2 per cent of the votes cast, securing two seats in Parliament under the proportional representation system. No RUFP person was appointed minister after the post-conflict elections.

2. Transitional justice

Sierra Leone's civil conflict had been characterized by unspeakable brutality. International war crimes of the worst type were routinely and systematically committed against Sierra Leoneans of all ages and the suffering inflicted upon the civilian population was profound. While all sides committed human rights violations, the rebel forces were responsible for the overwhelming majority of them. It is also significant that Sierra Leoneans had suffered a great deal of structural violence prior to the start of the civil conflict in 1991. Given these stark realities, the end of the war posed new challenges, the most immediate being the question of whether to punish those who had brought mayhem on the people, or to forgive them.

> Sierra Leone is in the unique position of experimenting with two types of transitional justice systems in parallel—the Truth and Reconciliation Commission, set up to establish the truth about the conflict and promote healing and reconciliation; and the Special Court, established to try those who 'bear the greatest responsibility' for serious violations of international humanitarian law and Sierra Leonean law during the war.

The Lomé Peace Agreement had made provision for a transitional justice system, the Truth and Reconciliation Commission (TRC), as part of the peace-building process. Subsequent events, however, necessitated the creation of another system, the Special Court. The government also established the Anti-Corruption Commission as part of its overall good governance programme.

2.1. The Truth and Reconciliation Commission

The Sierra Leonean Parliament enacted the Truth and Reconciliation Commission Act, 2000 on 22 February 2000. The objectives of the commission were:

- to create an impartial historical record of violations and abuses of human rights and international humanitarian law related to the armed conflict in Sierra Leone, from its beginning in 1991 to the signing of the Lomé Peace Agreement in 1999;
- to address the problem of impunity, to respond to the needs of the victims;
- to promote healing and reconciliation; and
- to prevent a repetition of the violations and abuses suffered (Truth and Reconciliation Commission Act, 2000).

The act also gives the commission the right to 'seek assistance from traditional and religious leaders to facilitate its public sessions and in resolving local conflicts arising from past violations or abuses or in support of healing and reconciliation' (Truth and Reconciliation Commission Act, 2000, para. 7.2).

The TRC became fully operational in mid-2002 and completed its work in 2004. During this period, it collected over 8,000 statements from victims, perpetrators and others working for a week each in the country's 12 provincial district headquarter towns—Kabala,

Makeni, Magburaka, Port Loko and Kambia (Northern Province); Bo, Moyamba, Bonthe and Pujehun (Southern Province); and Kenema, Koidu and Kailahun (Eastern Province), as well as in Freetown (Western Area). Thus, large areas of the country were left uncovered. The TRC's inability to cover the entire country was due mainly to funding constraints.

The commission involved traditional, civil society and religious elders in its truth-seeking and reconciliation sessions (including traditional rites of forgiveness), especially in the provincial areas. It did not encourage local rituals of cursing but it did, in concert with the local elders, establish monuments or memorials, particularly at mass grave sites in the districts, and supported traditional reconciliation ceremonies such as the pouring of libations and cleansing rituals.

The district hearings often failed to elicit detailed, truthful confessions from former combatants, largely because of time constraints. Nevertheless, the TRC and local communities considered vague expressions of regret sufficient as long as former combatants displayed humility towards the community during the hearings. The commission performed general reconciliation ceremonies where the perpetrators accepted their wrongdoings and asked for forgiveness, and the victims were also encouraged to accept and to gradually work towards forgiveness and reconciliation. Tim Kelsall, a lecturer in African politics who observed hearings of this commission, notes that the addition of a carefully staged reconciliation ceremony to the proceedings was extremely significant (Kelsall 2005: 363).

If the TRC's recommendations, as outlined in its final report, submitted to the Sierra Leonean Government in October 2004, are fully implemented, they would without doubt act as catalyst for the social and legal reform required to address impunity and establish a culture of respect for human rights in Sierra Leone, as well as helping the social regeneration of battered communities.

One important development in the consolidation of peace took place in August 2006 when the Sierra Leonean Government appointed the National Commission for Social Action (NaCSA) the implementing agency for the reparations. NaCSA, which started as a government ministry in 1996, is the main government body responsible for the reconstruction and rehabilitation of war-torn Sierra Leone. It has begun to receive grants from the government and international institutions to help pay the reparations.

2.2. The Sierra Leone Special Court

The establishment of a Special Court was the result of certain negative developments after the 1999 Lomé Peace Agreement. Segments of the RUF had continued flagrantly to violate the rights of citizens, in complete contravention of the provisions of the peace agreement. Some human rights groups therefore felt that such criminal offences must be punishable under Sierra Leonean law. The single most deadly violation that forced the government to initiate legal proceedings against the RUF occurred on 8 May 2000 when Foday Sankoh's boys fired at peaceful protesters, killing at least 20. The Sierra Leonean Government consequently approached the UN and requested the setting up of a Special Court. Pursuant to UN Security Council Resolution 1315 of 14 August 2002, the Special Court was established to try persons who 'bear the greatest responsibility' for serious violations of international humanitarian law and Sierra Leonean law committed during the war.

The Special Court has made some arrests since March 2003. Notable among the detainees have been Sam Hinga Norman, who was the leader of the pro-government Kamajor militia (a former deputy defence minister and, until his arrest, internal affairs minister), Foday Sankoh and Issa Sesay of the RUF, Kamajor high priest Aliu Kundorwa, and some former AFRC leaders. Foday Sankoh and Sam Hinga Norman have since died in prison. Former junta leader Johnny Paul Koroma and former Liberian President Charles Taylor were also indicted, but only the latter is in detention at The Hague, the Netherlands. It was feared that trying Taylor in Sierra Leone could have a destabilizing effect.

Sierra Leoneans seem to be divided over the ability of the Special Court to deliver, although it has sentenced three former AFRC leaders to long prison terms and the CDF leaders to shorter prison terms. Already the indictments it has made have been surrounded by controversy. Some opponents of the court think that the huge amounts of money spent on it could better be used to improve the lives of war victims and other vulnerable people. They also point out that sentencing the few people the court has in its custody will not be enough to deal with the culture of impunity in Sierra Leone. Only time will tell.

Sierra Leone has thus found itself in the unique position of experimenting with two types of transitional justice systems in parallel, the TRC and the Special Court. At one point there was some tension between the two because they were pursuing different types of justice. The Special Court seemed to be interested mainly in retributive justice. In spite of this tension, however, the two institutions have complemented each other.

> Sierra Leoneans seem to be divided over the ability of the Special Court to deliver, although it has sentenced three former AFRC leaders to long prison terms. The indictments it has made have been surrounded by controversy.

Addressing the twin issues of justice and reconciliation through the TRC and Special Court is necessary, but not sufficient. Of greater import, if peace is to be consolidated, is addressing the causes of the war, which by popular consensus lie in a combination of bad governance, the denial of fundamental rights, economic mismanagement and social exclusion in the context of any peace-building initiatives.

> Addressing the twin issues of justice and reconciliation through the TRC and Special Court is necessary, but not sufficient. Of greater import, if peace is to be consolidated, is addressing the causes of the war, which lie in a combination of bad governance, the denial of fundamental rights, economic mismanagement and social exclusion.

3. Traditional justice and reconciliation mechanisms

3.1. Background and description

The term 'traditional' with its Eurocentric connotations often tends to suggest profoundly internalized normative structures, patterns followed from 'time out of mind' in static economic and social circumstances. It must be borne in mind that African institutions, whether political, economic or social, have never been inert. They respond to changes resulting from several factors and forces. Thus, some would prefer the use of the word 'indigenous' rather than 'traditional'. The word 'traditional' as used in this chapter implies a dynamic process.

'Justice' here means seeking or establishing the truth without fear or favour, after allowing each party an opportunity to express themselves. It also denotes impartiality and fairness. It must be pointed out that truth telling, as is shown below in the case of the Mende, is an integral part of the justice system in indigenous societies.

'Reconciliation' is the act of reuniting groups or parties who have been fractured as a result of conflict. It may also involve the granting of some form of reparation to the aggrieved party. In the traditional context, justice and reconciliation are generally inseparable.

> African institutions, whether political, economic or social, have never been inert. They respond to changes resulting from several factors and forces. The word 'traditional' as used in this chapter implies a dynamic process.

> Truth telling, as in the case of the Mende in Sierra Leone, is an integral part of the justice system in indigenous societies.

> In the traditional context, justice and reconciliation are generally inseparable.

3.2. The features of and main actors in tradition-based practices

Traditional justice mechanisms have certain key features. They are generally male-dominated, although in the case of Sierra Leone some provision is made for female representation. Some truth-seeking mechanisms are actually headed by women. There is no place in them for young people, who are considered immature and not yet versed in the ways of the community. These tools are community-centred, open and transparent.

Belief in the supernatural (God, priests and priestesses, and ancestors) is quite strong and people credited with special gifts—diviners, 'medicine men' and the like—play a crucial role in the judicial processes. The mechanisms also involve rituals such as cleansing ceremonies, songs and dance.

> Traditional justice mechanisms are generally male-dominated, and there is no place in them for young people, who are considered immature and not yet versed in the ways of the community.

There are several actors. The principal actors include the chiefdom administrations, local courts, tribal headmen, community and religious leaders, and diviners. A formalized type of chiefdom administration in Sierra Leone (then called the Native Administration) came into effect in 1937. Each chiefdom unit is divided into sections, towns and villages, headed by section chiefs, town chiefs and village chiefs, respectively. The overall administrative leader of the chiefdom is the paramount chief and he/she is assisted by a council. The paramount chief and his/her subordinates are responsible for justice and law and order, and are custodians of the traditions and customs of the people in their domains. They are elected for life, although they could be deposed by the head of state for serious misconduct. Until 1963 the paramount chief and the sub-chiefs presided over court cases. Thereafter their jurisdiction was limited to minor civil cases. These cases are usually settled in the chief's *barray* (compound).

> These tools are community-centred, open and transparent. They involve rituals such as cleansing ceremonies, songs and dance.

The Local Court Act of 1963 created local courts headed by court chairmen. These courts are the most formalized structure of the customary justice system in the provincial areas. The vast majority of Sierra Leoneans (up to 80 per cent) fall under the jurisdiction of customary laws. Court chairmen are generally considered to be knowledgeable in customary civil cases. They are assisted by a panel of elders, clerks and other minor functionaries and are usually appointed for an initial period of three years; the minister of local government has the authority to remove them. No lawyers are present in the local courts although they are supervised by a customary law officer who is a trained lawyer. The customary law officer also trains court chairmen.

There are tribal headmen in most cities and towns. They became an integral part of local administration in the then Colony of Sierra Leone (now Western Area) following the enactment of the Tribal Administration (Colony) Ordinance of 1924. Some of their powers and duties were judicial (the administration of justice among members of their ethnic group) as well as social and administrative. Subsequent ordinances attempted to deprive them of the judicial functions as many were found wanting, but tribal headmen have continued to adjudicate in minor civil cases.

A new development in the judicial process is the emergence of certain lay people (called paralegals) who work with the poor and other disadvantaged groups to find solutions to problems. These paralegals have achieved outstanding success through their engagement with chiefs, the police and other law enforcement officials at the community level. Their interventions consist of advocacy and community education efforts. Most are very knowledgeable about customary law and institutions (Wojkowska 2006: 35).

3.3. The Kpaa Mende as a case study

Sierra Leone is a multi-ethnic country where some 18 ethnic groups reside. However, two major groups dominate—the Temne and the Mende. The Temne live mainly in most parts of the northern and western regions, and the Mende in the southern and eastern regions. They account for 29 per cent and 31 per cent, respectively, of the population. All the communities mix freely and there are no barriers to where people should reside.

Pettersson (2004), however, suggests that a certain tension appears to exist between the Temne and Mende which should be acknowledged. The Mende dominate the SLPP, while the Temne make up the majority of the members of the APC. The civil war was initiated by RUF leader Foday Sankoh (a 'northerner' and a Temne), although the first fighting took place in the heartland of Mende territory (Eastern Province). Many Mende therefore perceive the war as an invasion by the Temne from the north of the country. Meanwhile, the Temne often see the war as a south-eastern plot initiated by Sankoh as a paid agent, with the purpose of destabilizing the APC government.

It is reported that the RUF initially displayed palm fronds as a symbol of their 'revolution'. The palm frond has political significance among the Mende. The palm tree is the emblem of the SLPP. The RUF probably hoped that displaying palm fronds in a traditionally SLPP stronghold would attract people to their cause.

These ethnic divisions and interpretations of the war clearly have consequences for the reconciliation process.

Over the years each ethnic group has developed complex social systems, which include the administration of justice. Because of the diverse nature of the justice and reconciliation mechanisms of the different communities, and because of time and other constraints, it was not feasible to conduct field research among all of them. Consequently, only one group—the Mende—was targeted, and even among them only one subgroup (the Kpaa Mende) was studied in greater detail for the purposes of this book. Other Mende subgroups are the Sewama or Middle Mende, the Wanjama Mende and the Koo (Upper) Mende. The Kpaa Mende are the most populous subgroup and, more importantly, they have tried as far as possible to preserve many of their customs, even in the face of modernization and other challenges. They have a powerful secret society that unites them all, the Wonde. There is also a high degree of 'nationalism' among this group.

Kpaa Mende cultural life is controlled by certain codes of behaviour and their activities are sustained by religious beliefs. Fundamental to the cultural beliefs of the Kpaa Mende (and indeed the other subgroups) is the belief that the human being is a spiritual entity. Belief in the supernatural is therefore quite strong among them. Three main strands can be discerned in the concept of the supernatural. The first is the belief in a supreme being, the creator of the universe, the ultimate source of power, controller of the forces of nature, and the upholder of truth and justice. He is referred to as Ngewo. The second is the veneration of the ancestors and the third is a belief in natural divinities.

3.3.1. Transgression and justice

The Kpaa Mende have developed complex ways of dealing with crime and punishment. There are basically two interrelated ways of seeking justice—*restorative* and *retributive*. The form of justice used in a particular case may be determined by the gravity of the crime or the object of the punishment. Generally, tradition-based practices among the Kpaa Mende aim to repair and restore (restorative justice), even though some punishment could be meted out during the process. Restorative justice is largely dependent on an acknowledgement by the wrongdoers of their crime or action, an apology to the person who has been injured, and a genuine expression of remorse. It may also require assisting the victim to cope with their plight, for example, the payment of reparation.

A series of regulations control Kpaa Mende social life. These injunctions fall into two main groups—those relating to the family and those affecting the community as a whole. The human being is an individual but also part of a wider community. Thus his individual action may affect the well-being of the entire community. This is illustrated, for example, in the laws regulating sexual conduct, licit or illicit. Incestuous sexual relations are forbidden. The Humoi society, which is headed by a woman, regulates sexual conduct. The law on incest (*simongama*) forbids sexual intercourse with one's sister, the sister of one's wife and so on. It also forbids a brother to sit on his sister's bed and vice versa. Moreover, a man is not allowed to shake hands with the mother of any woman with whom he has had sexual dealings.

At the community level, it is illegal to have sexual intercourse with a girl under the age of puberty (or one who has not been initiated into the female secret society, the Bondo (Sande)), or with a person in the bush at any time, or with a pregnant woman (other than one's wife) or nursing mother. Such infractions (defilement) could lead to various kinds of illness and also affect the economic fortunes of the community.

A major wrongdoing such as having sexual intercourse in the bush requires a very complex cleansing ceremony, because such violations affect the community as a whole. The Kpaa Mende are a predominantly farming community. Their connection with the farmland is more than economic; it also has spiritual undertones. It is believed that sexual relations in the bush could annoy the ancestral spirits and consequently lead to poor harvests. The offenders and the bush where the deed was performed must undergo a rite of purification by the Humoi priestess.

Chiefs and other community elders generally adjudicate in civil cases such as land grabbing, seduction, '*woman palava*' (a situation where a man has illicit sexual dealings with a married woman and the woman later confesses or is forced to confess the act to her husband), and criminal offences such as arson, theft and violation of community sanctions. In civil cases the plaintiff and defender are encouraged to advance their cases together with their witnesses (if any) before the chiefs can take a final decision. Generally, some compensation is paid to the aggrieved party.

The justice system is heavily tilted against women, especially in husband–wife relationships, and against young people. It is not considered in the best interest of the family to wrong a husband even if his guilt is clearly evident. Instead, the elders would attempt to say soothing words to the wife and later privately rebuke the husband for his misdeeds. While this may look like an injustice to the woman, there is an important social element here. The main interest is to hold the marriage together, not to create a situation where the woman will 'win the war but lose the peace'.

Criminal offences require a range of punishments, ranging from public reproach and the payment of reparation to cleansing ceremonies. Where an alleged offender denies his guilt, the services of diviners, medicine men and other supernatural agencies are sought to help identify the culprit.

3.3.2. The diviner and the medicine man

The diviner is believed to be invested with supernatural powers and wields considerable influence in the community. He commands great respect because he is the only person capable of providing answers to situations beyond the powers of ordinary humans. He can invoke his oracular powers to identify a wrongdoer. If the person continues to deny his of her guilt, other methods can be resorted to, such as swearing ('*sondu*' in Mende) or a curse. It is important, however, to note that, although the oath or curse may be sworn on inanimate objects, as the example below shows, Ngewo (God) is the ultimate medium of the curse.

One of the most potent 'medicines' for swearing is the 'thunder-medicine' (*ngele gbaa*). The potency of the *ngele gbaa* derives from its origin, for it is supposed to have been sliced off from heaven by lightning. The *ngele gbaa*—a small axe (meteorite) dug from the ground together with an assortment of other small metal objects—is wrapped in a hamper of leaves and its owner is held in awe by the community.

If a theft has taken place and no one has confessed to it, the aggrieved person will 'beg the ground' from the chief and elders for a nominal fee and state his intention to curse the thief on the ngele gbaa. When the chief gives his consent, the ngele gbaa-moi (owner of the ngele gbaa) is sent for, most often from a nearby settlement.

A few days before he arrives, the town crier publicly informs the whole community of the reasons for the swearing of the intended curse, the kinds of 'medicine' that will be used and the place where the swearing will take place. He then invites everyone to attend the ceremony. To achieve maximum impact, the town crier narrates the efficacy of the 'medicine', including the number of people it has killed or who have confessed on their deathbeds. When the ngele gbaa-moi arrives, the town crier informs the whole community of his presence. All this is meant to give the thief or anyone who has knowledge of the theft a last chance to make a confession.

Before the swearing takes place, the ngele gbaa-moi places his medicine on the ground and leans it against the stump of a tree. The chief then asks the aggrieved person why he intends to utter the curse. He may say: 'I am going to curse the person who stole my goats; may the ngele gbaa kill him instantly and burn his house'. Sometimes the curse may be extended to anyone who aided and abetted the thief, or has some knowledge about the theft.

If no one answers, the ngele gbaa-moi can continue. He then places poma magbei (Neuboldia laevis) leaves, which are ordinarily used to drive flies away from corpses, near the ngele gbaa. This is to symbolize the impending death of the thief and any accomplices. Then the offender pronounces the dreaded words: 'O God, come down and let me give you your chicken. I am uttering these words against the person who stole my goats. You "medicine" lying here [referring to the ngele gbaa], may you hold every part of this body: his hands, legs, heart. Let him not escape; strike him dead and may you also burn his house'. The ngele gbaa-moi will then answer 'Ngewo jahun' ('by the permission of God').

A curse sworn on the *ngele gbaa* generally affects not only the culprit but also other members of his household, because if lightning strikes a house innocent people may be killed. For this reason, anyone who has information about the theft could come out and confess before the curse is sworn. If the thief confesses at the right time, he will be required to compensate the aggrieved person, including payment of all expenses previously paid to the *ngele gbaa*. The thief will also be publicly rebuked and ostracized before being accepted back into the community.

Powerful medicines like the *ngele gbaa* deter criminals because they threaten them and their accomplices and families with severe punishments, including death. However, provision is also made for curses or oaths to be revoked. If an offender falls ill or confesses his guilt, the curse may be lifted, usually in a public cleansing ceremony (Harris and Sawyerr 1968).

3.3.3. Reconciliation

The ultimate goal of the traditional justice system among the Kpaa Mende (and indeed among most African communities) is reconciliation. This is, for example, vividly portrayed in their Wonde ceremonies. During a ceremonial dance, done in a circle, a battle scene is enacted. The initial single group of dancers breaks into two concentric circles, representing the parties to the conflict. Later the peacemakers arrive. These are men dressed as women making characteristically feminine movements and gestures (symbolizing the important role of women in peacemaking). They come between the combatants and eventually all the dancers form a single circle again. The values reinforced in this ceremony reflect indigenous beliefs about complementarity and the importance of all segments of society in efforts to re-establish harmony and restore continuity (Alie and Gaima 2000).

> The ultimate goal of the traditional justice system among the Kpaa Mende (and among most African communities) is reconciliation.

3.3.4. External influences

The imposition of British colonial rule in Sierra Leone in the late 19th century had an adverse effect on the traditional mechanisms of justice and reconciliation. British colonialists reorganized the judicial system to suit their own ends. To this end, they established three types of court in the Sierra Leone hinterland—the Court of Native Chiefs, the Court of the (European) District Commissioner and native chiefs, and the Court of the District Commissioner. All criminal offences were henceforth decided by the district commissioner's court, while the chiefs decided minor civil cases affecting their local subjects. More importantly, emphasis was now placed on litigation. In addition, court fines and fees became an important mechanism for generating revenue for the local administration. Not surprisingly, miscarriages of justice slowly crept into the fabric of the justice system. The appointment of court chairmen also seems to have been politically influenced.

> Colonial rule had an adverse effect on the traditional mechanisms of justice and reconciliation. All criminal offences were henceforth decided by new courts and emphasis was now placed on litigation. The appointment of court chairmen also seems to have been politically influenced.

4. Tradition-based practices today

Although these practices play a major role in conflict resolution among the Kpaa Mende, they have been subjected to severe stresses, especially in contemporary times.

4.1. The impact of the conflict

The civil conflict brought untold disaster to all segments of Sierra Leonean society. It occasioned unprecedented mass movements of people. Thousands, particularly those in rural communities, were forced to abandon their settlements and seek shelter either in camps for displaced people or in the major towns, with adverse consequences for the indigenous social networks and institutions. Traditional leaders, who were the repositories of society's culture and traditions, were specifically targeted by the rebels since they were perceived as part of the corrupt and decadent system that the insurgents wanted to get rid of. Sacred places such as those where secret societies met in the bush and shrines were routinely defiled and their ceremonial objects destroyed. The impact of the conflict was incalculable, since these elders and institutions, which were methodically destroyed, were critical to the effective functioning of these mechanisms. They consequently lost their prestige and relevance.

> The impact of the conflict in Sierra Leone on the traditional justice system was incalculable. The institutions were methodically destroyed and the elders who were critical to the effective functioning of these mechanisms lost their prestige and relevance.

4.2. Traditional practices and grave human rights crimes

During the civil conflict the warring factions, and particularly the rebels, systematically committed heinous transgressions, including war crimes and crimes against humanity, such as sexual violence, sexual slavery and enforced prostitution, amputations, indiscriminate killings and torture. Naturally, the victims would demand justice and if possible some reparation. But what kind of justice would they want—retributive or restorative? Which of these forms has the potential to build the peace and which has the potential to disrupt it?

There are certain realities that must be faced. For example, those people whose limbs were amputated or women who were raped have to live with the scars forever. Although retributive justice may have the potential to act as a deterrent, it could at the same time create more societal problems as both the victims and the perpetrators may be living in the same neighbourhood. Restorative justice, on the other hand, aims to repair and create social harmony within the battered communities. Whatever the case, the justice that the victims desire would come at a high price, especially when one considers that in certain cases members of the same family fought for different warring factions, and many children were involved in the atrocities.

> Although retributive justice may have the potential to act as a deterrent, it could at the same time create more societal problems as victims and perpetrators may be living in the same neighbourhood. Restorative justice, on the other hand, aims to repair and create social harmony within the battered communities.

The TRC has actively encouraged reconciliation at the level of the family, the home community, the community where the individual has settled after the conflict, and the local church or peer groups, 'more specifically during the reconciliation ceremonies at the end of each of its district hearings. Many of these ceremonies focused on reconciliation between ex-combatants and the communities they currently live in. Others focused on the reunification of abducted children with their families and communities, or on the reunification of a "bush wife" with her family, or that of a chief with the community that he or she had abandoned during the war' (Sierra Leone Truth and Reconciliation Commission 2004, vol. 3b, chapter 7, section 21). The final report of the TRC also notes that many aspects of traditional dispute resolution, 'such as mediation, purification, token appeasement and the willingness to show remorse, are in harmony with the objectives of the TRC policy and have been sustained by the Commission during its hearings and beyond' (Sierra Leone Truth and Reconciliation Commission 2004, vol. 3b, chapter 7, section 36). A study by the non-governmental organization (NGO) Manifesto '99, submitted to the office of the United Nations High Commissioner for Human Rights in preparation for the TRC, argues that the 'strong traditional belief in swearing, cleansing and purification should be considered seriously by the TRC. In essence where the truth cannot easily come out voluntarily, these practices should be appealed to as a way of enhancing the truth and reconciliation process' (cited in Sierra Leone Truth and Reconciliation Commission 2004: 25).

The conflict had a particularly telling effect on children. They were at the centre of the crisis, for they sustained the rebel group as well as the civil defence forces. Young children were deprived of their childhood and forced to take on adult responsibilities, including combat roles, in contravention not only of the 1989 Convention on the Rights of the Child but also of traditional social norms. Boys as young as ten years were attracted to the rebel forces through their rhetoric; others were forcefully conscripted, drugged and brainwashed. These under-age boys killed, maimed and committed gross human rights violations. The young girls became sex slaves, cooks and porters. Many were brutally gang-raped and sexually mutilated. Some girls also committed acts of terror. Gender-based violence was the norm during the crisis. Children were thus exposed to experiences that were at variance with the social and cultural norms of Sierra Leonean society. These terrible experiences left them completely traumatized. It is estimated that 40 per cent of the approximately 20,000 rebel fighters were children between the ages of seven and 17. About 50 per cent of all the fighters during the conflict were under 18 years of age.

> The conflict had a particularly telling effect on children, and the reintegration of these children into their former communities was a major challenge.

The reintegration of these children into their former communities was a major challenge. Fortunately, Sierra Leoneans generally have immense capacity to forgive, especially children. Reintegration and reunification ceremonies were used all over the country. In the northern provincial town of Makeni, for example, an NGO, Caritas Makeni, successfully reintegrated ex-child soldiers into their families through a combination of the methods described below.

> When Caritas Makeni reunified child ex-combatants with their families, the latter sought to 'change the hearts' of their children through a combination of care, support and ritual action. Usually, the eldest member of the family prayed over a cup of water and rubbed it over the child's body (especially the head, feet, and chest), asking God and the ancestors to give the child a 'cool heart,' a state of reconciliation and stability in which the child is settled in the home, has a proper relationship with family and community and is not troubled by nightmares and bad memories ... Some parents then drank the consecrated water that had washed their child. The consecrated water now becomes the new physical bond between parent and child ... some parents also offered kola nuts ... Some parents, in addition, followed this up with liquid Quranic slate water ... Others again made a 'fol sara' to thank the ancestors and God, either dedicating a chicken and caring for it thereafter, or slaughtering and cooking it with rice as an offering to poor people, or to a Muslim ritual specialist to eat (Shaw 2002: 6-7).

Child protection agencies such as the United Nations Children's Fund (UNICEF), with support from the government of Sierra Leone, also used indigenous reconciliation mechanisms and resources in Mendeland. The emphasis was on rehabilitation, reintegration and fostering respect for the rights of others. In parts of Kpaa Mende territory, the parents of former child combatants dressed in rags and took to the streets as community members followed, singing and dancing. For reconciliation to be successful, meaningful and long-lasting, it has to be done at the community level and by the people of the community themselves.

> For reconciliation to be successful, meaningful and long-lasting, it has to be done at the community level and by the people of the community themselves.

4.3. Civil society initiatives

Civil society groups, including community, women's and religious organizations, all ably complemented the efforts of the international community to bring peace to Sierra Leone. The Inter-Religious Council (IRC), formed in Sierra Leone in 1997, regularly engaged the RUF rebels and the government. They even met rebel leader Foday Sankoh in his prison cell in April 1999 before the start of the peace talks in Lomé. Some of their members took great risks to venture into the bush to appeal to the rebels to release the children in their custody. The women of Sierra Leone were no less involved, and many of them paid dearly with their lives as they attempted to meet with the rebels.

The role of civil society in the reconciliation process was commendable. The TRC, during its final stage, invited the IRC, in recognition of the latter's familiarity with traditional methods of reconciliation, to initiate joint reconciliation activities in the districts and to set up structures that would continue operating beyond the life of the TRC. Together the TRC and the IRC trained IRC district coordinators and organized reconciliation workshops in all the 12 provincial districts. These were followed by the setting up of reconciliation support committees in the districts with representatives in the chiefdoms who would encourage, identify and fund local reconciliation activities conducted by the communities.

5. An assessment of traditional justice and reconciliation mechanisms in Sierra Leone

Tradition-based practices seek to bring social harmony to their communities, and to this end they use various methods and strategies, some of which have been discussed above. Here we examine the major strengths, weaknesses, opportunities and threats with specific reference to the Mende of Sierra Leone.

5.1. Strengths

1. Tradition-based justice and reconciliation mechanisms are *transparent and open*, and *the possibility of a miscarriage of justice is therefore greatly reduced*. Thus, many community people have great faith in the system—hence the high level of community participation.

2. They are *cheap and affordable*; anyone can seek justice irrespective of social class or financial status.

3. Decisions are generally arrived at after a lengthy process of *consultation and debate*, thus giving each aggrieved party ample opportunity to state their case.

4. Where *punishment* is meted out, this *is done with the view that it could act as a deterrent*, especially for crimes that affect the entire community.

5. Their ultimate goal in Mende culture is to *foster social harmony*, as is evidenced, for example, in the Wonde dance and ritual mentioned above.

These strengths are very important and must be exploited in any post-conflict community regeneration efforts, even though the Mende truth and justice systems have not been able to deal adequately with the crimes committed during the war. The social system of the Mende, and indeed all other ethnic groups in the country, was completely destroyed.

> The Mende truth and justice systems have not been able to deal adequately with the crimes committed during the war. The social system of the Mende, and indeed of all other ethnic groups in the country, was completely destroyed. The traditional justice mechanisms were not resilient enough to withstand the pressures of the war.

5.2. Weaknesses

1. The Mende *practices are applicable only to their communities* and, since there has been a great deal of mixing of the groups over the years (e.g. through intermarriage), they may not be suitable in settling disputes arising between Mende and non-Mende people within the community.

2. The *over-reliance on elders* for the settling of disputes and other problems could be disadvantageous to other groups, for example, young people. Moreover, currently, there appears to be an acute shortage of elders who are fully knowledgeable about the ways of their communities. In the long run these *practices may disappear completely.*

3. The justice mechanism appears to be *inflexible* and often archaic methods are used to address emerging issues.

4. The *use of the supernatural* in settling disputes among the Mende is problematic.

5. *The traditional justice mechanisms were not resilient enough to withstand the pressures of the war.*

Traditional justice and reconciliation instruments must take changing conditions into account and make provision accordingly for wider participation and inclusion, especially for women and young people. It may be difficult to reconstitute these tools to enable them to deal adequately with war crimes and crimes against humanity.

5.3. Opportunities

1. The conflict has generated a great deal of external interest, particularly among NGOs, in carrying out detailed studies as well as utilizing the traditional conflict management tools in community reconciliation efforts.

2. Many agencies seem willing to use these mechanisms in the reintegration of child combatants into their communities, as is indicated above.

5.4. Threats

1. Although there appears to be some interest in the potential of the Mende practices to settle communities and reconcile warring parties, *some people still view these mechanisms as backward and primitive.* This was probably the main reason why the Sierra Leone TRC did not make much use of such systems.

2. *Top–down approaches* to peace building from government and international agencies are making these mechanisms dysfunctional.

3. The *dislocation of families and the mass migration of young people* into urban centres contribute to making them less effective.

6. Conclusions

The deadly conflict which engulfed Sierra Leone from 1991 to 2002, and which was preceded by several years of political and social exclusion, economic mismanagement and organized corruption, was an unprecedented human disaster. It has left in its wake many difficult challenges, not least for the application of justice. The internationalization of the war, the involvement of external actors and players in the search for peace, and the nature and magnitude of the crimes committed during the war partly necessitated the use of 'top–down' peace-building strategies.

The war has again underlined the Sierra Leoneans' capacity for forgiveness and reconciliation. Sierra Leoneans are fully aware that they cannot turn the clock back. What has been done cannot be undone. This is more forcefully expressed in the Mende saying *'Kpande yia, ii yia'* ('When a gun is fired, it is fired'). In other words, one must look to the future.

The end of the conflict was followed by the setting up of transitional justice mechanisms, including the Truth and Reconciliation Commission and the Special Court. Although the TRC made use of traditional rulers in its truth-seeking and reconciliation processes, it largely eschewed local rituals of cursing, cleansing and purification, which may have limited its ability to induce confessions and effect reconciliation.

A multi-sectoral review and reform of the legal and judicial sector is well under way, and has the potential to consolidate peace in Sierra Leone. One must not, however, lose sight of the fact that what took decades to collapse cannot be rebuilt overnight.

Societal resources such as indigenous accountability mechanisms are very useful in peace building, especially after a violent conflict. They have the potential to facilitate the reintegration and healing process, since the community members can easily associate with them. Thus tradition-based practices have been used effectively to reintegrate child soldiers in Sierra Leone. That said, these tools can only complement the efforts of formal criminal justice systems, since only the latter are capable of dealing with complex issues such as war crimes and crimes against humanity.

References and further reading

Abraham, Arthur, 'Liberia and Sierra Leone: History of Misery and Misery of History', *International Journal of Sierra Leone Studies and Reviews*, vol. 1, no, 1 (fall 2000)

Alie, Joe A. D. and Gaima, E. A., *Conflict in Sierra Leone: Rising From the Ashes* (New York: United Nations Development Programme (UNDP), 2000)

Harris, W. T. and Sawyerr, Harry, *The Springs of Mende Belief and Conduct: A Discussion of the Influence of the Belief in the Supernatural among the Mende* (Freetown: Sierra Leone University Press, 1968)

Kelsall, Tim, 'Truth, Lies, Ritual: Preliminary Reflections on the Truth and Reconciliation Commission', *Sierra Leone Human Rights Quarterly*, vol. 27, no. 2 (May 2005)

Lord, David (ed.), 'Paying the Price: The Sierra Leone Peace Process', *Accord* (Conciliation Resources, London), issue 9 (2000), available at <http://www.c-r.org/our-work/accord/sierra-leone/contents.php>

Minneh, Kane et al., 'Sierra Leone: Legal and Judicial Sector Assessment', Legal Vice Presidency, World Bank, 2004

No Peace Without Justice and UNICEF Innocenti Research Centre, *International Criminal Justice and Children* ([Florence]: UNICEF Innocenti Research Centre, 2002)

Pettersson, Björn, 'Post-conflict Reconciliation in Sierra Leone: Lessons Learned', in International IDEA, *Reconciliation Lessons Learned from United Nations Peacekeeping Missions: Report Prepared by International IDEA for the Office of the High Commissioner for Human Rights (OHCHR)* (Stockholm: International IDEA, 2004)

Shaw, Rosalind "Remembering to forget: Report on local techniques of healing and reconciliation for child ex-combatants in Northern Sierra Leone" (USA: Tufts University, 2002), pp. 6-7

Sierra Leone Truth and Reconciliation Commission, 'Reconciliation', *Final Report*, 2004, Vol. 3B, chapter 7, available at <http://trcsierraleone.org/drwebsite/publish/v3b-c7.shtml>

Wojkowska, Ewa, *Doing Justice: How Informal Justice Systems Can Contribute* (Olso: UNDP and Oslo Governance Centre, 2006)

CHAPTER 6

CHAPTER 6

The institution of bashingantahe in Burundi

*Assumpta Naniwe-Kaburahe**

1. The Burundian conflict

1.1. The beginning of a bloody conflict

Burundi is a small country (27,834 km²) that has been independent since 1962. An administrative system of a dynastic monarchy had been in place for several centuries before it was colonized by Germany (1896–1912) and Belgium (1912–62). It is situated in the Great Lakes region of Africa with Rwanda to the north, the Democratic Republic of the Congo to the west, and Tanzania to the south and east. With agriculture accounting for 90 per cent of the economy and with one of the highest population densities in Africa (about 290 inhabitants/km²), the country continues to experience huge development difficulties. Its population consists of four groups that are usually qualified as ethnic groups (*ubwoko*)—the Bahutu, the Batutsi, the Baganwa and the Batwa. These ethnic groups speak the same language, share the same culture and history, and live in the same territory.

Despite this linguistic and cultural commonality, over four decades Burundi has experienced different violent conflicts of an ethnic and political nature. Since independence in 1962 it has gone through cycles of violence based on the issue of access to and retention of power, involving the manipulation and exploitation of the ethic groups by the political elite in their power struggles.

The Kingdom of Burundi, a former German colony, was placed under the mandate of Belgium by the League of Nations in 1919. The ethnic cleavages which were to tear Burundi apart did not exist under the monarchy, which had developed a considerable degree of stability. The monarchy was a highly complex system of government with an intelligent share of ethnic and clan elements in its working machinery.

*The original French version of this chapter can be found at www.idea.int/rrn

Immediately prior to independence, Burundi experienced intense political upheaval. There were at least 26 political parties, some of which, like the Union Pour le Progrès National (Uprona), were fighting for immediate independence while others, supported by the colonial power Belgium, were in no hurry to achieve this. Uprona, a party which succeeded in mobilizing the Bahutu and Batutsi under the leadership of Prince Louis Rwagasore, and which led the country to independence, gradually came to be dominated by the Batutsi and remained in power from independence, obtained on 1 July 1962, until the advent of multipartyism, heralded by the electoral victory of the Bahutu-dominated Front pour la démocratie au Burundi (Frodebu) in 1993.

On 13 October 1961, Prince Louis Rwagasore, the hero of independence, was assassinated. On 15 January 1965 Prime Minister Pierre Ngendandumwe, a Muhutu and a close companion of the prince was also assassinated. After the assassination of these two great political and nationalist figures the country entered into a period of political instability and ethnic hatred. The enfeebled monarchy was swept away by a military coup in 1966, led by Captain Michel Micombero, who was deposed by Colonel Jean Baptiste Bagaza in 1976. Bagaza was evicted by Pierre Buyoya in 1987.

The year 1972 saw the outbreak of hostilities and inter-ethnic massacres between the Bahutu and the Batutsi on a national scale. By their very intensity and the trauma they left in the minds of Burundians, many of whom—especially Hutu intellectuals killed or forced into exile—fell victim, the tragic events of that year were a key factor in the recent history of Burundi. The authorities' management of the 1972 crisis was catastrophic. The great democratic impetus which had led to independence was drowned in blood after just a few years. Attempts to overthrow the government and other real or imaginary plots widened the chasm between the Bahutu and the Batutsi. For three decades the country was governed by military rulers from the same province succeeding each other via military coups and depending entirely on the only political party, Uprona, to rule the country.

1.2. August 1988: a half-hearted call for democracy

22 August 1988 marked a turning point in Burundi's recent history. After a series of massacres in the north, a group of Hutu intellectuals addressed an open letter to President Buyoya in which they expressed the desire to see Bahutu included in the defence and political leadership of the party. This letter had a significant impact both within and outside Burundi. As a result Buyoya initiated a so-called national unity policy. He appointed a Hutu prime minister and the make-up of his government became balanced in terms of ethnic representation. 'National unity' was symbolized in many different ways. In February 1991 a 'unity charter' was adopted and a 'unity anthem' composed. A 'government of unity' was the talk of the day, a 'unity monument' was erected on the heights of the city of Bujumbura, a 'unity flag' was hoisted beside the national flag, and even 'unity caps' went on sale. For the first time Burundians started publicly to debate the issue of ethnicity. Thanks to this policy of openness, hitherto taboo issues related to ethnicity were openly tackled (if sometimes clumsily); the social atmosphere seemed to

become less tense and the democratic process began to move forward. Despite sometimes justified criticism, it cannot be denied that this policy defused ethnic tensions to some extent, even if only superficially. But, despite the new policy of openness, inter-ethnic antagonisms remained.

1.3. Burundi in the wind of democratization

The wind of democratization that was blowing through Africa in the early 1990s after the 16th Franco-African summit forced Pierre Buyoya to initiate a democratization process in Burundi. The country acquired a new constitution based on multipartyism and freedom of the press.

In June 1993 Burundians went to the polls to elect a president. Three groups contested the election—Uprona, Frodebu and the Parti pour la Réconciliation du Peuple (PRP), a relatively new minority party with no apparent ethnic dominance, but composed mainly of Baganwa and Batutsi. Frodebu won the election and for the first time in the country's history a Muhutu, Melchior Ndadaye, took office as president of the republic. The whole world hailed this alternation of power and the country's new democratic experiment. In the event, the 'democracy in brackets' lasted only three months. Ndadaye, together with some of his close associates, was assassinated by Batutsi soldiers in October 1993, triggering large-scale ethnic massacres. Civilians, mainly Batutsi, were killed on the basis of their ethnic identity, resulting in close to 300,000 deaths, while 800,000 were displaced or forced to seek refuge in or outside the country.

Burundi experienced massive destruction of its socio-economic infrastructure and a crisis of moral values, on the one hand, and, on the other, the organization of an armed struggle by two Hutu armed movements—the Front National de Libération-Parti pour la Libération du Peuple Hutu (FNL-Palipehutu), and the Forces pour la défense de la Démocratie (FDD), the armed wing of the Conseil National pour la défense de la démocratie (CNDD).

1.4. Civil war and negotiations

It was in 1998 that Burundi started to engage in negotiations in an attempt to stop the war. Major Pierre Buyoya, who had taken power again in July 1996 in what he called 'a coup d'état unlike any other' and an 'initiative to save the country', began talks with the Hutu rebel army, which was increasingly gaining control on the ground. However, his coup was not welcomed by the international community. A total embargo was imposed, the effects of which worsened a situation that was already critical following years of political instability, growing insecurity and worsening socio-economic conditions.

For the purpose of negotiations the first meetings were secret and were held in Rome under the auspices of the religious community of San Egidio. Negotiations became official in Tanzania with the involvement of former Tanzanian President Julius Nyerere, and finally of Nelson Mandela. The Arusha Peace and Reconciliation Agreement was signed on 28 August 2000. Under the terms of the agreement a transitional government was established, to be led by Buyoya, a Mututsi, for an initial period of 18 months, and by Domitien Ndayizeye, a Muhutu, for a second period of 18 months. As a follow-up to this process the United Nations Operation in Burundi (Opération des Nations Unies au Burundi, ONUB) was established on Burundian territory on 1 June 2004. It completed its mandate on 31 December 2006, with the creation of the United Nations Integrated Office in Burundi (Bureau Intégré des Nations Unies au Burundi, BINUB).

This mission was itself a response to the request of Burundian political stakeholders who, under the Arusha Agreement, protocol V, articles 7 and 8, and in line with the respective ceasefire agreements, spelled out the roles of the international community and the United Nations (UN) in terms of ensuring the implementation of the agreement.

From November 2003, after the signing of the Pretoria Agreement on power sharing between the government and the CNDD-FDD rebel movement, the security situation greatly improved, despite the absence of the FNL-Palipehutu, which finally joined the peace process in September 2006.

A series of reforms envisaged by the different peace agreements are currently being implemented, notably in the defence and security structures and the judicial system. Significant progress has undoubtedly been made both in terms of peace and security in Burundi and in the areas of democratization of the state institutions, the reform and reorganization of the defence and security forces, and the voluntary return of repatriated persons; but the situation remains precarious.

1.5. Stages in the development of transitional justice in Burundi

The different transitional justice mechanisms suggested for Burundi have changed several times since the August 2000 Arusha Agreement. That agreement provided for the establishment of a national truth and reconciliation commission (commission nationale vérité réconciliation, CNVR), and two international mechanisms—an international judicial commission of inquiry and an international criminal tribunal. The international judicial commission of inquiry and the CNVR would be mandated to investigate the cycles of violence that have plagued Burundi since independence in 1962, while the international criminal tribunal was to punish the guilty in cases where the commission of inquiry confirmed the existence of evidence of crimes of genocide, crimes against humanity or war crimes.

Although it was responsible for putting these mechanisms in place, the transitional government requested the UN secretary-general to set up the international judicial commission of inquiry on 24 July 2002.

Following a mission to Burundi, in May 2004 the UN assistant secretary-general, Tuliameni Kalomoh, submitted his report to the Security Council (the Kalomoh Report). It recommended that a national truth and reconciliation commission be established and that a special chamber be created within Burundi's judicial structure. This solution was intended to avoid duplication of functions between the CNVR and an international judicial commission of inquiry and to enable the Burundian judicial system to benefit from the international support expected for special chambers.

In its Resolution 1606 of 2005 the UN Security Council requested the secretary-general to start negotiations with the government, and to consult the Burundi people. The government formed a delegation of nine national experts with the task of negotiating the establishment of the proposed dual transitional justice mechanism. The first round of negotiations between the government and the UN delegation took place in Bujumbura in March 2006 on the basis of a memorandum (of 26 March 2006) put together by the government delegation. They reached several agreements but there was also much disagreement on some fundamental aspects of the proposed dual mechanism, namely the organization of broadly based consultations, the issue of amnesty, and the relationship between the proposed CNVR and the special tribunal.

In its Resolution 1716 (2006), the UN Security Council set up BINUB to replace ONUB and mandated it among other things to support the government in establishing transitional justice mechanisms for the promotion and protection of human rights and for the fight against impunity.

It should be noted that institutions that resulted from democratic elections are now operating at all levels, with a mandate of five years. However, there are still major challenges, particularly those facing the justice sector—impunity for offences and crimes; corruption in the judicial structures and other state services; the general propensity for popular revenge; the problem of truth; forgiveness and reconciliation; property problems; the rehabilitation of victims of war, and so on.

This (by no means exhaustive) catalogue of issues that must be addressed in order to restore the rule of law in Burundi calls for the involvement of all legitimate national institutions. After the period of violence the government, which has tackled the situation head-on, is struggling with the question of how to manage a past that is characterized by serious human rights violations in order to avoid the past negatively influencing the future, thereby perpetuating the cycle of violence. It is a question of analysing how the current system of government can respond to the imperative of upholding justice after a long period of impunity, by relying on both formal and informal judicial systems—such as the institution of *bashingantahe*.

The *bashingantahe* have always played an important role not only in traditional society but also during the crises that have regularly shaken the country. They demonstrated their influence particularly during the massacres of October 1993, when they intervened, interposing themselves as a barrier between the warring parties and attempting to save many lives. In areas where a strong and operational body of *bashingantahe* existed, the damage in terms of loss of human lives was relatively limited and the Bahutu and Batutsi remained united thanks to these elders. Who are they? How do they operate? And how can they help Burundians to handle both the country's difficult past and the challenging task of promoting justice, democracy, peace and security today?

2. Traditional justice mechanism: the institution of *bashingantahe*

2.1. Description of the institution

2.1.1. The concept

In current usage, the term *bashingantahe* (singular *umushingantahe*) refers to men of integrity who are responsible for settling conflicts at all levels, from the top of the hill to the courts of kings. Formed from a combination of a root verb, *gushinga* (to plant, to bolt down), and the noun *intahe* (staff of justice), the word literally means 'the one who bolts down the law'. These men are referred to in this way because of the staff of justice with which they hit the ground rhythmically and in turns to invoke the wisdom of the ancestors buried beneath and to highlight the power of the judgements they give when arbitrating on conflicts. The noun *intahe* is used metonymically and symbolically to refer to equity and justice. F. M. Rodegem in his Rundi–French dictionary of 1970 translates the word *umushingantahe* as 'magistrate, eminent personality, councillor, umpire, assessor, judge, the one invested with judicial authority and who wields the rod (*intahe*) symbol of his authority', and for Ntabona (1999) the term *umushingantahe* refers to 'A man responsible for good order, for tranquility, for truth and peace in his environment. And this is not by virtue of some conferred administrative authority, but by his very being, by the quality of his lifestyle recognized by the society and for which it confers such powers on him'.

2.1.2. The origin and selection of the bashingantahe

According to legend, the institution of *bashingantahe* goes back to the late 17th century and a certain Ngoma ya Sacega, a wise elder famous for his judgements rendered during the reign of the first king, Ntare Rushatsi, mythical founder of the Burundian monarchy. This indicates that the origin of the institution is essentially judicial. It is made up of elders, people of irreproachable morality, and has played an important role for many decades, particularly during the era of the monarchy. It presided over the judicial organization of the country at all levels and played the role of check and balance on power. In a sense the *bashingantahe* constituted a peaceful and independent authority that contained, limited and controlled the power of the king and chiefs, while also ensuring that arbitrary judgement and lack of justice were curbed.

It is this function of the institution that constitutes its main strength—a strength that is also seen in the selection of the *bashingantahe*. To be selected, as research carried out countrywide has confirmed, a candidate must exemplify certain essential qualities such as experience and wisdom; a high regard and love for truth; a sense of honour and dignity; a love of work and the ability to provide for the needs of others; a highly developed sense of justice and fairness; a sense of the common good and social responsibility; and sobriety and balance in speech and action. Other moral and intellectual qualities are also needed, such as discretion, a keen intelligence, self-respect and respect for others, a spirit of temperance, courage and dedication. These qualities guarantee the moral integrity and authority of the *bashingantahe* and are the basic guiding principles for their behaviour and their performance of their duties. By tradition, only men are admitted to this noble institution.

> The ancient institution of bashingantahe in Burundi is made up of elders, people of irreproachable morality. It presided over the judicial organization of the country at all levels and played the role of check and balance on power, ensuring that arbitrary judgement and lack of justice were curbed.

2.1.3. The investiture of bashingantahe and the meaning of the oath

The candidate for the institution of *bashingantahe* has to go through an initiation consisting of several stages during which he is observed, monitored and guided by the people around him, especially his mentor, whose role is to initiate and prepare the aspirant for his future duties (see box 9). The oath of loyalty represents not only the covenant between the people and the newly invested *umushingantahe* but also the commitment to fulfil the obligations that flow from it. It is an oath that integrates and fulfils the socio-political functions of inclusion and commitment.

Box 9: The investiture of an umushingantahe in Burundi

1. The aspirant at the beginning of his course. The candidate shows his desire to become part of the body of bashingantahe.
2. The first level. The candidate has to expressly request to be initiated. From then on he is carefully observed during his public speeches, in his behaviour and in his attitudes during official ceremonies at which he is assigned certain responsibilities, especially in relation to the sharing of drinks among the uninitiated men. The candidate is also authorized to participate in debates and to take the initiative of reconciling parties in conflict or to arbitrate in different cases.
3. The candidate awaiting investiture. A mentor monitors the candidate more closely, lavishing advice on him, initiating him into a deep knowledge of customs and skills of dispute settlement, which is the knowledge and information that he needs in order to perform his future duties.
4. The investiture. With the approval of his mentor the aspirant is accepted at an official investiture which is carried out during a grand festival that represents a ceremony of confirmation, affiliation and

elevation to the ranks of the bashingantahe. This ceremony is of great importance as it represents the candidate's strong commitment to this new status. The speeches delivered on this occasion deeply reflect the commitments and obligations to which the umushingantahe subscribes. The aspirant's membership of the bashingantahe is further concretized by the staff of justice that he receives and the oath he swears during the investiture.

2.1.4. The original structure and operation of the institution

Since the era of the monarchy, at all levels, every authority has had a body of *bashingantahe* which helped and advised it while playing the role of check and balance. Here, the structure is informal and it has a number of missions. On the other hand, in terms of jurisdiction, the institution has a formal structure, starting from family arbitration, continuing through local-level arbitration to arbitration of the deputy chief and from there to the arbitration of the chief and then the king's court. At these different levels of jurisdiction the *bashingantahe* settled various kinds of disputes relating to matters of succession and the sharing of property (land, livestock), family and social quarrels, neighbourhood conflicts or disputes on the hills, and so on. More important cases (murder or the theft of cattle) were resolved at the level of the tribunals of chiefs, while the tribunal of the king (*mwami*) handled disputes between higher chiefs and more serious cases, especially acts of lèse-majesté and cases calling for capital punishment. The institution worked according to a strict code with well-defined missions.

2.1.5. Basic missions and principles of the institution

The institution is assigned three essential missions—mediation, reconciliation and arbitration.

Mediation. By tradition, an *umushingantahe* was appointed to help the parties to a dispute to resolve their differences. Only if his efforts failed was the Council of Bashingantahe called in to find a compromise solution through conciliation. It should be noted here that conciliation is not exclusively linked to the resolution of a conflict; it is part and parcel of Burundian culture and is practised in other social settings such as the organization of ceremonies like marriages or even in rituals.

Conciliation. When a conflict or a dispute breaks out among members of the community, especially where members of the same family or neighbours are in engaged in a dispute, the *bashingantahe* try to bring the parties to a peaceful resolution by means of counselling and proposing mutual forgiveness and reconciliation instead of claims for damages. In this context, conciliation is perceived as a necessary preliminary to all court action and consists of finding a common basis of understanding between the parties involved, with the focus being primarily on reconciliation, peacekeeping, social cohesion and harmony.

Arbitration. This complements and prolongs conciliation if the latter proves not to be effective. A judgement is handed down by the *bashingantahe*, who are considered in situations of this kind as real judges whose decisions are binding on the parties. The success of conciliation and arbitration requires mutual understanding and a willingness on the part of the complainants to put an end to their differences, as well as the presumed neutrality of the arbiter, who is not from the side of any of the parties. Depending on the nature of the conflict, a party that is not satisfied with the outcome of the arbitration can take the matter to the upper hierarchy right up to the arbitration of the king. Today, the party who feels aggrieved goes to the courts, presenting a copy of the official minutes of the judgements pronounced by the *bashingantahe* (e.g. in cases of conflicts over land property).

> The institution of bashingantahe has three essential missions—mediation, reconciliation and arbitration.

2.1.6. The driving principles of the institution

These principles are reflected in the commitments undertaken by the *bashingantahe* during their investiture, and the leitmotif that guides their actions. They are as follows.

Neutrality and impartiality. These principles consist of giving equal treatment to all parties involved, a commitment not to be partisan in conflicts, which does not in any sense imply inaction or indecision. The *bashingantahe* have to listen to everyone, search for the truth and act with wisdom without allowing themselves to be influenced or take sides in any situation.

Collegiality. This principle has been given the force of law by Burundian tradition, which rejects the primacy of individual judgement in the course of a trial. Through regular consensus building, which is the mode of action of the *bashingantahe*, impartial judgements are handed down after a collegial deliberation that is free of any indiscretion. This method (see e.g. Ntahombaye and Manirakiza 1997b) is of great value in the quest to reveal the truth in a way that is consistent with objectivity and a basis in a verifiable reality that are fundamental to every sound system of justice. This collegiality is the basis of the official credibility of the judgements made by the *bashingantahe*—a view confirmed by the fact that currently over 70 per cent of them are confirmed by the resident tribunals (*tribunaux de résidence*, the state courts at the bottom of the judicial hierarchy) (Dexter and Ntahombaye 2005).

Transparency and respect for truth. Acting collectively, the *bashingantahe* bring progress reports on their work and the results expected or achieved to the attention of the public. They have to publish full information about their activities and therefore open themselves to observation and criticism. Moreover, both the *bashingantahe* and witnesses undertake to abide permanently by the truth.

Credibility. This principle helps to reinforce individual and institutional legitimacy. It requires of the *bashingantahe* not only that they build a positive image but above all that they be careful about the views and judgements of others on the individual and on the institution. Without credibility, the legitimacy of actions undertaken is seriously undermined.

Legality and legitimacy. The institution draws its legality from the fact that it derives from customary law. Its legality is guaranteed as long as customary law is not abolished. Today, that legality is protected by various statutory enactments, in particular the constitution (of March 2005, article 68) as well as by the law on local government, which lends the institution legitimacy by providing that: 'Under the supervision of the hill or suburb chief, the mission of the hill or suburb council is to . . . carry out arbitration, mediation, conciliation as well as the settlement of conflicts in the neighbourhood on the hill or in the suburb, with the *bashingantahe* of the entity' (Loi no. 1/016, 20 April 2005).

Equity. This principle focuses on non-discrimination and inclusion. Here, equity complements, corrects and humanizes the law. It is the sense of natural justice present in the appreciation of what is due to each person. It is also the virtue present in whoever possesses this sense of natural justice.

Discretion and impartiality. Every member of the institution is committed to secrecy in their deliberations and any contravention of this rule will attract moral and social sanction, involving exclusion from the group. This highlights the importance attached to the role the *bashingantahe* are called upon to play in settling conflicts between citizens without being partisan and without any bias towards one or another party.

Free social service. All the tasks the *bashingantahe* undertake—conciliation, arbitration and providing judicial rulings—are unpaid. In principle, there is no fee for court proceedings or remuneration of any kind. The exception is in cases where those who seek their services are asked to provide a certain quantity of beer, commonly called *agatutu k'abagabo*, which is shared by everyone and is a symbol that unity has been restored.

2.2. The evolution of the institution of bashingantahe *from the colonial era to the* republican regimes

The institution was an integral part of traditional Burundian society which, as is observed above, had clearly defined missions and played the role of check and balance. However, subsequent socio-political developments did not leave it untouched. In the course of its historical evolution it has both changed its form and lost some of its prerogatives.

2.2.1. Under the colonial regime

The colonial regime was the first to make significant changes to the traditional system of justice based on the institution of *bashingantahe*. From the early 1920s, the Belgian administration undertook a reform of the judicial system by withdrawing certain prerogatives, particularly from the *bashingantahe*, the most important reform being the abolition of certain sanctions that were considered barbaric, and the checking of judgements rendered. These actions of the colonial authorities, which 'arrogated the right to evaluate the authenticity of customs, for the first time denied the *bashingantahe* their fundamental mission of guaranteeing the continuity of traditional jurisprudence' (Deslaurier 2003).

The colonial authorities established courts under chieftaincies and sub-chieftaincies, and appointed judges with responsibility for resolving conflicts. This was a significant intrusion into the functions of the *bashingantahe*, particularly those of bringing aggrieved parties together and conciliation. This coexistence, in which the chiefs of the new courts had the blessing of the colonial authorities, considerably weakened the role of the *bashingantahe*, who increasingly lost their influence in the community. In reality the power of social control shifted from the collective to the administrative centre of the country. Even so, the institution of *bashingantahe* remained a symbol of equity and justice and managed to maintain its influence among ordinary members of the community, and the *bashingantahe* have continued to render their judgements.

Equally, missionaries contributed to the weakening of the institution through the introduction of what were called *abajenama* (counsellors). These men, who were very close to the missionaries and were recruited from among the clergy of the parish, Catholic school teachers, had increasing influence among the Christian community, to the detriment of the *bashingantahe*.

2.2.2. After independence

A law of 26 July 1962 abolished all customary jurisdictions and created a single order embodied in the establishment of magistrates and judicial personnel. However, the Council of Bashingantahe of the Hill (the lowest level in the administrative hierarchy) was retained to resolve conflicts by conciliation in matters where they were permitted to do so by the law, to maintain public order, peace and calm.

Under the First Republic (1966–76), Uprona engaged in politicizing the institution, thereby contributing to its becoming distorted. In effect the authorities started to invest civil servants as *bashingantahe* without taking into account the time-honoured criteria for investiture outlined above. From this period onwards the term '*umushingantahe*' was devalued and quite simply confused with the title of 'Mr' as used in referring to any male adult. This period ushered in the practice of conferring membership of the *bashingantahe* not on the sole basis of the criteria established by tradition, but rather on the basis of formal qualifications and intellectual status.

Under the Second Republic (1976–87), the practice of investiture was forbidden throughout the country because of the cost involved. Instead President Bagaza authorized community administrators appointed by the authorities to appoint individuals to play the role of *bashingantahe* on the hills.

In 1987 a law reorganizing the judicial system restored the Councils of Bashingantahe of the Hill with a mission to seek conciliation between contending parties before they resorted to legal action. This decision should in principle have rehabilitated the institution. Unfortunately, however, there were no accompanying measures to establish the criteria for investiture which would take into account the current political context and the evolution of Burundian society.

Thus, all through the different regimes, colonial as well as post-colonial, the institution of *bashingantahe* experienced many vicissitudes and distortions of its basic values in the sense that it has sometimes been oppressed and forgotten, and sometimes been used as a tool for the programmes and policies of successive administrations. It has been used and manipulated: the *mushingantahe* hat has been worn by political dignitaries or servants of the ruling regime who possessed nothing of the *bashingantahe* qualities in the real sense of the term but saw membership of the group as a means to climb the political ladder without having the corresponding commitment and conviction.

3. The institution of bashingantahe today

Despite this situation, the institution has not completely lost its credibility in the community it serves, which continues to resort to its wisdom. This section analyses the role it has been able to play during the various events the country has experienced over the past decade or so, the impact of these events on its functioning, and its overall place in society.

3.1. The impact of the 1993 crisis on the institution

The 1993 crisis was a further difficult test for an institution already seriously affected by the vicissitudes of the colonial and republican regimes. The role it played during the inter-ethnic massacres that plunged the country into mourning over a decade cannot be passed over. A study undertaken by the University of Burundi in collaboration with the Life and Peace Institute (Ntahombaye and Kagabo 2003) in ten different representative communities in different regions of the country showed that many *bashingantahe* who had been invested in the traditional way tried to play their full role as fathers within their own

> In the 1993 crisis many traditionally invested bashingantahe tried to protect persecuted individuals, save victims from the criminals and organize themselves to arrest killers and looters. Many are considered heroes in their local communities. Following the return of calm, in several areas these men started to organize themselves to engage in a process of reuniting and reconciling communities.

social setting by protecting persecuted individuals, saving victims from the hands of criminals and organizing themselves to arrest killers and looters. Numerous sources testify that many *bashingantahe* are considered heroes (*inkingi z'ubuntu*) in their local communities—a term comparable to 'The Just', the title of honour bestowed by the state of Israel on people from all over the world who have risked their own lives to save Jews from extermination.

Following the return of calm, in several areas these men started to organize themselves to engage in a process of reuniting and reconciling communities which had been tearing themselves apart along ethnic lines, and with the intention of restoring dialogue and progressive reconciliation among their members. Enquiries and interviews conducted by several experts (Ntahombaye and Kagabo 2003) report cases of public requests for forgiveness and reparation for wrongs being made as a result of the initiatives of *bashingantahe* in their communities. These initiatives are not isolated cases, but they were limited to certain places.

However, this mission of serving as custodians of morality and as mediators has not been easy for the *bashingantahe*, who often found themselves confronted with numerous obstacles. There are records of *bashingantahe* being assassinated for trying to save lives or for having taken custody of the property of victims; others suffered the same fate just because they were potential witnesses to atrocities. Some were even prevented from taking any action by manipulated and inflamed youths who considered anyone of their own ethnic group a traitor if they did not participate in the barbaric acts, which they termed a crusade (*isekeza*). Some invested elders gave in to temptation and participated in the atrocities that were being committed around them, while others failed to address the appalling situation out of fear or because of lack of resources.

All in all, eyewitnesses and media reports acknowledge that in places where the *bashingantahe* were still active, human lives were indeed saved. These men of integrity were able to stop atrocities before irreparable damage occurred, and they succeeded in restoring calm and peaceful coexistence in their respective social environments.

3.2. The rehabilitation of the institution

The revival of the *bashingantahe* institution was initiated in the wake of the National Reconciliation Policy which sought to create a framework for dialogue and consultation between the different factions of the Burundian people with regard to the basic challenges facing the country. The commission charged with studying the question of national unity had recommended that the institution be adapted to the current context: 'It does not have to be mythologized but rather to be revived and given back the honour it deserves while taking into account the new state of affairs in Burundian society' (Ntahombaye and Kagabo 2003). The rehabilitation process, which was of particular interest to the *bashingantahe* who had been invested in the traditional way, began at the time of the debate on the Charter of National Unity (1991–2) and of the democratization of Burundian institutions.

From 1996 onwards the *bashingantahe* enjoyed real support as much from the government as from Burundian civil society and the international community. The latter considered the *bashingantahe* as offering a way out of the crisis and built upon the capacity of the institution's members to mobilize their fellow citizens around the ideals of peace and harmony and the positive role that they can play in the life of society.

In its 'Support for the Promotion of Good Governance' project, carried out between 1999 and 2001, the United Nations Development Programme (UNDP) supported activities aimed at identifying *bashingantahe* who had been invested in the traditional way all over the country. In all, more than 34,000 households of traditionally invested and active *bashingantahe* were identified in the 17 provinces of Burundi. This operation made it possible to better understand the real situation of these *bashingantahe*, as well as their number (which would be around 64,000 if one bears in mind that most households consist of a man and a woman: normally women are invested with their husbands).

In 2002, the UNDP launched a second phase of implementation of the 'Support for the Rehabilitation of the Bashingantahe Institution' project. This achieved varied results, including support to the self-structuring of the institution from the lowest level (Conseil de Colline) right up to the top (Conseil National, National Council) and through the local and provincial structures, with democratic elections held each time at different levels. This project helped not only to facilitate communication among the *bashingantahe* but also to rectify certain operational mistakes that had been fostered by years of acting in isolation, and sometimes actions dictated by the government in contradiction of the traditional philosophies of the institution.

The different organs of the institution and their respective powers and duties were entrenched in writing in the Bashingantahe Charter, adopted in April 2002 at an extraordinary congress which brought together five elected representatives from the invested *bashingantahe* in each province.

The institution took the gender dimension into account by including 33 per cent of women in its management committees. The presence of women at management levels constituted a definite asset which helped to trigger positive reflection on the conditions for investiture of women in their own right—something which up until then Burundian tradition had not permitted.

Since 2002 the institution has been progressively recovering its former vitality. Investiture takes place in broad daylight, both in rural and in urban settings. According to available figures, today Burundi has nearly 100,000 *bashingantahe* (men and women) who have been invested in the traditional way ('Rapport de la Mission Indépendante' 2003: 24 ff.).

The evaluation report on the UNDP project notes the steps taken to rehabilitate the institution, and recommends that efforts be focused on activities aimed at reinforcing the capacity of the *bashingantahe* at the grass roots through training in different domains such as juridical function, general law, property law, family law, techniques for the prevention and settlement of conflicts, and basic literacy ('Rapport de la Mission Indépendante' 2003: 24). The implementation of these recommendations ought, however, to take the philosophy and ethics of the *bashingantahe* institution into account and to involve the members, some of whom have a good level of education in different areas and who should themselves be in charge of implementing the programmes of rehabilitation.

In addition, there is the issue of strengthening the technical capacities of the *bashingantahe* and their involvement in development work in order that they may learn to better apply the principles of gender equality and better manage issues related to succession and matrimonial laws, as well as support self-sufficiency in food and people's material well-being—important criteria for being invested as an *umushingantahe*.

Today, the institution has advantages which reinforce its legitimacy at the political and institutional level. The Arusha Agreement acknowledges that the *bashingantahe* constitute a unifying factor on the hills and that the institution is part of the judicial system.

As a customary jurisdiction, the institution of *bashingantahe* has always had a place in Burundian society, which accords it a certain authority. It has some strengths but also some weaknesses, which should be rectified if it is to play its role in the establishment of the rule of law in Burundi.

4. Strengths, weaknesses, opportunities and threats

We now analyse the strengths and weaknesses of the institution of *bashingantahe* in order to spell out the role it could play in establishing the rule of law in Burundi, at a time when it is critical to determine ways and means of helping Burundians to stop the infernal cycle of violence and put in place appropriate mechanisms of justice.

This also provides us with an opportunity to revisit the weaknesses and challenges inherent in the ethical basis and code of conduct of the *bashingantahe* themselves, since these could be an obstacle to the effective implementation of the institution's mission.

4.1. Strengths

The strengths of this secular institution, which has traditionally played a primary role in the organization of Burundian society, are found in the way it is organized, its mission and the principles that guide its actions.

4.1.1. A factor for social cohesion

On the social front, the institution was a factor for social cohesion, order, the resolution of conflicts, and reconciliation between individuals and families. It developed a complete code of behaviour which guaranteed social harmony and stability—'Security without the police, without the military, without prisons' (Ntahombaye and Manirakiza 1997a). According to Ntahokaja (1977), the *bashingantahe* are official representatives of the people and spokesmen for their constituencies. They are negotiators drawn into the problems that arise between rulers and the ruled.

At the moral and cultural level the *bashingantahe* were custodians of customs and practices and served as models in their environments for the promotion of the virtues of mutual respect, dignity, integrity and truth. At the political level, they represented the main pillar of the Burundian political system by means of a network of advisers reaching from the hill right up to the royal court. They represented a restraint on the exercise of power. In recognition of their values and moral integrity, the king and local chiefs alike were obliged to take note of the views of these wise men.

These advantages which were the strength of the institution in traditional society remain relevant today, or at least represent goals to be achieved through the rehabilitation of the institution. Currently, the institution is seeking to position itself as a point of reference to exercise a positive influence on society, and to 're-gild its coat of arms' by inviting its members to return to the values cited above. It has the capacity to do this and the resources needed to enable it to fulfil its mission.

4.1.2. Its national dimension

The institution has a national dimension: its members are active in all provinces right down to the hill (village) level, and membership is not limited to a particular ethnic group or clan. As a result, it can exercise moral authority and influence in society, and participate in the moral reconstruction of public life and in community harmonization. This will enable it to participate actively in the work of the CNVR and in strengthening the rule of law.

4.1.3. A democratic institution

The institution is also democratic from the standpoint of the modalities by which candidates accede to the ranks of the *bashingantahe*. The procedures prescribe consultation with the people, not nomination by the authorities. Investiture is and always has been a public affair. Opposition from any citizen, regardless of their age or rank, can contribute to an application for the status of *bashingantahe* being annulled.

It is also founded on universal values, especially the concern for justice, a high regard for truth and a deep respect for the common interest. Taking a comparative approach, Ngorwanubusa (1991) describes the *umushingantahe* as an 'honourable man', and demonstrates the existence of similar institutions across Africa and in the rest of the world. He cites the *silatigi* in Saharan West Africa, the *chaman* among the Indians of South America and the *imfura* of Rwanda and others as examples.

4.1.4. The justice of proximity

Its strength also resides in its capacity to render the justice of proximity in all its main missions, namely mediation, conciliation and arbitration. Citizens have always needed a permanent service of mediation, conciliation and arbitration. For a dispute to be settled and to end in a sustainable solution it does not necessarily have to be taken before the police, or to the courts or tribunals. These forms of formal, essentially repressive justice, do not always favour conciliation of parties in conflict. This function is often particularly important in rural contexts, where the *bashingantahe* arbitrate in conflicts of all kinds guided by a spirit of conciliation and peace.

> During a post-conflict period, the judicial and administration system is sometimes incapable of rendering justice, providing restitution for stolen property, or effecting reparations for victims. It is thus important to find mechanisms that are complementary to the judicial approach to delivering justice, restoring the rights of victims and defusing social tensions.

During the current large-scale repatriation of refugees and internally displaced persons, the institution of *bashingantahe* is widely sought after for the settlement of family conflicts and property conflicts resulting from the seizure of property by individuals, and in some cases by the state itself. In a post-conflict period, questions of justice, reconciliation and forgiveness surface regularly, yet the judicial and administrative system is sometimes incapable of rendering justice, providing restitution for stolen property, or effecting reparations for victims. It is thus important to find mechanisms that are complementary to the judicial approach to rendering justice, restoring the rights of victims and defusing social tensions. This is why the institution of *bashingantahe*, with its missions of mediation, conciliation and arbitration, can play a part in the establishment of a state of law.

For these reasons, and above all in the light of the fact that it is difficult for orthodox justice to provide adequate responses to the many issues raised by gross violations of human rights, it is important that transitional justice intervenes in a complementary fashion. In this context the *bashingtanahe* should be associated with and even play a potentially central role in any national transitional justice mechanism established to facilitate a return to peace and harmony in Burundian social life.

With regard to their judicial function, it is not easy to quantify how far the effectiveness of the *bashingantahe* has improved. However, information obtained from resident tribunals indicates that in 70 per cent of cases where the opinions of the *bashingantahe* has been sought, these have been upheld by official tribunals (Dexter and Ntahombaye 2005).

Those interviewed in the study conducted by the Réseau de Citoyens Network Justice et Démocratie (Réseau de Citoyens Network 2002) were of the view that the *bashingantahe* system has to be encouraged insofar as the *bashingantahe* are close to those who are to be tried. Moreover, they know the root causes of the conflicts which they are called on to resolve, both in general and in the minutest detail, and the truth is thus easily discovered. In the absence of this 'voluntary justice', formal tribunals would be choked with litigation and thereby prevented from performing their normal functions. In many instances cases are fully settled by the *bashingantahe* without the need to transfer them to the formal tribunals.

> The institution of bashingantahe is a factor for social cohesion, a national institution, democratic in nature and founded on universal values. It delivers a justice of proximity: litigation does not necessarily have to be taken before the police, or to the courts or tribunals.

The *bashingantahe* are also of great help to the tribunals with regard to the delicate task of executing judicial decisions, particularly in relation to land property litigation. In cases relating to the demarcation of property, legal tribunals often resort to the *bashingantahe*, who are both reliable witnesses and legitimate authorities in cases of relapse. Above all, they are there to ensure that the decisions made are respected and to guarantee their validity over successive generations.

4.2. Weaknesses

4.2.1. Weaknesses in judgements

In a few instances judgements made by the *bashingantahe* may not be in conformity with the law, or could be handed down without due consideration of the law by reason of ignorance of the law. Thus the legitimate rights of a person in terms of the written law may on occasion be infringed, and some judges confirm that it is sometimes difficult to rely on the arrangements proposed by the *bashingantahe*. The latter do not formally belong to the 'judicial world' and are guided mainly by common sense and fairness in relation to custom, without reference to written law. Certain magistrates prefer to treat them, if not as eyewitnesses, at least as witnesses capable of providing credible testimony.

These shortcomings do not, however, appear to outweigh the advantages of the institution. For example, the fact that the decisions of the *bashingantahe* are taken without direct reference to the law is not necessarily a disadvantage. In some instances it can be an asset in the sense that social peace is sometimes more easily attained through an equitable solution reached without strict regard for the formal legal norms in force.

In the light of this weakness, it would be helpful if a more detailed study could be undertaken of the various areas of civil and criminal law in which the *bashingantahe* are called upon to intervene, these proceedings being understood as preliminary to hearings in the courts under state jurisdiction. This analysis should relate both to the legal texts currently in force and to litigation that has been brought before the resident tribunals, the relevant jurisdiction of first instance. The outcome would support reflection on the direction of judicial reform with the end of giving voluntary justice the tools it needs to improve its functioning, and to remove ambiguities about its indispensable complementary relationship with formal justice.

4.2.2. The ambiguous position of women

Among the criticisms levelled at the institution is its exclusion of women, which tradition has established in contradiction to the modern-day principles of the equality of men and women and of equity. In effect, tradition does not accept the investiture of women in their own right and it has not set out the procedures for women to be invested as *bashingantahe* or to be prepared for this function.

However, the status of women must be understood in relation to culture and socially sanctioned values (the education of children, initiation into adult life, the patrilineal tradition, the respective rights and responsibilities of men and women, the division of labour, the system of taboos, proverbs and sayings, religious rites, funeral rites and so on) as well as the natural harmony envisaged by the country's institutions. The institution of *bashingantahe* is a link in the chain of traditional institutions. It would thus be mistaken to claim, for example, that the social practices which lend support to the exclusion of women were invented, protected and transmitted forward by the institution of *bashingantahe*. The element of male domination that is present in the institution stems from the cultural system described above, which the traditional woman accepts against her will. In our view, however, the current inferior status of Burundian woman compared to their male counterparts can be improved in the context of ongoing efforts to rehabilitate the institution of *bashingantahe*.

The Bashingantahe Charter adopted in 2002 stipulates that women are invested together with their husbands (article 3). They take the oath but do not receive the rod of wisdom (article 29). On the day of the investiture, women are recognized as persons of integrity on the same basis as their husbands. The *intahe* symbol is given to the head of the household, to be kept under the conjugal roof and to remind them of their common commitments—commitments which refer more to their responsibility to the community than to their individual social prestige. From this point onwards the couple are expected to serve as social role models, to receive complaints relating to neighbourhood conflicts and to intervene whenever the need arises in relation to the maintenance of social order. They are expected to act in solidarity with the circle of those invested, transparently and with unfailing collegiality. A woman thus has no place in the institution of *bashingantahe* except in her capacity as a wife. However, a widow can be nominated in her own personal capacity if she fulfils the requisite conditions.

With the process of rehabilitation of the institution, some women have been elected to the National Council of Bashingantahe. In 2005 the representation of women in the council stood at 35.48 per cent (National Council of Bashingantahe 2006b). Initially, these women are nervous when they sit with the *bashingantahe* on the hills and in the suburbs to participate in the deliberations. The opportunity for free expression exists, and the status of women can change as a result of their own dynamism and active participation. However, to increase their representation to 50 per cent in line with the complexity of the challenges of modern society and the proven efficiency of women in the field of conflict transformation, the conservative social climate will first have to be overcome.

> The weaknesses of the institution of bashingantahe are that their judgements may not always be in conformity with the law, or could be handed down without due consideration of the law by reason of ignorance, and that the position of women within it is ambivalent.

4.3. Opportunities

4.3.1. The process of self-rehabilitation of the institution

It is important that the institution is able to adapt itself to the modern context in order to participate fully in the process of reconciliation and of consolidation of peace, while taking into account the specificities of the political, social, economic and security context of the country.

Among the key controversies that require serious reflection are the ways in which the institution of *bashingantahe* can be rehabilitated in urban environments (HDPR-Shingarugume 2003), the selection of *bashingantahe*, the way in which they are invested, the precise definition of their areas of competence, their collaboration with other structures of conciliation (for example, company councils in the workplace) and, above all, how the institution can play its role in the current post-conflict period when the concern is to establish mechanisms of transitional justice that will promote peace and stability in Burundi.

Anxious to find responses to this imperative, the National Council of Bashingantahe embarked on a process of rehabilitation aimed at adapting the institution to the modern context. This rehabilitation starts with capacity building for its members so that they can respond adequately to the different needs of their environment, and to empower them to address current challenges in a context in which forgiveness, the healing of wounds, reparation and reconciliation are preconditions for the reconstruction of the country.

Burundian society has judged the activities of the institution in a positive light. According to an opinion poll, 73 per cent of those interviewed gave a positive evaluation of the work already done within the institution of *bashingantahe* (HDPR-Shingarugume 2003: 18). A study undertaken by CARE (CARE 2002) revealed that among the local structures responsible for resolving conflicts (heads of families, heads of the hill, zonal chiefs and administrators), the institution of *bashingantahe* is one of those most often applied to, despite a number of failures. Other research carried out, in particular by the International Crisis Group and the Africa Centre for Technology Studies, suggests that, apart from needing certain corrections in its general operational approach, particularly with regard to local participation in the rehabilitation process, the *bashingantahe* institution is viewed as capable of defusing the 'property bomb' that could explode in the wake of the large-scale repatriation of refugees (International Crisis Group 2003: 11–12).

4.3.2. Strong membership of intellectuals

The institution of *bashingantahe* has long been viewed as something essentially relating to rural people and intended for a rural setting. A few rare cases existed of intellectuals being invested by their village *bashingantahe* within their own villages, but not until 2002 did urban intellectuals began to take an interest in the institution. In 2002, some 50 such persons were officially invested with much publicity and, since then, the practice of investiture has gained currency in urban no less than rural areas. On the one hand, the investiture ceremonies have generated much interest among Burundians, particularly among the young people, many of whom had never previously heard of the institution. On the other hand, this development has also generated sharp criticism, especially from political actors. The criticisms levelled at the institution led to efforts to clean up the investiture procedure. Today a variety of *bashingantahe* councils include intellectuals who have been invested in conformity with the requirements of tradition and are resolutely committed to the institution. The membership of intellectuals can only boost its popularity and legitimacy, thereby enabling it to participate fully in the return to peace and stability in Burundi.

> The institution of bashingantahe is currently rehabilitating itself, aiming to adapt to the modern context. Burundian society has judged the activities of the institution in a positive light. The growing membership and commitment of intellectuals from urban areas can only boost its popularity and legitimacy.

4.4. Threats

Although the *bashingantahe* currently function within the sphere of civil society, they are confronted by many challenges—the conservatism of some members of the institution, the problem of leadership in an unfavourable political context, questioning of the institution's legitimacy, and socio-economic problems, to mention but a few.

4.4.1. Pointless conservatism

The institution of *bashingantahe* is strongly established in rural settings where the influence of tradition is in constant conflict with modernity. Examples include the gender dimension, the management of conflicts, the inclusion of Batwa as members, and the opening up of the institution to other African and international experiences. There are many important aspects to be considered but they face some resistance from conservatives who are determined to safeguard customs and find it difficult to tolerate any form of innovation. Today, however, the investiture of women and the inclusion of Batwa are occurring in drip-feed fashion in some regions of the country. This often triggers unexpected reactions from certain *bashingantahe*, who reject the changes and are ready to oppose all initiatives or decisions taken in this regard. The place of the institution in the modern world will depend on the pace at which the *bashingantahe* themselves embrace the principles of good governance in the rehabilitation process.

4.4.2. The relationship between the bashingantahe *and locally elected officials*

There is a problem of demarcation between the authority and mandate of the people who are elected locally and those of the *bashingantahe*. On the one hand, the institution of *bashingantahe* derives its legitimacy from both tradition and contemporary law, which has assigned it a place within the judicial apparatus (Law no. 1/004 of 14 January 1987, relating to the organization of judicial competences); on the other hand, locally elected officials draw their legitimacy from the ballot box. Consequently, both categories—the locally elected officials and the *bashingantahe*—exercise legitimate leadership and enjoy a mandate.

Even though the new law on local government, article 37, #2, stipulates collaboration between the hill council and the *bashingantahe* (without spelling out the modalities), people continue to consider the voluntary justice exercised by the latter as the resort of first instance, before going to the official courts. Moreover, the constitution of March 2005 requires all Burundian citizens to respect and promote the cultural values (article 68), and gives the National Commission on Unity and Reconciliation responsibility for proposing ways and means of rehabilitating the structure and making it an instrument of national cohesion (article 269).

The institution of *bashingantahe* has been affected by sudden and violent political and structural changes which have influenced its operation and on occasion contributed to weakening it. The advent of multipartyism in particular can be seen as a tempest that struck it and placed it in a politically controversial position. In some places those elected in the 1993 election quickly took to denigrating the *bashingantahe* of the hills, which they called 'Upronistes' (a reference to the Uprona party which ruled the country for decades), defeated and outmoded men, unfit and old-fashioned. The *bashingantahe* were completely lost in this situation: they were very disorganized and weakened by sheer lack of a platform for communication and expression. The crisis of 1993 came suddenly, and at a time when the *bashingantahe*, weakened by the vicissitudes of the colonial era and beyond, did not have the means or strength to face the resulting changes.

With the electoral propaganda of 2005, a similar phenomenon could be seen all over the country. An open leadership conflict broke out between the *bashingantahe* and locally elected officials. The latter refused to cooperate with the *bashingantahe* in some regions and denied them any legitimacy. More specifically, elected officials aimed to replace the invested *bashingantahe* in all areas of their traditional responsibility on the basis of the fact that they alone enjoyed the legitimate mandate of the people. The *bashingantahe*, however, considered their position as legitimate in their mission of conciliation and arbitration and as custodians of customary practices.

Following diverse initiatives taken by the Ministry of the Interior and Public Security, the reciprocal polemics are now beginning to die down. An example worth mentioning is the collaborative platform for the two groups established following a dialogue workshop organized by the ministry with the support of the United States Agency for International Development (USAID) and IFES (formerly the International Foundation for Election Systems) in March 2006.

The government is conscious of the need to properly define the place of the institution of *bashingantahe* within the overall organization of the country. In a letter referenced 100/CAB/115/2006, the head of state requested the Ministry of the Interior and Public Security to follow relations between local government officials and the *bashingantahe* closely. As a result of the laudable political will displayed and practical initiatives that have been implemented since March 2006, cooperation is gradually being restored between the councillors of the hills and the *bashingantahe* in the majority of local authority areas. Nonetheless, the need remains for the government to clarify the modalities of collaboration between the administration and the institution of *bashingantahe* by means of an organic law.

This conflict, the motivation for which can be partly if not exclusively explained in terms of the real or supposed material interests or political motivation of the parties, should not have arisen in the first place. In reality, ever since the era of the monarchy the *bashingantahe* have always existed side by side with the administration, serving as intermediaries between the leaders and the citizens while also attempting to safeguard the interests of the latter.

4.4.3. The impact of poverty

Poverty is a source of weakness and sometimes leads to behaviour that is contrary to the values of the *bashingantahe*, such as begging and weakness when confronted with attempts at corruption. The *bashingantahe*, like at least 81 per cent of the population of Burundi, live below the poverty line.

Traditionally, a certain level of well-being that was synonymous with the independence and stability given by honestly acquired material wealth, and in particular an occupation, were required for an individual to be accepted as a candidate for investiture. This did not mean that financial considerations were a criterion for investiture as an *umushingantahe*, but men had to be found who would be able to act in complete independence and without seeking any form of remuneration—in other words, men of integrity who were capable of providing for their own needs. Voluntary service was a fundamental value expressed in the oath pronounced by all candidates on the day of their investiture.

Nonetheless, some members of the institution (incorrectly) saw access to the function as the springboard to a better life and, contrary to the ethics of the institution, looked forward to the imagined material benefits of investiture.

The voluntary nature of the service, which is its most valued aspect, has diminished with monetization and the increasing spread of poverty at all levels of the society. Will respect for this spirit of voluntary service endure among the *bashingantahe* in an increasingly monetized world? This question must be addressed in order to avoid possible shortcomings in the institution or side-slipping. Realism forces us to reflect on alternative solutions that will preserve the spirit of voluntarism which has always characterized the institution while also adapting its functioning to the challenges and exigencies of modernity.

4.4.4. The permanent spectre of politicization

In urban centres, at the City Hall of Bujumbura and to a lesser extent in rural areas, some citizens accuse the present *bashingantahe* of having been invested without adequate preparation. There was even talk of alleged 'investiture inflation' in 2002, a year in which the institution saw unprecedented rehabilitation in Bujumbura, with heightened media coverage and public visibility. Some condemned what they called 'prestige *bashingantahe*', invested not for their exceptional qualities or not even possessing the qualities required for acceding to this distinguished function. Rightly or wrongly, some of the dignitaries invested have been called opportunists for seeking political position via the institution of *bashingantahe*. These criticisms point to a serious weakness not with regard to the institution as such but rather in relation to the criteria for investiture. *Bashingantahe* are called to serve their fellow citizens in a body of men that cannot be tainted by irregularities.

The members of the National Council of Bashingantahe should not ignore these criticisms but instead analyse them with a view to improving the position of the institution in contemporary society. Measures have thus already been taken, in particular extending the period of observation of candidates for investiture. This is fixed at at

> The bashingantahe face many challenges—the conservatism of some members, the relationship with locally elected officials, the impact of poverty, the impact of the monetization of society on the value of voluntarism, and the permanent threat of politicization.

least a year in order to give time for members of the community to express their views concerning the qualities of the aspirant, and to avoid developments that could sully the image of this noble and prestigious institution.

5. Conclusions and recommendations

The respected institution of *bashingantahe* is the crucible of national values. For a long time it has offered Burundian society a basis on which its communities could be held together and prevented from collapsing. The *bashingantahe* have served as lubricants to the wheels of traditional Burundian society. At the time of the monarchy the functions delegated to them went beyond the purely judicial: they served as custodians of tradition, and their mores were a force for social cohesion and the maintenance of order, and exercised a regulatory role within the politico-administrative system.

The evolution of the institution from the colonial era up to the Third Republic is marked by periods of darkness. With the intrusion of civil servants, the manipulation of the institution, its politicization and the forbidding of investiture, it has been denatured and has lost some of its substance. Happily, however, it has survived all forms of adversity and remained alive and vibrant up to this day. The time has come for it to be rehabilitated and modernized in order to adapt it to current challenges and needs so that it can contribute to the restoration of social harmony and the reconstruction of the country. This is a condition of its survival. It does not necessarily mean a revival of ancestral customs simply for the sake of remaining faithful to tradition. It is rather a question of drawing out the essential from tradition and integrating it with the positive dimensions of modernity in order to derive an organic synthesis from the process. It is a question of building something new upon the old, of adapting the institution to contemporary challenges.

Here, great efforts have already been made by the *bashingantahe* themselves, with the support of a range of actors drawn from civil society and the international community. In particular, the institution has been restructured from top to bottom, with *bashingantahe* councils established at all levels. Initiatives to enhance their capacity have been undertaken, in a number of instances with the assistance of donors operating in Burundi that are convinced of the important role this body can play in the current post-conflict period.

> The institution of bashingantahe has survived all forms of adversity, and has remained alive and vibrant. It is now being rehabilitated to adapt it to current challenges and exigencies.

The importance of this traditional mechanism, which has already proved its worth in the settlement of social conflict in both traditional and contemporary Burundian society, does not require further demonstration. In this regard, for example, the formal judicial system recognizes that the *bashingantahe* possess certain competences in local-level arbitration and conciliation.

Peace remains fragile in states that are recovering from conflict. As with all countries that have recently emerged from conflict, Burundi needs to establish benchmarks that will enable it to climb the path towards the full recovery of stability, and here the restoration of the rule of law is a prerequisite.

During the current post-conflict period the country is confronting many challenges. In this context it is particularly important that Burundians endeavour both to heal a past that is characterized by gross violations of human rights and to prevent this from negatively influencing the future, thereby perpetuating the cycle of violence. How can this past be addressed without causing undue hurt, at a minimum without destabilizing a society that is composed of both victims and perpetrators of gross human rights violations? The victims are calling resolutely, albeit without much hope of success, for justice, while the perpetrators wish to escape justice at all costs. How can these two points of view be reconciled?

Currently the preferred means of seeking a lasting solution to conflict is regional and international mediation, and Burundi has had recourse to such an approach. It is our conviction, however, that the wrongs committed in a particular country are best dealt with by those who are familiar with their root causes and the parties involved—those, in other words, who have suffered directly and have issued pleas for help to political leaders who are not always able to provide answers to the challenges at hand. Political transitions can sometimes appear like a no man's land where all kinds of evil practices go on behind the scenes, with crimes and a prevailing culture of impunity only serving to increase the number of victims. This in turn is why macro-political efforts should always be accompanied by initiatives that operate close to the people, on a human scale that enables the resolution of conflicts at the grass-roots level.

In Burundi transitional justice can serve as a complementary element to existing judicial structures that have either broken down or been rendered ineffective by the conflict and the painful experiences of many. As a traditional institution for managing conflict the institution of *bashingantahe* can act as a safeguard guaranteeing community harmony and reconciliation.

Increasingly, the *bashingantahe* see themselves as guardians of social cohesion. Moreover, as was noted in a public declaration of the president of the National Council of Bashingantahe, the institution hopes that Burundians will remain aware of the role that the *bashingantahe*, persons recognized for their integrity, can play in the establishment of transitional justice institutions, particularly the proposed CNVR and special tribunal. 'Everything possible must be done to ensure that truth, justice, reparation and reconciliation triumph' (Conseil National des Bashingantahe 2006a). Before the CNVR is set up, however, the National Council of Bashingantahe recommends an extensive awareness campaign aimed at preparing the minds of the people, and it expresses its readiness to provide a modern adaptation of traditional mechanisms for the resolution of non-judicial conflicts.

With regard to the proposed special tribunal for Burundi, the National Council of Bashingantahe proposes that the tribunal should draw inspiration from traditional justice mechanisms. 'In fact, the *bashingantahe* will very much be able to contribute to the special tribunal, as persons nominated and oath bound, thanks to their competence gained from tradition in the areas of restorative and reparative justice, which they are in the process of adapting to modernity in order to make contributions that go beyond punitive justice and aim to put a end to cycles of vengeance' (Conseil National des Bashingantahe 2006a).

However, the council laments the fact that Burundian society does not give sufficient credit to this illustrious institution, which has not as yet had the opportunity to give of its best and thereby contribute to the transformation of conflicts in the country. Accordingly, the council calls on the public authorities to 'take the institution seriously and allow it to contribute its maximum to the healing of the Burundian people' (Conseil National des Bashingantahe 2006a).

Major challenges remain, mainly involving a tendency to trivialize the institution and the development of sound collaboration between the authorities and the *bashingantahe*. Additional problems such as the integration of young people into the institution, and the investiture of women in their individual capacities, independently of their husbands, as well as the role they can play in the present context of a country recovering from crisis, also need to be resolved. These are significant challenges, but they should be tackled sensitively, without unduly disrupting an already fragile Burundian society.

Culture does not change overnight. Mindful of this, once it is back on its feet the institution of *bashingantahe* can play its full social and political regulatory role in the maintenance of peace and social cohesion and as a moral and cultural reference point. Additionally, it can play a significant role in the process of reconciliation in a society which has torn itself apart in the course of recent years, but is today committed to the path of reconciliation and reconstruction. To help achieve this goal, the following recommendations are put forward to relevant stakeholders.

5.1. General

1. Encourage the National Council of Bashingantahe to reconstitute itself so that the provincial, communal and hill representations are made up only of persons of proven exemplary behaviour who reflect models of positive values and do not hold a brief for any particular political party.

2. Within the framework of civil society, conduct inclusive dialogues regarding critical issues requiring the intervention of the political and administrative authorities.

3. Implement fully the positive initiatives already undertaken within the framework of rehabilitation of the institution of *bashingantahe*.

5.2. To the government of Burundi

4. Establish the CNVR as an independent commission, the composition of which should at all costs be non-partisan, and which will take care that article 269 of the constitution, relating to the rehabilitation of the *bashingantahe*, is applied.

5. Collaborate with the National Council of Bashingantahe on all questions relating to the rehabilitation of the *bashingantahe* institution as well as on the issues of pardons and national reconciliation that are pivotal to future national development.

6. Associate the *bashingantahe* with the work of the CNVR.

7. Recognize and protect the role of the *bashingantahe* in the management of property disputes.

8. Restore the central and important role of the *bashingantahe* in the management of litigation by voluntary justice mechanisms.

9. Educate the people of Burundi to respect cultural values (article 68 of the constitution).

10. Carefully develop an organic law regarding the application of the law on local government, article 37, #2, to define clearly the mode of collaboration between the *bashingantahe* and locally elected officials.

5.3. To the National Council of Bashingantahe

11. Preserve at all times the autonomy and non-political character of the institution of *bashingantahe*.

12. Improve the representation of women within the structures of the institution towards a target of 50 per cent.

13. Document and disseminate the experiences of conciliation, mediation and arbitration achieved at the community level.

14. Publish the declarations of the National Council of Bashingantahe in its ordinary and extraordinary meetings, and transmit the advice of the Council Secretariat to the relevant authorities.

15. Punish all *bashingantahe* who are guilty of corruption stemming from abuse of the practice of *agatutu k-abagabo* in a transparent way in order to maintain a positive image of the institution.

16. Increase the number of inter-provincial meetings of *bashingantahe* so that they can share experiences and correct possible operational errors.

17. Adopt all measures capable of putting collaboration between the *bashingantahe* and locally elected officials at the level of the hill on a sound footing without compromising the basic role and rationale of the institution.

18. Draw up a strategy which will enable the *bashingantahe* to exercise visible influence in the political arena in relation to ongoing efforts to inject a moral dimension into public and political life.

19. Develop promotional activities, for example, involving musical and theatrical performances, for the values advocated by the institution, particularly that of reconciliation.

20. Create a framework for interaction with civil society, including women's organizations, the academic community, human rights organizations, religious groups and youth organizations.

21. Popularize the official legal texts—the constitution, the code of persons and the family, the property code, the code of criminal procedure, the 1979 Convention on the Elimination of All Forms of Discrimination Against Women and so on.

22. Invested and fully trained *bashingantahe* should assist in educating and training their counterparts in rural areas to help them integrate democratic principles and values without compromising the ethics and philosophy of the institution.

23. Emphasize the need for the institution of *bashingantahe* to have the financial resources required to enable it to function efficiently.

24. Take note of the criticisms and recommendations already outlined by a number of civil society stakeholders and donors with a view to promoting a genuine process of reconciliation.

5.4. To the international community

25. Build the capacity of the institution through education, institutional support and the provision of knowledge tools.

26. Help it to open up to other African and international experiences of conflict management, local voluntary assistance and local governance.

27. Coordinate interventions intended to support the *bashingantahe* with a view to avoiding overlap.

28. Integrate the values promoted by the *bashingantahe* both within and across development assistance programmes.

29. In collaboration with the government and the National Council of Bashingantahe, participate in the process of rehabilitation of the institution.

30. Strengthen the non-remuneratory justice mechanisms provided by the *bashingantahe* in the areas of conflict management and reconciliation.

References and further reading

CARE, 'Projet Protection de l'Environnement dans les Provinces Karusi et Gitega' [Project on the protection of the environment in the Karusi and Gitega provinces], Bujumbura, CARE, 2002

Conseil National des Bashingantahe (National Council of Bashingantahe) (CNB), 'Déclaration du 29 Avril 2006: Mise sur pied de la Commission Vérité et Réconciliation et du Tribunal Spécial au Burundi' [Declaration of 29 April 2006: the national truth and reconciliation commission and the special tribunal in Burundi], Bujumbura, CNB, 2006 (2006a)

Conseil National des Bashingantahe (National Council of Bashingantahe) (CNB), 'L'Institution des Bashingantahe hier et aujourd'hui: Arbitrage, médiation, conciliation' [The institution of bashingantahe yesterday and today: arbitration, mediation, conciiation], Bujumbura, CNB, February 2006 (2006b)

Deslaurier, C., 'Le Bushingantahe au Burundi' [The *bashingantahe* in Burundi], in F. X. Fauvelle and C. H. Perrot, *Le Retour des Rois* [The return of the kings] (Paris: Khartala, 2003)

Dexter, T. and Ntahombaye, P., 'Le rôle du système informel de la justice dans la restauration d'un Etat de Droit en situation post-conflit: Le cas du Burundi' [The role of the informal justice system in the restoration of a state of law after conflict: the case of Burundi], Bujumbura, Centre pour le Dialogue Humanitaire, 2005

HDPR-Shingarugume, 'Sondage d'opinion sur les attentes de la population vis-à-vis du projet "Réhabilitation de l'institution des bashingantahe"' [Public opinion poll on public expectations of the 'Rehabilitation of the Institution of Bashingantahe' project], Bujumbura, August 2003

International Crisis Group (ICG), *Réfugiés et déplacés au Burundi: désamorcer la bombe foncière* [Refugees and displaced persons in Burundi: defusing the property bomb], Rapport Afrique no. 70 (Nairobi and Brussels: ICG, 2003)

Ngorwanubusa, J., 'L'Institution des Bashingantahe et le bel idéal universel de l'honnête homme' [The institution of *bashingantahe* and the universal ideal of the honourable man], in *La réactualisation de l'Institution des Bashingantahe*, Etude pluridisciplinaire, Bujumbura, Université du Burundi, 1991, pp. 285 ff

Ntabona, A., *Itinéraire de la sagesse: Les Bashingantahe hier, aujourd'hui et demain au Burundi* [The way of wisdom: the Bashingantahe in Burundi yesterday, today and tomorrow] (Bujumbura: Ed. Centre de Recherches pour l'Inculturation et le Développement, 1999), 303 pp.

— 'Les enjeux majeurs de la réhabilitation de l'institution des Bashingantahe' [The main stakes in the rehabilitation of the institution of *bashingantahe*], in *Au Cœur de l'Afrique*, vol. 1, no. 2 (2002), pp. 3–21

Ntahokaja, J. B., 'Imigani-ibitito' [Stories and tales], Bujumbura, Université du Burundi, 1977

Ntahombaye, P., Kagabo, L. et al., *Mushingantahe wamaze iki?* [The role of the *bashingantahe* during the crisis], University of Burundi, 2003, 211 pp. (with summary in Kirundi, French and English)

Ntahombaye, P. and Manirakiza, Z., 'La contribution des institutions et des techniques traditionnelles de résolution pacifique des conflits à la résolution pacifique de la crise burundaise' [The contribution of traditional institutions and mechanisms of conflict resolution to the peaceful resolution of the Burundi crisis], Unesco, Bujumbura, 1997 (1997a)

Ntahombaye, P. and Manirakiza, Z., 'Le rôle des techniques et mécanismes traditionnels dans la résolution pacifique des conflits au Burundi' [The contribution of traditional techniques and mechanisms in the peaceful resolution of the conflicts in Burundi], Unesco, Bujumbura, December 1997 (1997b)

'Rapport de la Mission Indépendante d'Evaluation du Projet "Appui à la Réhabilitation de l'Institution des bashingantahe"', BDI/02/B01, 5–25 juillet 2003

République du Burundi, Loi no. 1/016 du 20 avril 2005 portant organisation de l'administration

Réseau de Citoyens Network Justice et Démocratie (RCN), 'Etude sur l'harmonisation du rôle des Bashingantahe avec celui des instances judiciaires de base (tribunaux de résidence) dans les provinces frontalières avec la Tanzanie' [Study on harmonizing the role of the *bashingantahe* with that of the resident tribunals in the provinces bordering Tanzania], Bujumbura, RCN, December 2002

CHAPTER 7

Conclusions and recommendations

Luc Huyse

Section 1 of this chapter pulls together the information as to where on the scale of judgement traditional justice practices have to be placed. The second section then moves towards a cautious analysis of their strengths and weaknesses, and the chapter ends with a list of recommendations for national and international stakeholders.

1. The two faces of tradition-based practices

An assessment has to start with the question of what the goals and objectives of a particular institution are. Chapter 1 identifies two sets of goals in the case of traditional justice practices. The healing of the survivors, social harmony and the prevention of new violence are general ambitions. Accountability, reconciliation, truth telling and reparation are the instrumental objectives that pave the way towards broader targets, thereby establishing a framework for the building of sustainable and effective democratic processes and institutions. Do indigenous mechanisms achieve these goals in times of transition from civil war or genocide? The question then is how to identify the strengths and weaknesses that ultimately determine the outcome.

A Penal Reform International report on informal justice systems in Sub-Saharan Africa lists several strong points of such arrangements:

> They are accessible to local and rural people in that their proceedings are carried out in the local language, within walking distance, with simple procedures which do not require the services of a lawyer, and without the delays associated with the formal system.
>
> In most cases, the type of justice they offer—based on reconciliation, reparation, restoration and rehabilitation—is more appropriate to people living in close-knit communities who must rely on continuous social and economic cooperation with their neighbours...

They help in educating all members of the community as to the rules to be followed, the circumstances which may lead to them being broken, and how ensuing conflict may be peacefully resolved.

The fact that they employ non-custodial sentences effectively reduces prison overcrowding, may allow prison budget allocations to be diverted towards social development purposes, permits the offender to continue to contribute to the economy and to pay reparation to the victim, and prevents the economic and social dislocation of the family (Penal Reform International 2002, by kind permission).

This catalogue of strengths offers references to factors that sustain the domestic credibility of traditional practices, for example, easy access and an appropriate type of dispute resolution in close-knit communities. It also points to aspects that increase their effectiveness—the simplicity of the procedures, the reduction of delays, and low cost. The problem with this list is that it presents the model, not the reality. It is, moreover, not focused on a post-conflict context. This section, therefore, starts with a description of obstacles, handicaps and shortcomings in the war-torn countries that are part of our project.

> The healing of the survivors, social harmony and the prevention of new violence are general ambitions. Accountability, reconciliation, truth telling and reparation are the instrumental objectives that pave the way towards these broader targets, thereby establishing a framework for the building of sustainable and effective democratic processes and institutions. Do indigenous mechanisms achieve these goals in times of transition from civil war or genocide?

By looking first at the weaknesses, not the strengths, we may avoid unfounded expectations.

1.1. Obstacles and shortcomings

Reparation, our case study authors write, is an important dimension of most indigenous justice and reconciliation systems. The perpetrator or his clan has to pay damages to the victim or his community. But the nature of the conflict in these countries has been such that victims often do not know who is responsible for what happened to them. In such a situation rituals will be difficult to perform. In addition, even if victim and perpetrator are both identifiable, payment of the reparation will often be impossible given the total impoverishment the war has brought to them.

The example shows that problems exist in two critical areas: traditional mechanisms have a limited range of action and effect; and process conditions are tricky.

1.1.1. Limited range

In their chapter on Mozambique (chapter 3), Victor Igreja and Beatrice Dias-Lambranca observe that the *gamba* spirit ceremony is a regional phenomenon, that Christian members of the community despise it and that it carries a bias against women. The authors thus identify three factors that determine the social space in which this ritual is applicable—ethnicity, religion and gender.

Ethnicity

The Ubushingantahe in Burundi and the Gacaca in Rwanda cover all national ethnic groups. Tradition-based mechanisms in Mozambique, Sierra Leone and northern Uganda, on the other hand, are culture-specific and are, consequently, almost inflexible. James Latigo writes in chapter 4 on the Acholi practices in northern Uganda that 'It is often difficult for people who do not belong or subscribe to the particular culture to respond positively to the traditional justice processes. There is very little leeway and no possibility of changing or bending the rules hitherto prescribed to suit particular circumstances'. The *mato oput* rite, for example, is in all probability not available as a justice and reconciliation technique to be applied in the case of crimes committed between the Acholi leaders of the Lord's Resistance Army (LRA) and the survivors of their raids in the neighbouring Teso and Lango districts. There are even cultural differences between the different Acholi communities. The range of indigenous mechanisms is thus significantly restricted in ethnically diverse countries where each group has developed its own complex systems of dispute resolution. In the case of Sierra Leone, Joe Alie in chapter 5 notes that over the years ethnic mixing has taken place in the Mende region so that the existing traditional practices may not be suitable for handling disputes between Mende and non-Mende people.

Religion

In his anthropological description of the case of Amelia in central Mozambique (see chapter 3), Victor Igreja demonstrates that applying the *gamba* spirit approach is impossible because her father, who is a Christian, refuses to participate. Igreja writes: 'the problem of the Christian religious groups is that they neither encourage discourse and practices that revisit the violent past nor demand any form of responsibility of people involved in war-related conflict… Christian religious groups in Gorongosa rely entirely on unilateral forgiveness since God is considered to be the most important figure in the resolution of conflicts'. In northern Uganda, too, some Christian believers reject traditional practices outright, although new techniques have emerged that tend to hybridize with Christian religious beliefs and rituals.

Gender

Tradition-based systems of dispute resolution are usually male-dominated. The most critical assessment comes from Victor Igreja. The gender bias in the content of *gamba* is very apparent: 'the women killed during the Mozambican civil war are unable to return as spirits to the realm of the living to claim justice. Only the spirits of men can do this. In this sense, although *magamba* spirits break with the silence of the past, structurally the justice they offer helps to reinforce patriarchal power in a country that is struggling for gender equality'. In Burundi women are not allowed to become members of the Ubushingantahe *à titre individuel*. They can only participate in the deliberations as the wife or the widow of a member. The justice system in Sierra Leone is also heavily tilted against women, especially in husband–wife relationships.

Recently changes have been introduced. In Sierra Leone some provision is made for female representation in dispute settlement cases. Joe Alie notes that certain truth-seeking mechanisms are actually headed by women. According to Assumpta Naniwe-Kaburahe in her case study on Burundi (chapter 6), efforts to increase the participation of women are being held up by the conservative reflexes of men. Bert Ingelaere (see chapter 2) concludes that women have taken up an important role in the Gacaca proceedings in Rwanda. This court system, however, remains 'biased against women because of its inadequacy to fully address sexual crimes. Provisions have been made to allow women to testify on sexual crimes, for example, through in camera sessions. But the embedding of the Gacaca in a local face-to-face community makes it difficult to tackle these crimes'.

Other shortcomings

Traditional justice mechanisms tend to exclude young people. They are viewed as immature or as not sufficiently socialized into the local mores. Joe Alie's view is that the over-reliance on elders is causing this type of exclusion.

Another source of exclusion is of a political nature—the tendency to protect certain crimes or certain perpetrators from the accountability and reparation dimensions of indigenous practices. The Rwandan Gacaca tribunals lack the authority to deal with the violence the Batutsi-dominated Rwanda Patriotic Front committed against the Bahutu. In northern Uganda, middle- and high-level commanders of the LRA have been beyond the scope of *mato oput* ceremonies. So are most members of the Ugandan Army.

> Traditional mechanisms have a limited range of action and effect in terms of ethnicity, religious group, and societal groups. Certain crimes or certain perpetrators may be protected from the accountability and reparation dimensions of indigenous practices. Some of these conflicts have crossed national borders or have been fuelled by neighbouring countries.

Finally, some of these conflicts have crossed national borders or have been fuelled by neighbouring countries. This also limits the radius of action of the instruments we discuss here. As James Latigo writes about the *mato oput* ceremony, a fundamental weakness of its application as a remedy is that 'conceptually, it wrongly projects the LRA insurgency as a local Acholi affair. In reality this war had inherent national and international dimensions'. The dynamics of the conflict and its legacy, just as in Sierra Leone, go far beyond the territorial and personal reach of domestic tradition-based mechanisms.

1.1.2. Difficult process conditions

Two questions lead this part of our evaluation. First, are these indigenous tools able to deal with war crimes, genocide and crimes against humanity? Second, do they have the capacity to restore years and sometimes decades of material and social destruction of their biotope?

The scale of the wrongdoing

Traditional justice systems are designed to deal with relatively small numbers of cases of wrongdoing. Erin Baines, a researcher working on informal justice mechanisms in northern Ugandan communities, cites 'a 2005 study on traditional justice and reintegration in which dozens of elders across Acholiland almost universally expressed the opinion that there was little sense in pursuing *mato oput* on a case-by-case basis as too many people had been killed and it was therefore difficult to trace who had killed whom and which clans to engage' (Baines 2007: 105). The authors of the present book are not opposed to the introduction of a tradition-based approach to justice and reconciliation after transition—quite the contrary. But they also share the doubts of the interviewees in Acholiland. The Acholi traditional justice system, writes James Latigo, was in its original form 'not conceptualized as a method for adjudicating over war crimes and crimes against humanity, because in pre-colonial Acholiland these never occurred. Hence it is not well suited to being applied as the sole reconciliation measure to the LRA architects of terror'. And Joe Alie concludes that these mechanisms can only complement the efforts of national and international criminal justice systems.

> Traditional justice systems are not designed to deal with great numbers of cases of wrongdoing, or with war crimes and crimes against humanity.

A wounded biotope

The case studies describe the devastating effects of genocide, civil war and oppression on the form and substance, status and potential of tradition-based instruments in their respective societies. The scale and degree of violence and repression vary, but all countries share the experience of having their traditions deeply injured. Material conditions and political constraints are highly unfavourable. In addition, the social fabric has broken down, greatly damaging the natural biotope of traditional practices.

Material obstacles

Large numbers of the victimized population and of returned perpetrators have lived or still live in refugee camps—environments that are too artificial for the effective use of cleansing, reintegration and reconciliation ceremonies. The dislocation of families is another handicap. In Sierra Leone, mass migration of young people to the cities makes the traditional practices less effective. In addition, urban settings are not the natural biotope of ritualistic-communal procedures, as the experience with Gacaca courts in Kigali demonstrates. Moreover, the resources that are needed to fulfil the reparation dimension of these rites are lacking because of extreme poverty.

Political constraints

Joe Alie notes that the top–down approaches to peace building adopted by the Sierra Leonean Government and international agencies alike have rendered tradition-based mechanisms dysfunctional. The chapter on Rwanda argues that, although local authorities are not overtly active in the Gacaca process, 'they form the framework within which the Gacaca functions. In Hutu perceptions this often means that the combination of the

Gacaca, with its reference to the pre-colonial past, and a power structure that is occupied by a politico-military movement dominated by members of the Tutsi minority is perceived as a return to the feudal period when Hutu servants were subordinate to Tutsi lords in all domains of life'.

Erosion of social capital

Civil war and genocide have brought in their wake mutual mistrust in small-scale communities, and this may limit the willingness to be reconciled. Taboos have been disregarded and sacred places defiled. The legitimacy of traditional leaders has been greatly harmed, particularly in their relations with the younger generations. The spontaneous socialization of young people has almost disappeared, especially in the case of abducted children. How can healers and elders successfully perform rituals if their authority is disputed?

> Genocide, civil war and oppression may have had a devastating effect on the substance, status and potential of tradition-based instruments. They bring in their wake mutual mistrust. The social fabric and the spontaneous socialization of young people have broken down, and the legitimacy of traditional healers and elders has been greatly harmed.

1.2. Strengths

This chapter started with a brief overview of the strong points of tradition-based practices. The section on obstacles and shortcomings, however, brought in doubts and queries about their actual or potential performance in countries that have been plagued by civil war and genocide. We now turn to a closer scrutiny of this rather bleak picture and list the positive effects these tools can have in the context of dealing with a legacy of grave human rights violations.

1.2.1. Accountability

Accountability is one of the instrumental objectives of most transitional justice policies. Systematic prosecutions are the most direct way to establish guilt and punishment. Chapter 1 argues that this strategy is highly questionable in contexts where regime change is an extremely delicate and/or complex operation. Full-scale trials may endanger a fragile peace or even make it impossible to put an end to a violent conflict—as is currently the case in northern Uganda. However, a blanket amnesty or an imposed silence is not an acceptable policy choice. It lacks legitimacy if it involves explicit impunity. Nor will a culture of denial (the Mozambican implicit preference) lead to the repairing of broken relationships or heal the victims. There is a growing belief that non-state mechanisms may act as an (often interim) alternative to trials. They are less threatening to the forces that dread prosecutions. They have, in addition, a dimension of acknowledgement of responsibility. Their proximity to the victims and survivors is a further asset, since it becomes possible for people to see that partial justice has been done—in distinct contrast to the procedures and outcomes of far-away criminal courts. Bert Ingelaere notes that in Rwanda formal tribunals are 'both physically and psychologically remote institutions' for the ordinary peasant.

> Systematic prosecutions are a highly questionable strategy in contexts where regime change is an extremely delicate and/ or complex operation. Non-state mechanisms have a dimension of acknowledgement of responsibility. There is a growing belief that they thus may act as an interim alternative to trials. Their proximity to the victims and survivors is a further asset.

1.2.2. Revealing the truth

Formal truth commissions may not be the most appropriate option in societies where the public revealing of the truth is not strongly rooted in the local culture. The case studies on Burundi, Rwanda and Sierra Leone indicate that this is a problem there. Precisely because they are rooted in established local values and traditions, ritualistic-communal practices may be better suited to creating a collective atmosphere that opens the heart and the mind and delivers parts of the truth.

1.2.3. Reconciliation

Victor Igreja's chapter on the *gamba* spirit ceremony in central Mozambique is a strong demonstration of the reconciliation such a practice can bring about. The *bashingantahe* in Burundi are considered to have the same potential, although they have not yet been operational in the context of dealing with a very painful legacy. Cleansing and reintegration rituals, particularly if they deal with ex-combatants and returning abducted children, have succeeded here and there in restoring family and clan relations. Serious doubts exist, however, with regard to the reconciliation capacity of the Gacaca proceedings in Rwanda. According to Bert Ingelaere's case study, the Gacaca courts are mimicking the ancient institution but with reduced potential to achieve real reconciliation.

The *gamba* spirit practice creates social spaces where the past can be worked through. This healing aspect is not specific to the particular ceremony Victor Igreja describes. Other tradition-based mechanisms too open up such curative spaces. In addition, access is not confined to victims. Many more survivors, perpetrators included, are involved in these ritualistic scenarios.

> Tradition-based mechanisms can produce reconciliation and restore family and clan relations. Their healing elements open curative spaces. Perpetrators as well as victims are involved in these ritualistic scenarios.

1.2.4. The restoration of broken communal relations

After a devastating conflict this is an extremely intricate undertaking. The authors of the country studies on Burundi and Mozambique argue convincingly that local mechanisms have the capacity to renew damaged social capital. Another added value lies in the creation of situations where a natural, spontaneous socialization of people as to norms about good and bad may arise. Finally, instruments like the Ubushingantahe are in principle able to deal with the often forgotten fallout of civil war, such as property conflicts when refugees return and an increase in marital violence.

> Tradition-based mechanisms are in principle able to deal with the often forgotten fallout of civil war, such as property conflicts when refugees return and an increase in marital violence.

It is much more problematic to judge whether these tools are well enough equipped to prevent the *recurrence of grave human rights violations*. In Gorongosa, central Mozambique, violence at the level of communities has remained absent. According to Victor Igreja this is the product of the rituals he discusses in his chapter. Elsewhere, however, all the cases are too recent for an assessment of their medium- and long-term achievements to be possible.

> With the possible exception of the case of Mozambique, all the cases of traditional justice mechanisms being used are too recent for an assessment of their medium- and long-term achievements to be possible.

2. A cautious analysis of strengths and weaknesses

The case studies presented in this book have brought realism to the ongoing discussion on the role of tradition-based practices in post-conflict societies. Our authors see strengths and weaknesses. Section 1 of this chapter has summarized their arguments. The following is an attempt to arrive at a set of what unavoidably must be called cautious conclusions.

Our analysis will use two yardsticks in weighing the actual and potential performance of the mechanisms in focus. The first is *effectiveness*—their impact in terms of the desired effects. The other is *legitimacy*—their degree of credibility, domestically and internationally.

2.1. Partial effectiveness

The effectiveness of a social institution depends to a great extent on how far it can influence individual behaviour and the future of a society. The question, therefore, is whether the reach of tradition-based instruments is wide enough to produce sufficient healing, social repair and durable peace after violent conflict. Several circumstances limit the scope of traditional tools of justice. They are culture-specific and, as a consequence, almost always limited to the ethnic, religious and regional communities in which they are applied. In the case of northern Uganda, for example, the Acholi have succeeded in using their own cultural heritage to cope with the legacy of widespread bloodshed. But war crimes have often been committed between Acholi and Langi, and between people of the north and of the south of the country. In those cases some of the victims or perpetrators are out of reach of the Acholi *mato oput* ceremony. A similar result is to be expected where a conflict has acquired an international dimension. In addition, forms of intended exclusion of stakeholders reduce the radius of action. Women and young people may be marginalized. Moreover, tradition-based practices are not immune from political manipulation, with the result that certain categories of offenders (e.g. middle- and top-level military or rebel commanders) are sometimes shielded from the accountability and reparation dimensions of non-state mechanisms.

> Traditional justice mechanisms are culture-specific and almost always limited to the ethnic, religious and regional communities in which they are applied. Moreover, they are not immune from political manipulation, with the result that certain categories of offenders are sometimes shielded from their accountability and reparation dimensions.

They will also be less effective if the process conditions are unfavourable. The case studies have demonstrated convincingly how war, genocide and oppression have a devastating effect on the capacities of traditional leaders to perform justice and reconciliation rituals. This development also casts doubts on their ability to adapt the original design of the mechanisms to the intricate task of dealing with mass human rights violations.

Judging the potential and/or actual performance of these instruments also requires that we pay sufficient attention to some broader aspects of their workings. What do they achieve at the micro level (individual victims and perpetrators), the meso level (clans, communities) and the macro level (national, regional and international)? In many cases we do not even have the most basic data that we would need to deal with this question. There is also the problem of their long-term impact. This is a very difficult issue, as most cases are too recent to be assessed on that particular point—the case of Mozambique perhaps being an exception.

For all that, the preceding chapters also include examples of the relative effectiveness of traditional mechanisms. Some of the rituals, such as the cleansing ceremonies in Sierra Leone and northern Uganda, seem to be successful in reintegrating and reconciling surviving victims and ex-combatants, particularly former child soldiers. In Mozambique, in spite of the government's explicit neglect of the need for a transitional justice policy, 'war survivors living in the former epicentres of the civil war in Gorongosa have neither resorted to violent revenge … nor gone along with the official authorities, who urged survivors to "forgive and forget". Instead, inspired by their own cultural wisdom, the

> Some of the rituals, such as the cleansing ceremonies in Sierra Leone and northern Uganda, seem to be successful in reintegrating and reconciling surviving victims and ex-combatants, particularly former child soldiers. Traditional mechanisms can act as interim instruments in cases where an official transitional justice policy is absent, delayed or crippled by political constraints.

survivors in Gorongosa managed to develop their own socio-cultural mechanisms to create healing and attain justice and reconciliation in the aftermath of the civil war' (chapter 3). The Gacaca proceedings in Rwanda are speeding up the backlog of genocide-related cases. More importantly, traditional mechanisms can act as interim instruments in cases where an official transitional justice policy is absent, delayed or crippled by political constraints.

According to the Burundi case study, members of the Ubushingantahe were active after the gruesome incidents between Bahutu and Batutsi in 1993. In Rwanda, Gacaca meetings were held immediately after the genocide ended, years before the government determined its policy. Finally, tools such as the *gamba* practice in Mozambique have shown that they are able to deal with the often forgotten effects of civil war, such as property conflicts when refugees return and the increase in marital violence.

2.2. Partial legitimacy

In Rwanda, presence at the meetings of the Gacaca at the local level is compulsory for all adult inhabitants. Chapter 2 notes that, after fatigue set in, 'Fines and coercion have come to replace voluntary participation'. Force and intimidation are indeed techniques that are often used to increase the effectiveness of a social institution. Patronage—buying

> The legitimacy of traditional justice mechanisms—their credibility in the eyes of the population and the trust they enjoy—is a much stronger source of compliance than the use of force and intimidation.
>
> The authority of traditional leaders has suffered from the general fallout of civil war and oppression, as well as from colonialism, migration to the cities, and manoeuvring by the national political establishment.

conformity through the personalized allocation of goods and services—is a 'softer' alternative. However, legitimacy—the quality of being credible, justified and worthy of trust—is a much stronger source of compliance. Legitimacy not only supports the effectiveness of institutions such as tradition-based practices; it also guarantees their survival.

Their degree of credibility, domestically and internationally, is the second benchmark in our evaluation.

2.2.1. At the local level

All the country studies present a mixed picture of the position of informal justice and reconciliation mechanisms in terms of their legitimacy. In Gorongosa, central Mozambique, '*Gamba* is part of the development of a well-established local tradition of settling accounts with histories of individual and collective violence' (chapter 3). Its credibility is high. But the authors of chapter 3 add that from a political perspective it 'is not a response to the failure of the state institutions to provide accountability measures as part of transitional justice process in the aftermath of the civil war'. Bert Ingelaere writes that ordinary Rwandans prefer the Gacaca courts over the national courts and the International Criminal Tribunal for Rwanda (ICTR) to deal with the genocide crimes. However, most Bahutu no longer see the Gacaca institution as conforming to standards of equity.

The Northern Uganda Peace Initiative (NUPI), a network of associations, has strongly supported the use of *mato oput* and cleansing ceremonies. The argument is that survivors of the civil war trust these practices to a high degree. Other local non-governmental organizations (NGOs) in the region disagree. They refer to surveys carried out in the camps for displaced persons the findings of which suggest that the legitimacy of local techniques is only partial, as they do not fill people's need for accountability. Assumpta Naniwe-Kaburahe is convinced that the majority of the population in Burundi see the Ubushingantahe as a credible instrument of dispute resolution, even in the context of dealing with crimes committed during the country's civil war; but there is a clear aversion towards it in most contemporary political circles in the country. In Sierra Leone, reintegration and cleansing ceremonies, particularly if addressed to former child soldiers, are viewed as reliable, but at the same time great doubt exists as to their role in handling more complex issues of the legacy of the war.

This ambiguity in the local vision is also intimately linked to the broader problem of the damaged authority of traditional leaders. They suffered from the general fallout of civil war and oppression. Their position has also been endangered by colonialism, migration to the cities and manoeuvring by the national political establishment.

2.2.2. The international community

Existing lists of the weaknesses of informal justice mechanisms have often been written from the Western perspective of consideration for the rule of law. The general perception is that the rules associated with them are very often imprecise and unwritten and that procedural safeguards are insufficient. This is the procedural aspect of the legitimacy gap that the international community, both in its state and in its non-state form, has identified as seriously problematic. In addition, many actors on the international field are convinced that these tools do not respect the duty under international law to prosecute genocide, war crimes and gross violations of human rights.

The spirited debate over this second problem is still unresolved. Some participants argue that a post-conflict society may refrain from the duty to prosecute if certain strict conditions are met. Blanket amnesty is not acceptable. All alternative strategies must thus have an accountability dimension. Perpetrators should confess and express regret. This must guarantee the unveiling of the truth and favour reconciliation. Reparation for

> The international community, both in its state and in its non-state form, has identified a serious legitimacy gap. Many actors on the international stage are convinced that traditional conflict resolution tools do not respect the duty under international law to prosecute genocide, war crimes and gross violations of human rights.

victims must be part of the transaction. And, finally, survivors should be involved in the decision to resort to non-prosecutorial instruments. In this view the legitimacy of tradition-based practices depends on the extent to which these conditions are met. The information brought together in section 1 of this chapter points to the occurrence of elements of accountability, truth telling, reparation and reconciliation.

Other international stakeholders, however, admit no exceptions to the international obligation to prosecute. Large NGOs such as Human Rights Watch and Amnesty International are the most outspoken upholders of this position.

The discussion has recently focused, as could be expected, on the northern Ugandan peace process and the intervention of the International Criminal Court (ICC). Some of those in favour of conditional amnesty, through local rituals, for the LRA leaders refer to article 53(1c),(2b) of the Rome Statute of the ICC. According to them this article creates an opportunity to accept local practices as an alternative. The problem is that this interpretation is based on the notion of 'interests of justice', an extremely technical and diffuse concept.

A recent conference on 'Building a Future on Peace and Justice' (Nuremberg, June 2007) has rightly advanced the idea that legitimacy is not only problematic in the case of tradition-based mechanisms. The conference report remarks that for too long 'the International Criminal Tribunal for the former Yugoslavia considered the issue of legitimacy only vis-à-vis the international community and not with respect to the local constituency'. It also notes that the ICC 'must close the legitimacy gap that may exist in respect of affected populations' (*Building a Future on Peace and Justice* 2007: 6, 5).

2.3. Summary

Do indigenous conflict resolution tools have an added value in times of transition? The answer is a cautious 'yes'. They are not sufficiently effective, and their legitimacy locally and internationally is not assured. The case studies have, however, demonstrated that tradition-based practices have the potential to produce a dividend in terms of the much-needed post-conflict accountability, truth telling and reconciliation that is not negligible. Consequently, positive effects may be expected with regard to the more general transitional justice goals of healing and social repair.

Nowhere in the real world has challenging state-based models of justice after transition been more discussed than in the northern Ugandan context of today. James Latigo, the author of our case study (chapter 4), has convincingly summarized the possible role of traditional conflict resolution instruments. 'Neither glorifying [them] as the only cure nor relegating them to the realm of the devilish is helpful to people seeking assistance in their suffering. It is only prudent to acknowledge the positive potential of traditional rituals and beliefs, not as contradictory to or competing with other approaches but as complementary to them. To ignore or discard traditional ways that have been seen to work in the past makes no sense. On the other hand, they cannot provide the cure for all ills'.

> The case studies have demonstrated that tradition-based practices have the potential to produce a dividend in terms of the much-needed post-conflict accountability, truth telling and reconciliation that is not negligible.

In 2005, a local network of NGOs (the Gulu District NGO Forum), the cultural institution of the Acholi (Ker Kwaro Acholi) and a Canadian research institute (the Liu Institute for Global Issues) joined forces to sum up the current debate. Their report concludes that a double false dichotomy has been created—local versus international approaches, and justice versus peace. Such a juxtaposition is misleading because traditional practices are being adapted to the Western vision of fair justice and 'in some instances, cleansing ceremonies and other rituals are already setting the foundation for justice' (Baines et al. 2005: 72). Removing them from the transitional justice toolkit is thus not an option.

Erin Baines, who has closely observed the many dilemmas that arise in northern Uganda, writes: 'The Juba talks are thus not only a historic opportunity to achieve peace in the country; they also provide a unique opportunity to begin to resolve how local approaches to justice and reconciliation can better inform and shape international approaches. This might involve adapting

> Traditional practices are being adapted to the Western vision of fair justice, but many challenges await if local and international stakeholders want in earnest to adopt and adapt tradition-based practices in their dealing with the legacy of civil war, genocide and oppression.

aspects of local justice that meet international standards, but will also require that international strategies be transformed to fit local sociocultural and economic realities' (Baines 2007: 114). This view reminds us of the many challenges that await if local and international stakeholders want in earnest to adopt and adapt tradition-based practices in their dealing with the legacy of civil war, genocide and oppression. It is in that context that part 3 of this chapter presents a very tentative list of recommendations.

3. Policy recommendations*

So far, this chapter has been predominantly descriptive. However, this book also aims to present ways in which the performance of tradition-based practices in the context of post-conflict societies can be improved. The policy recommendations that follow underscore that aspiration. Their range is limited as they are based on five case studies which cover one part of one single continent. We hope, nonetheless, that they will facilitate decision making in the area of justice during and after political transition.

Social engineering in this field is an intricate operation. It should be aimed at consolidating and, where practicable, increasing the actual strengths of indigenous justice and reconciliation practices. It must try to exploit existing opportunities, such as the growing interest in these tools. Answers must be sought to the problem of how to overcome their present shortcomings and weaknesses to the greatest degree possible. In addition, almost all post-conflict countries combine traditional instruments with other strategies for dealing with the legacy of civil war and genocide. This in turn is a source of difficult questions. How can and should these strategies interrelate? In particular, how can interpersonal and community-based practices live side by side with state-organized and/ or internationally sponsored forms of retributive justice and truth telling?

In short, the challenge of integrating traditional justice mechanisms into broader reconciliation and transitional justice strategies requires imagination, wide consultations, consensus building and capacity building, technical support, research and time. Our list of recommendations is conceived as one step in that complex process.

3.1. General rules

1. In the aftermath of regime change or civil war, do not limit the approach adopted and actions undertaken to 'hard reconstruction' (economic stability, disarmament and demobilization, security sector reform and so on), but give sufficient attention to the range of 'soft reconstruction' measures available (restorative justice through informal practices, survivor-oriented programmes, reconciliation, the restoration of local traditional authority).

2. When adopting or promoting tradition-based mechanisms and practices as part of a national transitional justice strategy, be aware that they should ideally serve as a complement to official judicial structures as opposed to being brought under state control.

3. Develop and deploy initiatives that reflect the wider trend of conceiving 'dealing with the past' as an intrinsic and unavoidable part of any peace negotiation process.

4. Be aware that transitional justice instruments and broader governance and democratization challenges are intimately interlocked.

5. Be attentive to the political, economic, cultural and international contingencies that play a role in decision making on transitional justice in general, and tradition-based practices in particular.

*This section co-authored by Mark Salter

6. Develop and implement political, legal, social, economic and cultural reforms that tackle the root causes of conflicts that provoke extreme violence or have done so in the past.

7. Devote sufficient time and energy to a careful, contextualized assessment of how best to blend the different state and non-state justice and reconciliation strategies available. Understand and utilize all chosen approaches in ways that complement each other synergistically, rather than work against each other.

8. 'Understand the times', that is, make a full and nuanced reading of the forces that exert an influence on both the overall transition agenda and specific transitional justice policy choices.

9. Accept the need for interim measures if formal justice and reconciliation policies are impossible to plan and implement immediately after a transition. In contexts where they are available, support the role of tradition-based mechanisms as an indispensable short-term alternative.

10. Be conscious at the same time of the importance of measures designed for long-term impact.

11. Make local ownership of policies and strategies the rule.

12. Give priority to the interests and perspectives of the most vulnerable population groups (children, internally displaced persons and refugees).

13. Give female war victims and survivors complementary opportunities that can give them both voice and agency in overall post-conflict policy formulation.

14. Establish a political agenda that is informed by local and international socio-cultural knowledge to address the gender bias present in many tradition-based practices.

3.2. To local stakeholders

15. Launch initiatives designed to enhance the procedural fairness of traditional dispute and conflict mechanisms.

16. Engage in efforts to sensitize the African Commission, the African Court on Human and Peoples' Rights and other relevant regional bodies to the need to recognize and upgrade the role of indigenous conflict management techniques.

17. Intensify efforts to enhance awareness and understanding of the role of traditional justice and reconciliation mechanisms among international agencies in general, and human rights NGOs in particular. In this context, emphasis should be placed on the

degree of truth, accountability and reparation they are capable of delivering, and their comparative effectiveness and legitimacy vis-à-vis classical 'formal' (criminal) justice instruments.

18. Increase wide consultations with constituencies (displaced persons' camps and urban settings included) on the choice of transitional justice policies in general, and the use of tradition-based practices in particular.

19. Create social spaces where victims and perpetrators can come together to address their war-related grievances and conflicts.

20. Endeavour to safeguard the role that traditional mechanisms play in the settlement of 'ordinary' disputes not directly connected to the legacy of violent conflict, and ensure that their efficacy is not undermined by radically adapting them for transitional justice purposes without appropriate prior local consultation.

21. Develop an outreach strategy that aims to help restore the authority and integrity that traditional leaders and/or traditional justice and reconciliation mechanisms may have lost among their local communities during the course of the conflict.

22. As refugees and internally displaced persons prepare to return to their original homesteads, pursue the revival of the core tenets of traditional justice and reconciliation mechanisms (e.g. social education received in the home and in the community through teachings surrounding the rituals involved).

23. Be attentive to the fact that survivors often bring their unresolved civil war-related conflicts (e.g. property disputes, marital violence) to informal traditional courts. Develop training programmes for lay judges, traditional leaders and healers on basic principles of transitional justice. Engage the international community in providing funding and technical assistance for these programmes.

3.3. To international stakeholders

3.3.1. General rules

24. Respect the following 'rules of engagement': be aware of the specific political, cultural and historical forces at work in a transitional society; accept that a process of post-conflict recovery must be locally 'owned' in the first instance; and be sensitive to such issues as the appropriate timing and tempo of external interventions intended to support such processes.

25. Sustain education and outreach programmes that increase both local and international understanding of the full range of transitional justice strategies available.

26. Be aware of the overarching need for inter-agency and inter-organizational coordination in post-conflict programming. The absence of a clear structure or framework for coordinating programmes and actions undertaken on the ground can at best complicate their impact, at worst critically undermine it.

27. Learn more about the range of traditional mechanisms and practices available in specific post-conflict contexts. This knowledge can serve to facilitate a contextually sensitized application of the norms and standards of international humanitarian and criminal law.

28. When facilitating a justice reform agenda, pay sufficient attention to local non-state, indigenous institutions. Facilitate the production of an audit of the informal justice sector.

29. Direct capacity-building programmes in the area of transitional justice in general, and the potential role of traditional mechanisms and practices in particular, towards the establishment of South–South networking initiatives and reciprocal exchanges of expertise.

30. Promote external monitoring of tradition-based practices that is based on peer review.

3.3.2. To the United Nations and other international institutions

31. Restructure internationally supported programmes of justice sector reform in post-conflict countries, for example, those initiated by the United Nations Development Programme (UNDP), the United Nations High Commissioner for Human Rights (UNHCHR) and the World Bank, in ways that effectively integrate the informal justice sector. Apply the same approach to audits of the justice sector.

32. Consider the establishment of an international panel of experts tasked with clarifying (a) in general, how traditional justice and reconciliation mechanisms can be better recognized under international law insofar as they contribute to implementation of the right to the truth, the duty to prosecute and the right to reparation; and (b) more particularly, how the notion of 'interests of justice' as defined in the ICC Statute can accommodate this important contribution to the international pursuit of truth, justice and reconciliation.

3.3.3. To donor countries and international NGOs

33. Collect information regarding the actual and potential impact of traditional justice and reconciliation mechanisms that will enable both a minimal cost–benefit analysis and funding decisions based on criteria of comparative effectiveness and legitimacy. Further

research in this area is much needed and should receive increased donor support in the future.

34. Provide financial and logistical support to the efforts of post-conflict countries to increase the actual strengths of indigenous justice and reconciliation practices and to overcome their present shortcomings and weaknesses.

3.4. Finally

35. Contexts and local situations vary. 'Translate' these recommendations by reading them through the lenses of the particular case in focus, also keeping in mind criteria such as the current phase of the conflict (ongoing or ended); the degree of internationalization of the conflict; the nature of the legacy of violence; the type of transition; and the degree of legitimacy of tradition-based justice and reconciliation practices.

References

Baines, Erin K., 'The Haunting of Alice: Local Approaches to Justice and Reconciliation in Northern Uganda', *International Journal of Transitional Justice*, vol. 1 (2007), pp. 91–114

Baines, Erin et al., 'Roco Wat I Acholi. Restoring Relationships in Acholi-land: Traditional Approaches to Justice and Reconciliation', Vancouver and Gulu: Liu Institute for Global Issues, Gulu District NGO Forum and Ker Kwaro Acholi, September 2005, available on the Liu Institute for Global Issues website, <http://www.ligi.ubc.ca>

Building a Future on Peace and Justice: Report on Major Findings of the Workshops, Nuremberg, 25–27 June 2007, <http://www.peace-justice-conference.info/download/Zeid_Synthesis.pdf>

Penal Reform International (PRI), *Access to Justice in Sub-Saharan Africa: The Role of Traditional and Informal Justice Systems* (London: PRI, 2002)

About the authors

Joe A. D. Alie is associate professor of history and dean of the Faculty of Arts, Fourah Bay College, University of Sierra Leone. He holds a BA (Hons) and MA degrees in history from the University of Sierra Leone, and a PhD in African History and Certificate in African Studies from the University of Wisconsin at Madison, USA. Dr Alie is a leading textbook writer in Sierra Leone and his published works include *A New History of Sierra Leone, Sierra Leone Since Independence: History of a Post-Colonial State* and *A Concise Guide to Writing College and Research Papers*. He has also published many articles in refereed journals.

Beatrice Dias-Lambranca obtained her MA degree in philosophy and French language teaching at Rouen University, France. She has carried out extensive field research on the social lives of women survivors of the civil war in central Mozambique.

Luc Huyse holds a PhD in political and social sciences. Until his retirement in 2000, he was professor of sociology and sociology of law at the University of Leuven Law School, Belgium. He has written and taught extensively in Dutch, English and French on the various dimensions of justice after transition (in post-World War II Europe, in the post-communist transitions in Eastern and Central Europe and in Africa). He has been a consultant to governments and non-governmental organizations in Burundi, Ethiopia, South Africa and Zimbabwe, and was co-editor of *Reconciliation After Violent Conflict: A Handbook* (Stockholm: International IDEA, 2003).

Victor Igreja is a fellow at the Netherlands Institute for Advanced Study in the Humanities and Social Sciences (NIAS). He obtained his PhD at Leiden University, the Netherlands, on the intersections of medical and legal anthropology. His multidisciplinary research focuses on the long-term consequences of the Mozambican civil war and the availability of community resources to engage in post-war reconciliation, justice and healing.

Bert Ingelaere studied philosophy and social and cultural anthropology at the Catholic University of Leuven (K. U. Leuven), Belgium. He has worked as a consultant for the World Bank in Rwanda and China, and is currently researching the experience and perception of political transition(s) and transitional justice at the local level in both Rwanda and Burundi. His research is funded by the Research Foundation Flanders and hosted by the Institute of Development Policy and Management (IOB-UA) and the Centre for Peace Research and Strategic Studies (CPRS) at K. U. Leuven.

James Ojera Latigo is a research fellow of the Marcus Garvey Pan African Institute (MPAI) and a fellow of the International Center for Transitional Justice (ICTJ). Formerly the director of the United States Agency for International Development (USAID) funded Northern Uganda Peace Initiative (NUPI), he is now the programme director of the

Uganda Historical Memory and Reconciliation Council, as well as secretary to the National Reconciliation Committee of the Council, and is actively researching indigenous African knowledge and culture.

Assumpta Naniwe-Kaburahe is vice-president of the Conseil National de l'Institution des Bashingantahe. She is active in the battle for broader rights for women and for their more effective integration in the Bashingantahe. She is a university professor and an independent consultant with several international organizations. Her research has focused on the social condition of women and children as victims of war violence. She is currently involved in the Burundi peacemaking process as gender programme officer of the local United Nations office.

Mark Salter, the project manager for this publication, is Senior Programme Officer in the Democracy Assessment and Analysis Unit at International IDEA. He has previously managed the institute's work on issues of reconciliation in several regions, including South Asia, West Africa, Latin America and the Western Balkans. He was formerly director of communications at the Life and Peace Institute (LPI) in Uppsala, Sweden. In 2006 he initiated the establishment of the Reconciliation Resource Network (RRN), an online resource and meeting place for the global community of reconciliation policy makers and practitioners.

About International IDEA

What is International IDEA?

The International Institute for Democracy and Electoral Assistance (International IDEA) is an intergovernmental organization that supports sustainable democracy worldwide. Its objective is to strengthen democratic institutions and processes. IDEA acts as a catalyst for democracy building by providing knowledge resources, expertise and a platform for debate on democracy issues. It works together with policy makers, donor governments, UN organizations and agencies, regional organizations and others engaged on the field of democracy building.

What does International IDEA do?

Democracy building is complex and touches on many areas including constitutions, electoral systems, political parties, legislative arrangements, the judiciary, central and local government, formal and traditional government structures. International IDEA is engaged with all of these issues and offers to those in the process of democratization:

- knowledge resources, in the form of handbooks, databases, websites and expert networks;
- policy proposals to provoke debate and action on democracy issues; and
- assistance to democratic reforms in response to specific national requests.

Areas of work

International IDEA's notable areas of expertise are:

- *Constitution-building processes.* A constitutional process can lay the foundations for peace and development, or plant seeds of conflict. International IDEA is able to provide knowledge and make policy proposals for constitution building that is genuinely nationally owned, is sensitive to gender and conflict-prevention dimensions, and responds effectively to national priorities.

- *Electoral processes.* The design and management of elections has a strong impact on the wider political system. International IDEA seeks to ensure the professional management and independence of elections, adapt electoral systems, and build public confidence in the electoral process.

- *Political parties.* Political parties form the essential link between voters and the government, yet polls taken across the world show that political parties enjoy a low level of confidence. International IDEA analyses the functioning of political parties, the public funding of political parties, their management and relations with the public.

- *Democracy and gender.* International IDEA recognizes that if democracies are to be truly democratic, then women—who make up over half of the world's population—must be represented on equal terms with men. International IDEA develops comparative resources and tools designed to advance the participation and representation of women in political life.

- *Democracy assessments.* Democratization is a national process. IDEA's *State of Democracy methodology* allows people to assess their own democracy instead of relying on externally produced indicators or rankings of democracies.

Where does International IDEA work?

International IDEA works worldwide. It is based in Stockholm, Sweden, and has offices in Latin America, Africa and Asia.